W9-DEP-839

The United States and Britain

The United States in the World:
Foreign Perspectives
Akira Iriye, Series Editor

H. G. Nicholas

The United States and Britain

The University of Chicago Press
Chicago and London

0726169

37390

The University of Chicago Press,
Chicago 60637
The University of Chicago Press,
Ltd., London

© 1975 by The University of
Chicago. All rights reserved
Published 1975. Printed in the
United States of America

Library of Congress Cataloging in Publication Data

Nicholas, Herbert George.
   The United States and Britain.

   (The United States in the world, foreign perspectives)
   Bibliography: p.
   Includes index.
   1.   United States—Foreign relations—Great Britain.
   2.   Great Britain—Foreign relations—United States.
   I.   Title.
   E183.8.G7N489   327.73′041   74–16681
   ISBN 0–226–58002–4
   ISBN 0–226–58003–2 pbk.

*H. G. Nicholas is Rhodes Professor
of American History and Institutions
at Oxford University. His
publications include* The American
Union *and* The United Nations as a
Political Institution.

Contents

0726169

37390

87830

Foreword

This book is a volume in the series entitled The United States and the World: Foreign Perspectives. As the series title indicates, it aims at examining American relations with other countries from a perspective that lies outside the United States. International relations obviously involve more than one government and one people, and yet American foreign affairs have tended to be treated as functions of purely domestic politics, opinions, and interests. Such a uni-national outlook is not adequate for understanding the complex forces that have shaped the mutual interactions between Americans and other peoples. Today, more than ever before, it is imperative to recognize the elementary fact that other countries' traditions, aspirations, and interests have played an equally important role in determining where the United States stands in the world. As with individuals, a country's destiny is in part shaped by how other countries perceive it and react to it. And a good way to learn about how foreigners view and deal with the United States is to turn to a non-American scholar of distinction for a discussion of his country's relations with America.

Professor Nicholas is too well known in the United States to be labeled simply a foreign scholar. Yet this book could not have been written by an American historian, born and brought up in his country. The insights the author brings to bear upon a discussion of familiar episodes, the intimate knowledge of British society and politics, and a unique view of Anglo-American shared experiences—these distinguish the book as a work of a British scholar who looks at the history of American-British relations as a drama in the larger Atlantic world. He thus contributes enormously to a more balanced understanding of the subject. Together with other volumes in the series, the book adds significantly to historical literature.

AKIRA IRIYE
Series Editor

1

History and geography have combined to endow the foreign relations of Britain and the United States with strikingly analogous characteristics. The mother-daughter bond of metropolis and colony, though complicated by other strands of colonizing nationalities, guaranteed that the thirteen colonies at the moment of nationhood would be peopled overwhelmingly by British stock. And though this element experienced progressive dilution as every year of immigration brought an additional influx from other European or African or Asiatic cultures, it was destined to remain until very recent times the dominant force in the shaping and directing of American public policy. A shared language and a common historical inheritance of "Anglo-Saxon" polity created, for British and Americans alike, a set of immediately recognizable and axiomatically accepted habits of thought and behavior—especially in the conduct of public affairs. This led not merely to the formulation and invocation of a common set of principles about foreign policy[1] but, perhaps even more important, to a common cast of mind, parallel styles of action and reaction at both the popular and the higher levels of government. Thus the evolution of what Arnold Wolfers aptly called a "philosophy of choice" as opposed to a "philosophy of necessity"[2] is matched by a pervasive disposition to judge issues of foreign, as well as domestic, policy by moral criteria. Moreover the inescapable concomitant of such a disposition, the conviction of being the exclusive repository of moral standards, has been further intensified by the development of an Anglo-American consciousness, a kind of paranationalism which, however much given to internal rivalries, has yet often felt itself superior to "lesser breeds" and non-Anglo-Saxon cultures.

Superficially the British islands and the North American landmass are very different entities, in scale and location. The unity of communication and government which had been attained in the United Kingdom of George III was in striking contrast to the state sovereignties and sectional divergencies of the United States of America, further intensified by vast distances and physical obstacles—so that eighteenth-century Maine could be twenty days' distance from Georgia by hard overland travel. The lead thus given by geographical compactness was shortened, but not eliminated, by the technological developments of the nineteenth and twentieth centuries. Britain remains an intimate, America even now an extended, society. Moreover, in their external relations, the twenty-odd miles which separate Britain from mainland Europe are mathematically minute by the scale of the three thousand miles of Atlantic or the six thousand miles of Pacific that float between North America and the nearest other landmass. Yet mathematical discrepancies may not be fairly reflected in the distorting mirror of men's thinking. Historically the ditch which is the Channel has conferred a feeling of otherness and impregnability hardly less strong than that which is imparted by the "steep Atlantick main." Nor is the insularity of the United States sensibly diminished by the coexistence on the same landmass of northern and southern (and, for much of her history, western) neighbors. Thinly populated and intractable terrain has always been a buffer limiting contacts between even the southern states and Mexico, while Canada, so far from being a menace to United States security, has generally been a hostage for Britain's good behavior. Thus, whatever the map may say, the United States since the moment of her inception has felt like an island and behaved like one. A peculiar kind of island, of course, which for most of its history has been expanding itself toward the setting sun. But one has only to reflect on the distinctive American usage of "frontier," to mean the edge of settlement, rather than a boundary between national sovereignties, to realize that in relation to the rest of the world the American feels insulated by space as well as differentiated by history.

Out of physical and historical pressures have come both in Britain and in the United States certain ways of looking at the rest of the world which have a good deal in common. Both countries have had, at the heart of their being, a conviction that they were free to choose, not once and for all, but repeatedly and indeed afresh on each occasion, how much or how little they would have to do with even their nearest neighbors—"establishing," as George Washington said, but as the Pitts or

Palmerston or Salisbury would have echoed, "conventional rules of intercourse, the best that present circumstances and mutual opinion will permit, but temporary and liable to be from time from time abandoned or varied, as experience and circumstances shall dictate." The label *isolationism* frequently applied to this disposition is inaccurate if it implies a settled withdrawal or abstention from foreign contacts. Britain acquired an empire, organized Europe against Napoleon, fought in alliance the Crimean War, participated in various manifestations of the Concert of Europe—all before its official abandonment of "splendid isolationism" at the end of the nineteenth century. The U.S.A. similarly allied herself with France to win her independence, erected and maintained a Monroe Doctrine behind the bulwarks of the British fleet, forced her way into Asia, acquired imperial possessions in the wake of the Spanish-American War, participated in European diplomacy before and during World War I—all without any explicit repudiation of the teachings of her Founding Fathers. Since World War I, of course, the suctions of commitment have proved irresistible for Britain and the U.S.A. alike, involving them willy-nilly in the affairs of the entire world and leaving the U.S.A., with whatever intermittent misgivings, inescapably implicated across the globe.

The explanations of the paradox of involvement coexisting with insularity are various and not, for the two countries, identical. But one predisposing factor they have in common—a sense of mission. In Britain this took two forms: in relation to Europe she conceived herself as the custodian and champion of what was variously described as "constitutional government" or "liberty"; in the mother country's relations with the Empire there was a doctrine of "trusteeship" which subsequently developed into a Commonwealth doctrine of self-determination and partnership. In the U.S.A. there was from the first a messianic vision of the new nation which, being founded on universal principles of justice and liberty, would be the forerunner of comparable commonwealths across the globe, while at home there was a "manifest destiny" to fill out the empty spaces of Zion with all who fled the contamination of Europe. Nor need this manifest destiny stop at the western waters' edge: it could suffer an easy transmutation into an imperial vision or an obligation to confer or guarantee a rebirth of freedom elsewhere across the world.

Thus the freedom to choose led inevitably, in Britain and America, to a conviction that the morality which exalteth a nation is a necessary touchstone of foreign policy. For some the moral imperative would point to deep and permanent involvement. For others, perhaps even more logically, it would dictate an avoidance of all "permanent entanglements" and a conviction that the nation must remain free to make each decision operate on the basis of a separate moral tally. In this way the pendulum could swing between commitment and withdrawal, with each having an equal claim to moral validity and, as time went on, to historical precedent.

To the extent, then, that common postures and predispositions create a mutual understanding, Britain and the United States have been uniquely placed to comprehend each other. And indeed the history of Anglo-American relations is fortunately replete with occasions when the course of public policy in either or both countries has been constructively modified by an instinctive understanding of the wellsprings of each other's behavior. Indeed one can say more: it is doubtful whether there has ever existed, since Yorktown, a sustained incomprehension in Britain or America of any major course of policy on which the other has embarked—such, for example, as existed in Britain of Nazi Germany in the thirties or in the U.S.A. of China in the forties and fifties. The closest parallels would be in the sluggish realization in Britain of the true character of the American Civil War or the long-delayed recognition in America of the idealistic elements in British imperial policy. But even on these issues neither country ever lacked informed expositors of what the other was doing.

But of course common attitudes and predispositions need not breed agreement. The family quarrel can have its own exclusive bitterness. Of this the Anglo-American relationship can bear eloquent testimony. Indeed one by-product of our admixture of morality with diplomacy has been a hypersensitiveness of each to the moral criticisms of the other and, of course, an uncanny skill in knowing where the moral stiletto can be inserted to best effect. This has often invested trivial dissensions with an undue significance and charged technical or accidental differences with an electrical shock of misplaced moral judgment. Precisely because we persist in being each other's keepers to a degree that we would think improper or pointless elsewhere, we often exacerbate our relations. We expect more of each other than we expect of third parties and are proportionately chagrined when we fail to find it. Public opinion in each country talks and thinks of the other not as a sovereign state with its own Hobbesian compulsions to seek first its national interest and security but as a moral being who can and should allow sentiment and altruism to determine its behavior.

One consequence of this has been a disposition to overlook the element of power which inevitably enters into our mutual relations. This disposition has been assisted by the breadth of the Atlantic. Until the coming of the airliner we did not rub shoulders, day by day, as two European neighbor states did. We were able to indulge our quarrels and reproaches without much risk that a careless word or a hasty movement of troops might start a conflagration that would get out of hand. During most of our history it took weeks, not hours, to cross the Atlantic, and although such delay sometimes contributed to ignorance or misunderstanding, it more often allowed time for tempers to cool or wiser heads to prevail. We have thus seldom felt obliged to treat all disagreements, however minor, as tests of strength involving an investment of prestige which neither side could afford to see lost. Yet, of course, power and an awareness by policymakers of the realities of power (however much underrated by the opinion makers) have always been present in the relations between the two states, and one of the tasks of the following pages will be to bring these underlying realities to the surface.

The relations of any two sovereign states are affected in some degree by their relations to the rest of the world, their place in the total complex of interstate relationships. This holds true of Britain and the U.S.A. Young America's relationship with France when France was in a life-and-death struggle with Britain was a crucial factor in securing and consolidating American independence. Yet significantly this was the last occasion on which the U.S.A. and France found themselves members of an alliance directed against Britain. At the time of the American Civil War, Britain and France had diplomatic understandings which in the earlier stages of the conflict promoted the formation of a common policy, but it never put them in outright opposition to the U.S.A., nor indeed did it long survive the restless ambition of Napoleon III. When the Anglo-Japanese alliance looked like becoming a cause of friction between the U.S.A. and the U.K., it was dropped. In all this, of course, the detached postures, the "isolationist" predilections of each country, have been a major determinant. There have been fewer external constraints on their mutual relationship than are generally found in the world of sovereign states. There has, of course, been the issue of Canada—first a British possession, then a dominion, and later still a sovereign ally. She has always been the third point in a triangular relationship, whether, as the Founding Fathers feared, as a constraining relic of imperial power, or, as Canadians felt through much of their history, as something between a pawn and a hostage, or, in sunnier moments of the triangular relationship, as a bridge or mediator between her neighbor and her motherland. But in all these respects Canada has been unique. Neither Mexico nor the islands of the Caribbean have been serious third parties in relation to any major Anglo-American issue. Nor, despite American expansion across the Pacific, has any Asian or Australasian power much complicated relations between London and Washington, at least until the outbreak of World War II. Rather, the Asian landmass has seemed literally to lie on the other side of a globe which Britain and the U.S.A. have approached from opposite directions and with nonconflicting interests in trade, territorial acquisition, or economic penetration. The fact that the American West allowed ample outlet at home for American energies during the period of maximum British overseas expansion undoubtedly reduced Anglo-American friction. The one area where serious clashes might have been expected to develop, Latin America, was in fact one of the least contentious once the Monroe Doctrine won acceptance as a projection of the principle that freedom to trade, not the acquisition of territory, was the basic interest of both Britain and the U.S.A. in this hemisphere.

Where basic attitudes and substantive issues are not in conflict, forms of government seldom constitute serious matters of disagreement. For most of their two hundred years of relationship Britain and the U.S.A. have differed as monarchy and republic and, more realistically, as aristocracy and democracy—with, to be more realistic still, tinges of what Walter Bagehot called a "deferential" disposition and European critics of America called a "business civilization." However, these differences were mitigated at every turn by the interpenetration of the two cultures, the two economies, even the two social structures, as British immigrants thronged Ellis Island and American heiresses married British peers. More serious perhaps were the differences in the actual machinery for conducting foreign relations. Under the British parliamentary system a British minister put his signature to a document and, provided he had the backing of the cabinet in so doing, that was that; the nation stood committed. Under the presidential system of divided powers a secretary of state or even a president could only give a provisional undertaking until the Senate, or, in case of a declaration of war, Congress, had given its endorsement. Again, the British foreign minister had at his command a department and a foreign service of well-organized professionals who seldom perverted his policy objectives (though they might err by failing to adjust to the non-European features of American diplomacy). By contrast the American secretary of state, himself generally less experienced in office, was served by less reliable administrative instruments, particularly in the field, where diplomatic appointments were especially liable to be treated as patronage plums. Yet, when all this is said, it is significant that these differences seldom proved crucial. Each nation recognized the dominant importance of its relationship with the other; public opinion on each side of the Atlantic saw that, in a real sense, Anglo-American relations were too important to be left to the diplomats—or to the senators, or to the journalists. At the great moments they involved the life of the nation and the major decisions were, in consequence, the decisions of the people themselves.

The relations of Britain and the United States, in general so conspicuous
for their amicability, have their beginning in war. The American War of
Independence was not a very long war, nor a very bloody one. But its
seven years were neither short nor devoid of suffering and bitterness. At
the end the Loyalists were left with the harsh taste of exile and ill treatment at the hands of their kinsmen and the victorious colonists had to
make good the loss and damage which they had sustained not merely at
the hands of fellow Britons but from hired Hessians as well. In Britain
the humiliation and shame at the "loss of America," while falling most
directly on the King and his supporters, was an inescapable national experience. But whereas for Britain the war itself, however painful, was
just another war, for the United States it was the furnace in which nationhood had been forged. The great moments of the war became the symbols, so indispensable to a young nation, of its own identity, the memo-
rials which would be so sedulously cherished in the years to come, to
inspire, to comfort, and to warn—the Shot Heard round the World,
Washington crossing the Delaware, Valley Forge, "I only regret that I
have but one life to lose for my country," "I have not yet begun to fight,"
"Times that try men's souls," "Put none but Americans on guard tonight."

The historic consequences of this are obvious. Whereas for Britain the
War of Independence was an inglorious episode, quickly turned into an
appropriate topic for the exercise of her great national gift for selective
amnesia, for the United States the earliest, most precious, and most tenacious memories were those which derived from a war against Britain.
Thus for Englishmen it is the act of separation which has to be forgiven
or forgotten, for Americans it is the actual birth pangs of the nation which
have to be transcended, if past conflict is not to foster future animosity.

Yorktown, and the ensuing need for peace, were nonetheless bitter pills for Britain to swallow at the time. The war had divided Britain: the depth of the division reflected the importance of the issues which each side felt to be at stake. George III was undoubtedly genuine in his early and classic statement of the domino theory: if America got independence, "the West Indies must follow them. . . . Ireland would soon follow the same plan. . . . Then this island would be reduced to itself and soon would be a poor island indeed."[1]

The fact that peace was made, despite such profound misgivings, is attributable not to any change of heart on the part of the King and those who felt like him, but to the patent impossibility of any other early solution in North America and to the menace of France, Spain, and Holland in the seas of northern and western Europe.

Peace once made, however, hopes revived. It was the same George III who in the speech from the throne five days after the signing of the provisional articles of peace told his Parliament: "Religion—language—interest—affections may, and I hope will, yet prove a bond of permanent union between the two countries." The language reflected the vain and short-lived aspirations of his Prime Minister, Lord Shelburne, who envisaged a settlement in which everything would be staked upon a mutual recognition that, when all was said and done, Britons and Americans were economic men. Seventeen seventy-six had not merely been the natal year of American independence. It had also seen the publication of the great manifesto of the economic Enlightenment by which nineteenth-century Britain was to live and prosper—Adam Smith's *Wealth of Nations*. The hopes of Shelburne and his supporters rested on the belief that the future of Britain lay with Adam Smith and free trade and that the enlightened Americans would see their future in similar terms. So Britain should discard outmoded mercantilism and treat Americans for trade purposes as if they had never broken away. The natural unity of the North Atlantic economy would reassert itself and would bring in its train a mutual rapprochement, perhaps even some degree of political reunification. For this it would be well worth abandoning any territorial claims in the Canadas or fishery demands in North American waters.

The Shelburne plan did too little justice to America's determination to make a clean break and anticipated by at least a generation the victory of Adam Smith's philosophy in Britain. Britain in the 1780s could not afford to abandon the navigation laws which were the expression of mercantilism because she could not trust her salvation to economics alone. She had lost Amercia, strategically, because she was too weak at sea. This same weakness made it impossible for her to be generous in the peace. Britain's navy was dependent on its merchant marine, for its men and for many of its ships. That marine, in turn, depended on the protection it derived from the navigation laws. Allow Americans a full share of the carrying trade, and their more cheaply built ships and locally recruited seamen would drive their British rivals first out of the lucrative West Indian trade and eventually perhaps out of the North Atlantic. As it was, the two were often interdependent, it being the return trip between North America and the West Indies that frequently paid for the journey between North America and Britain. So commercial prosperity seemed bound up with naval security. It was a shortsighted argument, but countries that lose wars are even less likely to take a long view than those who win them, and in 1783 it was the short view that carried the day.

Hence the terms of the Treaty of Versailles—or, to be precise, the silences of the Treaty of Versailles. For the treaty bought peace largely by imprecision, about boundaries and debt settlements in particular, and also by omission: commercial relations were left to be otherwise regularized. In fact they were regularized, in the failure of agreement, by British orders in council which produced friction for twenty years and more. In effect the rich West Indies trade was reserved for British ships, although the principles of mercantilism were weakened to allow Americans to trade directly with Britain, provided they brought only American produce. The result was to facilitate Anglo-American trade, but at the price of continuing American frustration.

The truth was that the war's end left, not a clean break, but a line of ragged connections. It took time for Britain to accept, emotionally and psychologically, the fact of American independence. George III told the Americophile Charles James Fox that "a Minister accredited from America would never be agreeable" to him and that he would have "a very bad opinion of any Englishman that can accept being sent as a Minister to a revolted state."[2] So it was two years before John Adams presented his credentials at the Court of St. James. George III in fact received him with a creditable, if illogical, courtesy, but his refusal to make a reciprocal appointment to America obliged Adams to withdraw in 1788. It was 1791 before George Hammond was appointed minister from Britain, to be matched in 1792 by Thomas Pinckney from the U.S.A.

Fortunately this reluctance to accommodate forms to realities did not extend in comparable degree to the economic activities of the two countries. Here was most clearly evident how little difference war and political independence had made. Indeed the immediate postwar rush to reopen old trading connections and restock with British goods led to the American depression of 1784–85 with its inescapable backwash in Britain. Though this was followed by a diversification of American trading—with France, Holland, even China—that would have been impossible before independence, the Anglo-American commercial connection remains basic. British houses were best able to extend the indispensable credits. British goods were most in demand, British investors were readiest with their capital. In consequence approximately a third of United States imports came from Britain in the years down to 1801. There was always an unfavorable trade balance. What America sent Britain varied from a half to a quarter of what she sent everywhere, and seldom rose above a twentieth of what Britain imported from around the world. Moreover the dominance of British capital persisted after the war as before. By 1798 half the stocks of the U.S. National Bank were held in Britain. By 1803 50 percent of all American securities were British owned. Thus there developed the paradox that one and the same class, that of businessmen and merchants, which had the most frequent disagreements with British policy was also the most intimately dependent upon the British connection.

The imprecisions of peacemaking at Versailles led in 1794 to the second attempt at tying up loose ends, which went by the name of Jay's Treaty. Britain's retention of the forts along the American-Canadian boundary and in the Northwest was a thorn in America's side because, as a continuing and active expression of the British connection with the Indian tribes, it seemed to present just the same kind of barrier to American westward expansion as the hated Quebec Act of 1774, that powerful propellant of independence. Britain justified her retention by the American failure to honor the obligation assumed at Versailles to settle the claims of the Loyalists, to which the U.S.A. had replied by invoking for the first (though not for the last) time the convenient argument of a federation—that this was a matter for the individual states.

By 1796 the British had evacuated the frontier posts and by 1798 a commission had settled the most pressing boundary dispute, that of the

Saint Croix River. The debts, claims, and counterclaims proved more intractable; the treaty had referred these problems to commissions meeting in Philadelphia and London, but these commissions failed to agree and it was not until 1804 that the last of the disputes was settled. But the Jay treaty involved more than this. There was a concession to Britain in the free access granted to British fur traders in the hinterland of the Canadian-American border and one to the U.S.A. in respect of trade with India, hitherto the monopoly of the East India Company; this monopoly was breached to permit American ships to trade direct provided they did not seek to steal the carrying trade between India and anywhere else. This same concern to protect the carrying trade marred an otherwise concessionary article of the treaty giving Americans direct access to the West Indies. At such a price the concession turned out to be unacceptable to the United States Senate and the article lapsed.

In all this Jay's Treaty might be thought (though seldom *was* thought at the time) to strike a roughly equal balance between the two parties. But what stuck most in American throats were provisions regarding neutral rights, omen of worse troubles to come. Britain's long war with Napoleonic France which broke out in 1793 required for its conduct two maritime practices which directly violated American sovereignty as an independent state and flouted the hypersensitive pride of a new nation. These were impressment and search.

In retrospect it must appear extraordinary that Britain should claim the right, and be willing to face war in defense of the right, to take by force sailors from American ships and to compel them to service in the Royal Navy. But impressment itself, of course, was such an extraordinary practice that those who accepted it regarded this application of it as a natural and logical corollary. The press gang was hallowed by usage but found its day-to-day justification in the determination of the British taxpayer to buy his maritime defense at the cheapest possible rate. This meant a small navy in peacetime with low pay and harsh discipline. When war required expansion, there could be no hope of recruitment by voluntary enlistment. Indeed even the retention of the existing crews was difficult enough. Admiral Nelson once estimated the total of desertions in the decade 1793–1803 at 42,000. Even for a merchant sailor American pay and conditions were a serious temptation; how much more for a naval rating. At Independence it was often uncertain who was an American and who was a subject of the King; after

Independence the temptation of deserters to pass themselves off as Americans did not diminish. So the officer of a British press gang could justify any violation of American rights with the excuse of recovering "deserters," while his superiors, concerned only with keeping their Hearts of Oak manned for a life-and-death struggle, would ask no questions provided he produced his tally of able-bodied seamen.

The right of search as applied to neutrals in a war was not intrinsically novel or outrageous. A belligerent was generally entitled to seize contraband of war bound for enemy ports. But the enforcement of this right could hardly fail to give offense, especially when it meant seizures of neutral vessels and delays, harshness, and sometimes downright injustice in admiralty courts, plus, of course, considerable disagreement as to what constituted contraband, with a persistent British determination to define it as widely as possible.

On these issues Jay's Treaty in effect secured no concessions. Hence in large part the extremely violent criticism that greeted it, despite its ratification by the Senate, twenty to ten. But the fact was that the French war had transformed the character of Anglo-American relations. No longer was their dominant feature the comparative status of ex-colony and ex-imperial power. Now for Britain the problem was how to fit America into the strategy of victory over France; for the United States it was how to utilize the European war to maximize her own advantage or, negatively, how to avoid sustaining injury from a conflict in which she wished to remain neutral. France, bound of course to the U.S.A. by the alliance of 1778, entertained hopes of receiving active support from the country whose independence she had made possible. She failed because her intrigues overreached themselves and she mistook Francophilia for a willingness to risk a resumption of conflict with Britain. Britain indulged no such expectations; her only oscillations were between seeking a benevolent neutrality and ignoring America's feelings provided she secured America's compliance. She could always count on an Anglophilia based on a combination of economic self-interest and social and cultural affinities. But she did not rest her policy upon what American Anglophiles would support. She rested it upon the harsh determinants of what victory over France required; American reactions had to accommodate themselves to that as best they could.

In fact the decade after Jay's Treaty was, as the most notable historian of this diplomacy well describes it, a period of mutual "rapprochement."[3]

This was due to the firm course set by Washington, with the aid of Hamilton, aligning the fortunes of the U.S.A. much more closely with conservative England than with revolutionary France. But Jefferson's succession marked no change, partly because the French had overreached themselves by their own sweeping confiscation policy at sea and partly because Jefferson found that if he was to turn Spain's and France's misfortunes to America's advantage, he needed, at the least, Britain's interpository presence in the North Atlantic. Thus his grand design of the Louisiana Purchase depended for its realization on Britain's ability to prevent France reasserting her traditional presence in the North American hinterland. Jefferson made his oft-quoted assertion that "from that moment we must marry ourselves to the British fleet and nation" with reference to the eventuality of a French repossession of the mouth of the Mississippi. The British, for their part, were considering a possible seizure of New Orleans on America's behalf when Napoleon, on a quick impulse, closed the deal. But perhaps a more significant indication of the longer-term intersection of British and American interests was provided by the fact that it was Baring Brothers, the British banking house which specialized in American business, that concluded the financial details of the purchase and arranged the payment in Paris—after hostilities between Britain and France had recommenced, at the end of the Peace of Amiens.

The resumption of the Napoleonic Wars brought a fresh set of strains and frictions. The first phase of the war, grim as it was, had not been a conflict to the death. It had thus been prosecuted by Britain without the full rigors of economic warfare waged at sea across the whole face of the Atlantic as well as the Baltic and the Mediterranean. Thus Britain's belligerent practices had in fact given less offense to American neutrality than had those of France. After the Peace of Amiens things were different. Unable to gain a foothold on the European continent, Britain found herself alone against the French genius who conquered Austria at Austerlitz, Prussia at Jena, and Russia at Friedland and Tilsit, until his sway extended from the Pyrenees to the Urals. Napoleon, for his part, triumphant on land, was, after Trafalgar, incapable of breaking through the cordon of the British navy to launch the invasion that was to complete his conquests. Thus the island redoubt and the continental armed camp, unable to come at each other by any of the methods of conventional warfare, turned in a manner hith-

erto unprecedented to the economic weapons of trade, seizure, and
blockade. Less bloody than armed conflict, the economic struggle was
far more pervasive and penetrating. To a degree unequaled until World
War I, this was total war.

From such a war no neutral could hope to escape unscathed, least of
all the greatest neutral sea power and trader, the United States. A succession of British measures soon made this clear. There was a tightening
up—partly mercantilist, partly strategic—on the highly lucrative American carrying and reexport trade with the West Indies, British, Spanish,
and French. In 1806 there was the quite unprecedented imposition of
a British blockade of the whole coast of Europe from Brest to the Elbe.
These measures, coupled with an aggravation of the standing American
grievance over impressment, led to the passage of the American Non-
Importation Act. Nonimportation, already dear to American patriots for
its association with the revolutionary struggle, rested upon an idea valid
enough in the context of a business-as-usual world—namely, that a ban
on American imports from Britain would so wound British commerce as
to make the mercantilists realize that measures aimed at American trade
would not pay. But there were two fallacies in the concept: first, the world
of the Napoleonic Wars was becoming with every year less of a business-
as-usual world as purely economic considerations were being subordinated to those of national survival; second, the United States, being more
dependent on trade with Britain than Britain was on trade with her,
was liable by this weapon to do more harm to herself than to Britain.

Immediately, in 1806, the American threat (because the act was
suspended pending negotiation) resulted in a compromise, the Monroe-
Pinkney Treaty, with some easement of British pressure over the reexport trade (though on little else). But then came the complication,
recurrent throughout these twenty years of war, that the French were
resorting to the economic weapon too. In November 1806 Napoleon
issued his Berlin Decree, prohibiting all trade with the United Kingdom
and theatening with seizure all vessels which had even called at a British
port. This in turn provoked a group of British orders in council outlawing all neutral trade between any ports in Napoleon's control. From
then on the deterioration in relations was rapid. In May 1807 Jefferson
rejected the Monroe-Pinkney Treaty and in June there occurred one of
those incidents to which impressment would predictably give rise, when
H.M.S. *Leopard,* fresh from the hospitality of an American port, at-

tacked the U.S.S. *Chesapeake,* killing three of her crew and removing four alleged British deserters. British warships were banned from American waters, but five years of negotiations failed to secure reparations. Meanwhile events took their predictable course. The Non-Importation Act went into effect, to be followed swiftly by Napoleon's Milan Decree (1807) making all ships that submitted to British search or regulations subject to confiscation.

In these circumstances, denied reparations for the *Chesapeake* or any abatement of impressment, and with American ships and commerce made the sport of belligerent powers, Jefferson got Congress to pass the Embargo Act, forbidding all American trade to any foreign port but aiming its blunderbuss especially and obviously at England. England in fact suffered little, though the West Indies sustained some damage. But it was the U.S.A. which suffered most, materially and in terms of morale, because the embargo aggravated dissension between Republicans and Federalists and encouraged the latter's widespread flouting of its provisions. When in 1808 Jefferson tried to use the embargo as a bargaining tool, offering to lift it against any power which respected United States commerce, George Canning, the foreign secretary, rejected the proposal with a sneer, confident in the knowledge that British losses were slight and that the U.S.A. would have to unload some of its blunderbuss before it exploded in its own face. Modification in 1809, by the Non-Intercourse Act, left the U.S.A. free to trade with neutrals but still maintained the hopeless posture of threatening the two belligerents with a weapon they did not fear. Britain's reply was indeed to offer some concession—an opening of the Baltic trade to Americans. D. M. Erskine, the new minister in Washington, sought to conciliate the new Madison administration by an agreement which dropped the British orders in council in return for a suspension of the Non-Intercourse Act. In so doing he exceeded his instructions in several particulars. The transatlantic telegraph, had it existed, would have made impossible the false dawn which the Erskine agreement created, with its rejoicings in Washington and fury in London; it might have made possible the working out of a compromise which did not violate principles each side deemed essential. As it was, Canning repudiated his envoy, a classic case of ambassadorial zeal outrunning ambassadorial discretion. Details and technicalities apart, what really separated the two parties was that Britain wanted a U.S.A. whose neutrality would leave her a commercial ally against Napoleon while the U.S.A. wanted to make the oceans safe for neutral commerce. Predictably, hopes dashed intensified resentment. The road from the failure of the Erskine agreements to 1812 is a clear one.

Behind much of the British intransigence lay the conviction that the country was not only fighting for its life but was also the world's champion against a universal tyrant. "The strength and power of Great Britain," said Canning in reply to an offer to repeal the United States embargo, "are not for herself alone but for the world." There were Americans who agreed, like Timothy Pickering with his famous Boston toast, "The World's last hope—Britain's fast-anchored Isle." Even Rufus King, who supported some limited resistance to Britain, avowed in 1808, "If England sinks, her fall will prove the grave of our liberties."[4] The sentiments, from whichever side uttered, were not insincere or absurd, but their validity was impaired by the fact that other than moral issues were at stake. Federalists did not fear merely Napoleon's tyranny: they were concerned about their trade. Britain did not seek merely to defeat France: she sought to preserve and promote her commerce as well. Thus she sought not so much to stop all trade with France as to control and profit from it. Hence the licensing system—some 15,000–20,000 licenses issued a year between 1809 and 1812 for trade with France, despite the blockade, and very few available to Americans.[5]

It was in this confused and contradictory clash of motives and interests, internal as well as international, that events moved toward war. Napoleon, taking advantage of America's embroilment with Britain, stepped up his trade war; the Rambouillet Decree of 1810 ordered the seizure of all American ships in French ports. The Embargo Act was replaced by the Mason Act, which feebly offered to restore total nonintercourse against either belligerent if the other would respect American commerce. James Madison found in Napoleon's ambiguous diplomatic dispatches assurances that the Berlin and Milan decrees had been lifted, and so secured from Congress authority to lift the ban on France while continuing it on British commerce until the orders in council were removed. The British position remained, with some justice, unchanged, on the grounds that Napoleon's advances were deceptive.

On this frustrating situation the news of Tippecanoe fell like a spark on tinder. To Whitehall and Westminster, Tippecanoe was as remote and insignificant as it was outlandish. To many Americans it was the kind of irrelevance that best proves conspiracy. If the British were not behind the new belligerency of Tecumseh and his Indian league, who were? And if Governor William Henry Harrison of Indiana could bring luster to American arms by killing upwards of three dozen Indians at the confluence of the Wabash and the Tippecanoe, what might a properly roused republic not do?

It has never been easy for the British to take the War of 1812 seriously. When it was declared, the struggle with Napoleon was still at its height. When peace was signed, Waterloo still lay ahead. By comparison, what happened in North America was of little consequence and why it happened of even less. Lord Castlereagh, whose foreign secretaryship spanned the war, would have read with a sardonic smile of the volumes of controversy that the war's causes have provoked among scholars. "Perhaps as many as fifty historians have offered original explanations of the war in the past seventy five years."[6] But indeed Castlereagh's smile and what lay behind it provide as good a clue as any to this most absurd and unnecessary of wars. It occurred, basically, because Britain would not take America seriously, because armored in distraction, self-righteousness, and an assurance of her overwhelming superiority, Britain would neither attend to America's substantive grievances nor provide the modicum of diplomatic emollient which might have made them tolerable. The French in general behaved no better, but they misbehaved with less condescension. Moreover, behind every British injury or insult lurked a distinctive relationship. Britain could have treated any other country as badly without the treatment's giving such offense. America was ex-colonial, newly and insecurely independent. Determined to be herself, she found Britain behaving as if Yorktown had gone the other way. Hence the peculiar causation of the war—proceeding not from any single irremediable, intolerable, novel outrage but from an accumulation of frustrations at last spilling over. The bizarre consequence was that Britain belatedly revoked the offensive orders in council in ignorance of Congress's declaration of war and negotiations for peace began their sluggish progress almost as soon as hostilities commenced.

Yet it is very doubtful whether the war could have been averted had transatlantic communications been better and had the British revocation of the orders come a little earlier. Madison's war message listed four main grievances and of these the interference with United States commerce accounted only for one. Impressment headed the list, British harassment of shipping within American waters came next. The last, like an unconvincing addendum, was "the war just renewed by the savages on one of our extensive frontiers." The message concluded that all this amounted to Britain being "in a state of war against the United States."

The course of the war, with its frontier skirmishes and Great Lakes encounters, belongs more to the connoisseur of naval and military maneuvers than to the diplomatic historian. In general, despite the burning of York and Washington, it is notable for the comparatively little damage and slaughter that the combatants inflicted on each other. But for Americans the war had another, larger significance. It was a second installment, so to speak, of the War of Independence and one in which the nation again proved its fledgling manhood against the greatest power in the world. It added its own postscript of glory and legend to those left by 1776. Commodore Oliver Perry and Captain Stephen Decatur, Captain Thomas Macdonough and General Andrew Jackson, "Don't give up the ship," "We have met the enemy and they are ours," "Oh say, can you see . . . ?"—these all meant a far greater increment of confidence and inspiration to the young nation than of humiliation and depression to the old. And since to the third party to the conflict, the infant Canada, the war brought a special recognition of its distinctiveness, it is even plausible to argue that the War of 1812, for all its absurdities, left in the actual relations of the North Atlantic powers a balance of profit over loss. It did not even seriously impede Britain's struggle against Napoleon; thanks to Federalist aversion to Madisonian regulations, American wheat continued to feed Wellington's soldiers in the Peninsular War throughout the conflict.

When peace came, as it formally did at Ghent on Christmas Eve, 1814, it was thus the consequence of both sides recognizing that war was too costly a method of resolving their differences and that it had brought about certain lasting changes in their mutual relations. It had served notice on Europe in general and England in particular that the U.S.A. would fight rather than see her interests violated or her newfound identity impaired. In this sense it was an essential step in the road that led to the proud affirmations of the Monroe Doctrine nine years later. It left Britain with a keen awareness that although relations with her ex-colonies remained subordinate to any struggle for balance in Europe, those same ex-colonies had a power to harass and, in certain circumstances, to tip that balance against her. And of course Canada remained—loyal, but also a hostage for Britain's good behavior. Thus, beyond its inescapable residue of bitterness, the conflict had bred a new prudential and mutual respect, the precondition of peaceful relations for the rest of the century and after.

There was little in the actual terms of the Treaty of Ghent to suggest that
it was about to usher in a period of Anglo-American pacification. Agreement was reached only when each side realized that it would have to
abandon its sine qua non; in the event, time secured what negotiations
could not. The Americans could not get a concession from the British on
impressment, since, for all they knew, they were going to need it to cope
with the escaped prisoner from Elba, but in fact no more Americans were
impressed then or later. The British had to abandon their design of getting an Indian state included in the treaty as a "permanent barrier" between the United States and Canada. The red man's alliance was sacrificed
in the interests of a paleface compromise. America's hopes of securing
some recognition of her neutral maritime rights were dashed; this had to
wait until, in a wholly European context, Britain signed the Declaration
of Paris in 1856. This declaration embodied almost all the principles for
which America had been contending—notably that "free ships make free
goods" and that "blockades to be binding, must be effective"—although,
by one of history's odder ironies, the United States declined the invitation to adhere. Two other silences in the treaty were eloquent reminders
of how the world had changed since 1783, when the Treaty of Versailles
had guaranteed to Britain the right to free navigation of the Mississippi
and to America the privilege of inshore fishing off British North America. Both claims lapsed at Ghent, reflecting the way in which United
States sovereignty had expanded in the West and Canadian identity had
consolidated in the East.

Wars create issues as well as resolve them. After 1812's fighting and
raiding, what were the boundaries of British North America and the
U.S.A. to be? Sensibly, the negotiators did not try to settle them at 3,000

miles distance and while the fighting was still in progress. Once the British abandoned, as they had to, the attractive idea of *uti possidetis,* keep what you've got, compromise was reached on the setting up of three joint commissions as in Jay's Treaty. This left the way clear for one of the more farsighted corollaries of the treaty, the Rush-Bagot agreement of 1817 by which both Great Britain and the United States pledged themselves not to maintain any armed forces on the Great Lakes—a notable pioneering example of disarmament by international agreement. What it has meant in the history, not only of North America, but indeed of the whole North Atlantic community, is beyond assessment, especially when it was almost imperceptibly accepted as applying to land fortifications as well as water.

There was one other corollary of Ghent, the commercial treaty signed in London six months later. The right to trade had been a cause of the war; trade, licit or illicit, had persisted throughout the war; trade bounded upward as soon as the ink was dry on the peacemakers' pens. In 1815 America and the British Empire shipped more goods to each other than in any other year since 1807. The significance of this was not lost on London or Washington. Initially what they agreed to was virtually an extension for four years of the commercial articles of Jay's Treaty. From 1816 onward there was full reciprocity in the transatlantic carrying trade. But the agreement of 1815 was followed in the ensuing decade by what in retrospect appears a peculiarly pointless and self-contradictory series of measures and countermeasures by Britain and the U.S.A. which reflected the rise or fall of conflicting pressures in each country—industry, agriculture, shipping, finance, the old habits of mercantilism dying hard in Britain and a countermercantilism feeding on rising nationalism in the United States, and each country trying to use its legislative controls to enable it to get an economic advantage over the other. Much of this maneuvering revolved around the old problem of access to the West Indies, but in 1830, when the principal antagonists in these maneuvers, John Quincy Adams and Canning, had disappeared from the scene, their successors, Andrew Jackson and Lord Aberdeen, negotiated an arrangement by which the West Indian trade was opened to the Americans while the U.S.A. opened her ports to British vessels coming from anywhere in the Empire. This signified the end of the British system of colonial monopoly; though the last of the mercantilist laws was not repealed until 1849, the triumph of Adam Smith was now assured.

The key indicator of what lay ahead in the North Atlantic relationship was provided not by the post-Ghent tit-for-tat but by the opening
in 1817, which Professor Albion rightly hails as an *annus mirabilis*,[1] of
a "packet-line" between New York and Liverpool of vessels with announced times of departure. From 4 January 1818 there were regular
fortnightly sailings of the Black Ball Line, to be succeeded by the Red
Star, the Swallowtail, and others, and then in 1840 by the Cunard.
Henceforth the gray wastes of the North Atlantic take their place be-
side the English Channel and the Mediterranean as a great highway of
maritime and economic intercourse, a uniting, not a dividing, expanse
of sea. This is reflected in the upward curve of transatlantic commerce,
a steady growth until the American panic of 1837 interrupted it for almost a decade, but then from 1846 soaring to new heights each year up
to the outbreak of the Civil War. And of this the great bulk was between
Britain and the U.S.A., with Britain providing a fairly consistent two-
fifths of American imports and taking a steadily increasing percentage
of her exports—from some 35 percent in 1830 to 50 percent and more
in the 1850s. A turning point in the balance of trade occurred around
1829; after that year Britain imports more than she exports. Cotton accounts for a large part of the change, as the mills of Lancashire consume
ever more of the products of Southern plantations. But there is also the
fact that the United States is developing her own industries and is thus
diversifying her own internal commerce.

But such shadings should not obscure the basic pattern of economic
relationships in the years between Ghent and Fort Sumter. The essential characteristics of this period are, as Frank Thistlethwaite has shown,[2]
first that there was an "Atlantic economy" and second that within this
the U.S.A. was a classic "underdeveloped country" and the United Kingdom a relatively mature economy, on the basis of which the one looked
to the other for capital, skills, and (initially) manufactured goods and
labor, while in return supplying raw materials and an outlet for enterprise. This is obscured, but not substantially modified, by the decision of
young America to develop its "American system" and shelter infant industries behind tariff walls. The tariffs were seldom high enough for long
enough to keep out the imported goods which were the essential payments for the surplus raw materials of America's plantations, prairies,
forests, and mines. On the British side these forty-five years cover a period of crucial transition, from reliance on a jealously guarded imperial

economy, breached but not destroyed by 1776, to an infinitely more profitable, if also more precarious, position as the dominant free-trading power of the world. In effect what Britain, emboldened by her leadership in the Industrial Revolution, did in this half century was to gamble her daily livelihood upon her ability to buy her food and her materials abroad and to pay for them by selling what she manufactured at home. In this gamble the United States played a decisive part. It was from her that Britain bought 80 percent of the cotton which accounted for two- to three-fifths of her total exports by the 1850s. What this dependence could mean was dramatically demonstrated during the Civil War. To the well-being of the United States as a whole no single import or export was as crucial as cotton was to Britain, though to the South the British market was the basis upon which not only the economy but, until Emancipation, its social structure depended. Yet the impact of the cotton connection was not confined to the South, since its plantation demands for food stimulated the development of America's breadbasket on the Great Plains. In turn, as the farmer of the Northwest depended more and more on cash crops, he looked to England and Europe to consume the surplus that made his profit. In another way the British economy was deeply relevant to American development. As capital surpluses piled up in Britain, the United States, despite political differences, assumed first place as the recipient of British credit. Her government, however democratic, did seem to be stable; her potentialities for development were rightly seen to be prodigious; and there existed a network of commercial and financial affiliations which independence and war had not broken.[3] Enormous quantities of American bonds were sold in Britain, the proceeds of which went to finance the canals, turnpikes, and railways which opened up trans-Allegheny America to the East and to the world. Between 1821 and 1837 foreign capital estimated at $125 million was invested in the United States. And most of that came from Britain. The 1837 crash, which provoked the Reverend Sydney Smith to his celebrated protest against American defaulting,[4] frightened the British investor off for a while, especially since he had his own decade of railroad mania in the forties, but within ten years the lure of railroad stock, conspicuously that of the Illinois Central Railroad in which poor Richard Cobden invested to such little profit, was drawing in British capital once more in something very like its previous volume.

Fundamentally more significant for the Anglo-American relationship

but a good deal harder to measure or chart is the other remaining form
of transatlantic traffic—the emigrant, as seen from Britain; the immigrant, when he arrives in America. He has his economic significance, of
course, sometimes quantifiable, as when he serves as a kind of fee-paying
human ballast on a timber- or cotton-carrying freighter on its return
voyage to North America, more often past measurement, as when he
contributes not only muscle but inherited or acquired skills to the American work force, at every level, from the mine to the boardroom. The
mercantilists, in their crude calculus, recognized the transference of economic resources that the emigrant represented by devising restraints on
his departure, but between 1825 and 1827 the last legal restrictions on
emigration were removed. Laissez passer actually preceded laissez faire.
The result was remarkable. Before 1815 the statistics are sketchy. But of
course the British base had been well and truly laid before Independence
and the British were probably (though not certainly) the largest element in the quarter of a million persons reputed to have entered the
United States between Yorktown and 1820. But from 1815 to 1826 the
flow of British emigrants to the U.S.A. seldom fell below 5,000 a year;
it then quickly accelerated and from 1830 to 1840 ran at nearly 30,000
a year. By 1847 it had risen to 142,000 and did not fall off again until
1854. Between 1815 and 1860 approximately 2,877,000 immigrants in
all entered the U.S.A. from Britain, substantially more than those entering from all other countries combined. What this meant for the political
and social makeup of the United States, what it represented in terms of
attitudes favorable or hostile to the country left behind, is a matter beyond the reach of certainty. One or two things may be noted. Of the
British total something like two million came from Ireland, many as a
result of the famine, and presumably had no kindlier feeling for England than did those of their fellow countrymen who remained behind.
Moreover, despite the alternatives open to emigrants, e.g., in the English-speaking colonies, it is significant that the United States attracted
by far the largest number—more indeed than all alternative destinations
combined. And this held true not only for the Irish but for all categories
of British emigrants.

Thus, in the whole complex interdependent economic world woven
mainly by British enterprise and the pound sterling, labor was fluid to a
degree hardly known before or since, and within this world it was the
British-American nexus which was dominant. For Britain, the United

States was her principal frontier of settlement, serving in large measure the same economic and social function as Frederick Jackson Turner's frontier served for the United States. For the U.S.A., Britain was, so to speak, its further East—London its super–Wall Street; Ireland and the teeming Midlands and the emptying Highlands its ultimate reservoir for the labor supply that unloaded on the quays of Boston, New York, and Philadelphia; Manchester, England, the dominant destination for almost all the southland cotton even after Manchester, New Hampshire, had gone into business as its American replica.[5]

In early Victorian Britain two attitudes toward this North Atlantic connection stand out clearly. The first is found in its purest form in those spokesmen for the new forces in economics and poltics who, in one form or another, echoed Cobden's conviction that "the cause of industry is the cause of humanity." They believed essentially that the machine, by creating a new abundance, would also, if allowed to draw its raw materials and distribute its products worldwide according to Manchester School criteria, maximize universal well-being and create a brotherhood of economic men whose mutual interests would smother the passions of nationalism and militarism. The United States they saw as the new country destined to give these beliefs their fullest embodiment, ahead of Britain in its democracy, in its freedom from antique social trammels, in its ready welcome to industry and enterprise. They welcomed every link which bound the two nations and especially the two economies closer together. In their advocacy of reform in British politics and society, the U.S.A. was their favorite exemplar and text. The multiplicity of associations which the Age of Improvement spawned in Britain for promoting human betterment and freedom had its counterpart, in nearly every instance, in the America of the Jacksonian Age and after, and the closest connection, through correspondence and personal contact, was maintained by each organization with its transatlantic opposite number.[6] Only two features of the United States stuck in the throats of these natural citizens of the Anglo-American community: slavery and protection. In consequence, despite old ties of blood and bible and existing bonds of cotton, this form of Anglo-American connection stopped at the Mason-Dixon line. The tariff, because its burden fluctuated and because most of the time it was not fully effective against the flood tide of British exports, was a less rigid impediment in the thinking of most of these reformers.

Internationalist, pacifist, and laissez faire, the Manchester School in the pre–Civil War years never actually got their hands on the levers of foreign policy. Nevertheless the translation of their ideas into diplomacy and especially into the diplomacy of Anglo-American relations was easy and clear enough. It was on all occasions to eschew resort to force, to emphasize the long-term identity of interests, to represent at court, as it were, the case for the United States—and, it may be said, in accordance with proper laissez faire principles, to be willing in all territorial disputes to cede to American claims, since territorial empire by definition was viewed as a vanity of pre-economic, militaristic man. And that held good for Canada too.

No such ideological unity marked the attitude which throughout the period stands in general opposition to Manchester School liberalism and informs, in varying degrees, the actual holders of political and diplomatic power. Viscount Palmerston, in view of his long tenure of the Foreign Office an appropriate spokesman, came near to summing up the prevalent anti-Cobdenite philosophy when he said, "Increased commercial intercourse may add to the links of mutual interest . . . but commercial interest is a link that snaps under the pressure of national passions."[7] Those who held this cautionary doctrine, however much they might embrace, as Palmerston did, the economic tenets of Adam Smith, even to the extent of holding with the young Disraeli that colonies were "millstones round our necks," would nonetheless view relations with the U.S.A. through rather differently colored spectacles. Their liberalism, no less revolted at slavery, would be even less likely to overlook the tariff, while their innate conservatism would see in American institutions poor or dangerous models for England and in American nationalism a force not sensibly different from nationalism everywhere else. They might welcome opportunities of joint action but they would be neither optimistic nor anxious about any longer-term alliance. They would be keenly alert to any conflict over territory in a continent where Britain and the U.S.A. were the principal elbowing neighbors. At the same time, while eschewing any pacifism, they would plan policy on the general assumption that differences would be settled peacefully. And they would be only one degree less aware than their radical opponents of the vital significance of the U.S.A. in Britain's world-based economy. It was in hands such as these that the British diplomatic relations with the U.S.A. rested between 1815 and 1860, hands made confident and shrewd by the dominant position which Britain occupied in the seas and markets of the world. By comparison British radicalism, for all its vitality, was, diplomatically speaking, an intermittent and interstitial force.

The unfinished diplomacy of Ghent hinged largely upon ticklish territorial adjustments. Of the three commissions appointed in the treaty the first completed its work in 1817, allocating the ownership of islands in Passamaquoddy Bay. The second had a more difficult task; it was 1821 before it agreed on a boundary line from the Saint Lawrence to Sault Sainte Marie, but it could not carry its agreement west of the Lake of the Woods because this involved the disputed question of the ownership of Oregon. The third, which had to delineate the frontier around northern New England to the sea, ran into profound disagreement over the boundary of Maine and adjourned in 1822. Meanwhile the question of Oregon got thrown into the same basket as the old question of fishing rights, to form the substance of negotiations in London in 1818. Out of these came a fairly generous concession by Britain, giving Americans fishing rights "for ever" off parts of Newfoundland and Labrador in return for their giving up claims in Nova Scotia and elsewhere. On Oregon an open-door policy to settlers from either side was accepted for ten years while the agreed boundary on the forty-ninth parallel was to run only to the Rockies from the Lake of the Woods. It was a bid by each side to buy time.

But larger issues impended. The Spanish Empire in South America was seen to be going the way the British had gone in the North when in 1820 insurrection in Spain weakened still further her grip on her colonies. To Britain, under the vigorous lead of Canning, this posed a challenge and an opportunity—a challenge to resist the baneful designs of the Holy Alliance and an opportunity to prize these rich territories out of the clutches of Spanish mercantilism. Britain had already acquiesced quite cheerfully in America's acquisition of Spanish Florida by the Adams-Onís Treaty of 1819 and had disavowed any interest in territories discarded by Spain. Her aim indeed was not to acquire territories in either the northern or the southern hemisphere. Her concern with the newly independent republics of Latin America was to attach them to that far more intangible and profitable sovereignty which was represented by British trade and the British pound—that, and a desire, to which Canning gave eloquent expression, to use the moral weight of constitutionalism and liberty against the autocratic principles of the Holy Alliance. In the spring of 1823 the French intervened in Spain and restored the reactionary King Ferdinand to full power. Would this be followed by a Franco-Spanish attempt at the resubjugation of Latin America? Canning, determined that it should not, proposed to Richard Rush, the American minister in London, the issuance of a joint declaration which recognized the independence of the former Spanish colonies, disclaimed any idea of acquiring them, but affirmed that "we could not see any portion of them transferred to any other power with indifference." It was, as Bradford Perkins says,[8] an offer of "a limited alliance," proceeding from the fact of certain common interests. The common elements were a desire to keep out other powers and a desire to have access to trade. In Canning's eloquence it was "the mother and the daughter" standing "together against the world." But the daughter was less interested than the mother in the anti–Holy Alliance element in Canning's diplomacy, and when it came to trade with Latin America, Britain and the U.S.A. were, after all, rivals. Nonetheless only British sea power could really keep European autocracies out of Latin America. It was Canning who extorted from France, in the Polignac Memorandum of October, the reluctant admission that the recovery of Spanish America was "utterly hopeless" and a consequent disavowal of territorial designs.

At the same time Britain and the U.S.A., despite their differences over Oregon, had been pursuing similar lines of protest against Russia's pretentious claims to control the West Coast from Alaska down to the fifty-first parallel. (This, incidentally, bore fruit in 1824 and 1825 when Russian treaties with the U.S.A. and the U.K. respectively accepted a southern boundary for Alaska at 50°40'.) The question for the Monroe administration, in face of these pressures, was whether to accept the offer embodied in the Canning-Rush proposals or not. Strong voices, including those of Jefferson and Madison, urged acceptance. John Adams, secretary of state, was cannier. He had the substance, in Britain's public pronouncements and commitments, but saw no reason for conceding the appearance. The American cockboat would not come in the wake of the British man-of-war. So President James Monroe issued his own, or at any rate John Adams's, "Doctrine," declaring:

1. that "the American continents are not to be considered as subjects for future colonization by any European power";
2. that the U.S.A. had nothing to do with the internal disputes of Europe;

3. that any interference by Europe with the independence of American
   states would be taken as manifesting an "unfriendly disposition"
   toward the U.S.A.

The anticolonization principle which was thus grafted onto Canning's
original proposals was not accepted by him; he made it clear that Britain
maintained her full rights to colonize any "unappropriated parts" of
America. To the affirmation of American isolation from the broils of
Europe he could have no objection and, despite the implied rebuff in
Adams's decision to go it alone, he could still claim subsequently to have
called in the New World to redress the balance of the Old. But for any
British observer of a later age, especially one who has witnessed the
American Laocoön wrestling with coils of isolationist dogma in relation
to two world wars, John Adams's astute suppression of the British role
in underpinning the Doctrine invites some reassessment. Perhaps it was
a necessary stage in the process by which a young nation learns to stand
on its own feet. But like all pretensions it was bought at a price; the
price was a widespread American illusion as to how far, to use Richard
Olney's later phrase, "the United States is sovereign on this continent"
and how far America's capacity to keep designing Europeans at bay was
due, first to the hearts of oak, and then to the ironclads of the Royal
Navy.

It was the late thirties before serious Anglo-American disagreement
broke out again. Maine, stubbornly insistent on her state sovereignty,
would not accept the award which in 1831 looked like concluding the
unfinished business of 1822; sporadic border conflict, "the Aroostook
War," dragged on into the late thirties. Then it got caught up in a larger
issue, the Papineau rebellion in Canada, which excited the hopes of
American annexationists once more. The Niagara incidents, with the Canadian destruction of the supply ship *Caroline,* could easily have developed into a serious conflict. But Palmerston in London and President
Martin Van Buren in Washington kept cool heads, while the reforms
embodied in Lord Durham's report on the Canadian troubles established
Canadian nationhood on a path from which not even the magnetic pull
of the U.S.A. would subsequently be able to shift her. The whole bundle
of Anglo-American irritations was disposed of in a classic exercise in
Anglo-American diplomacy, the Ashburton-Webster Treaty of 1842. The
elements of success included a British negotiator deeply committed to
the Anglo-American cause, Lord Ashburton of the House of Baring (see

p. 14 above); an American not above a little bamboozling of his own war hawks, Daniel Webster, with his *suppressio veri* and *suggestio falsi* over the maps of the Maine boundary; also a general willingness to split the difference where necessary and to settle on a paper formula where real agreement was impossible. This last was in relation to the slave trade. In theory the Americans were as committed to stopping this as the British; in fact Southern maneuvers had meant that nothing was being done. But of course the obnoxious British right of search was not made any more tolerable by being invoked in the moral context of freedom for Negroes. So American pride and British morality were traded off in a clause which established a largely illusory naval patrol off the coast of North Africa.

Though Britain would no doubt have welcomed an independent Texas (she sent consuls there in 1842), she was in no way disposed to erect serious obstacles in the way of American annexation, still less to get involved in the Mexican War that followed. Britain also stood down, in an equally unequivocal manner, as soon as American intentions and determination in California were fully evident. But Oregon was a slightly different matter. Here there were the claims of rival bands of settlers and an extravagant electioneering demand of James Polk ("Fifty-four Forty or Fight") which would have joined the U.S.A. to the southern boundary of Russia's claims and cut Canada short at the Rockies. In fact the British misplayed their hand. When Polk after election scaled down his demand to the far more reasonable 49° line, Richard Pakenham, the British minister, foolishly rejected the offer out of hand. It then took a year of threats, counterthreats, bluster, and eventually concession before a settlement could be reached in the form of a compromise which, as America's premier diplomatic historian well puts it, "was essentially surrender, surrender of territory to which his [Aberdeen's] government had the better claim."[9]

There remained one area in which the claims of manifest destiny and British imperialism might clash, that peculiarly ill-organized and strategically tempting zone south of Mexico which the fast developing technology of the nineteenth century marked out as the potential setting for an isthmian canal. In 1846 the Americans began the long process by securing treaty rights to construct a canal across the Isthmus of Panama. This spurred British interest further north where Belize (British Honduras) was already their territory; encouragement was given to forces on the "Mosquito Coast" to establish independence of Nicaragua, while the navy seized Tigre Island, which commanded the Caribbean approach to what was a very promising alternative canal route. Nicaragua appealed to the United States and ceded her exclusive rights to an isthmian canal. The new British minister to Washington, Sir Henry Lytton Bulwer, the brother of the novelist, was given instructions to negotiate. The outcome was the Clayton-Bulwer Treaty of 1850, which, behind deliberately ambiguous phrases governing the British position in Honduras and the Mosquito Coast, did embody a precise and cooperative solution of the canal question. Both parties agreed to facilitate the construction of a canal and bound themselves not to fortify or exercise exclusive control over it. Other states were invited to accede to the treaty on similar terms. It was a surprisingly forward-looking document for the construction of an international waterway. In fact it was too forward-looking. What it really reflected was a momentary balance of British and American power in this area. When that changed, the treaty would not survive.

Indeed, even as it was, the treaty's ambiguities proved troublesome. In 1852 the British made the disputed Bay Islands a crown colony, leading in 1854 to a protest invoking the noncolonization principle of the Monroe Doctrine. From Lord Clarendon, then at the Foreign Office, this elicited the riposte that the Doctrine "could be viewed only as the dictum of the distinguished personage who announced it, and not as an international axiom which ought to regulate the conduct of European states." Thus did the man-of-war retort to the cockboat which had declined its wake. But it was also significant that negotiations followed, which, though protracted, led at the end of the fifties to the conveniently face-saving arrangement by which Britain made treaties with Honduras ceding her the Bay Islands and with Nicaragua relinquishing claims to the Mosquito Coast.

Thus mid-Victorian Britain and "manifest destiny" America were learning to live and let live when America's own sectional conflict tore the fabric of her nationhood apart. The forty-five years after Ghent had been years of clashing exuberance on each side of the Atlantic, a period to which the cartoonists' images of confident John Bull and cocky Uncle Sam had been singularly appropriate. The old country was conscious of having completely recovered its poise after the loss of the thirteen colonies and the duel with France; she felt herself striding the world, all the more securely because her power rested even more on progress and industry at home than on territory abroad. The young country had found outlets for her energies within the natural limits of her continent and had won the most emphatic endorsement possible for her great experiment of independence and democracy in the thousands that fled from Europe to her receptive shores. Thus, for all their exuberance, the two great Atlantic powers had found the world large enough to accommodate them both. But this had not been done primarily by the establishment of exclusive spheres of interest. Though boundaries had been drawn for the avoidance of the cruder forms of conflict, the end of this period found the two countries more interdependent than at the beginning. They were component parts of a North Atlantic community—in trade, development, ideas, and endeavors. England was still the cultural capital of Anglo-Saxondom, but "the flowering of New England" reflected a self-confidence in the American muse that was transcending provincialism. From the days of Sydney Smith's "Who reads an American book?" to the best-seller triumph of *Uncle Tom's Cabin* is, in cultural relations, equivalent to the transition from impressment to the Declaration of Paris—and covers almost exactly the same generation of Anglo-American experience. It is an experience of reacquaintance, of kindred on either side of the Atlantic getting to know one another again, on terms of equality and mutual respect. Perhaps the truly Atlantic figure of the period is Charles Dickens, triumphantly successful in Britain and the United States, yet in permanent protest against the inhumanities of both, feted in the States (and defrauded of his royalties), idolized in London but at no ease in Victoria's Zion, a cornucopia of genius whose creations enhance the common heritage of both worlds.

4

For the smooth working of any international system the outbreak of a
civil war is bound to be a complicating factor. Not only does it impair
the efficient functioning of the state affected; it also in most instances
impairs the relations of that state with its principal neighbors. If those
neighbors are predatory, it offers them dangerous temptations to fish in
troubled waters; if they are innocent of such designs, the preservation of
their neutrality may still expose them to pressures from either or both
of the parties to the civil conflict. The American Civil War, as the largest internecine conflict of the nineteenth century, and indeed one of the
bloodiest wars to date, displayed these features to an unusual degree.
Britain, as the principal guarantor and regulator of the nineteenth-
century international system, and also as the closest and most important
of the United States "neighbor" powers, found herself willy-nilly and
despite the illusory buffer of distance swiftly and intricately caught up
in the consequences of the war. Whatever any dabbler in realpolitik
might imagine to be the long-term advantages for Britain of having the
dominant North American power split into two, there could be no disputing the immediately painful and embarrassing effects of the struggle
for the United Kingdom. She found herself in a situation where each
warring party regarded her as having a greater obligation of friendship
than in fact she had. And since on each side of the Atlantic opinion was
free, free to express itself in speech and writing, free to elect, demote,
and instruct its leaders, it was certain that the tasks of the policymakers
would be complicated by an uprush of opinions on every side, abrasive
as well as emollient, without any very clear indication for much of the
time which sentiment really represented the majority view.

There is still a good deal of controversy about the exact condition of

British public opinion on the war. Apart from the built-in difficulties, at all times and places, of "measuring" public opinion, there is a special difficulty in the Britain of the 1860s. Here was indeed a free society, in that open expression of opinion on political issues was possible and habitual, but it was also an aristocratic society in which the representation of the people lagged far behind the political awareness. The Reform Act of 1867 was grossly overdue. Thus opinion in Parliament was far from being a mirror of opinion in the country, while opinion in the press, closely tied to the existing system of property representation, was an almost equally chancy reflection of what its readers thought.

Moreover, opinion on the war on both sides of the Atlantic was at the mercy of a remarkable set of cross-pressures, of conflicting factors resulting from the paradoxes of the conflict and the internal contradictions of British and American societies. Thus in America the North was industrial, liberal, protectionist, and democratic, while the South was rural, increasingly illiberal, free trading, and, at least in certain important respects, aristocratic. In most people's eyes the North was antislavery and the South dedicated to its peculiar institution. Britain too was in many respects divided—into an aristocracy and a rising, self-assertive democracy, into liberals and tories, into an industrial North and a rural South, into protectionists and free traders. Did this mean that British aristocrats and agrarians favored the South? Only if they were able to suppress their antislavery feelings. Did it mean that northern industrialists and workers favored the North? Only if they forgot the spread-eagle-ism of the forties and fifties, overlooked the Morrill Tariff of 1861, and made light of the fact that the South was the indispensable source of supply for their principal raw material, cotton. And what of the Whigs, aristocratic but liberal, straddling the two Englands, still the dominant force in British politics? They were bound to deplore slavery, but they were equally committed to self-determination; they had espoused the cause of America in 1776; was not the South merely asserting the same claims in 1861?

These contradictions were intensified, for Britain, by the particular circumstances surrounding the actual outbreak of the war. Had it broken out immediately on the election of Abraham Lincoln, its character as a war for the Union would have been clearer. Even so, it was not immediately apparent to British onlookers why the Southern "sisters," however erring, should not be allowed "to go in peace." The peculiar set of constitutional and moral values which a leader like Lincoln identified with the preservation of the Union was too intricate and too American for its immediate apprehension across the Atlantic. When, moreover, the war followed, not immediately upon secession or other violations of the Constitution, but with apparent deliberation after the attempted provisioning of Sumter, British incomprehension easily shaded into cynicism. The role of slavery as an issue was obscured by Lincoln's acceptance, indeed active wooing, of the support of the border slave states and by his denial of any intention to interfere with slavery in states where it already existed. The passage of the Morrill Tariff offended a free-trade public and encouraged the illusion that the war was at least as much about commercial policy as about human liberty. Finally, whatever might be thought of the long-term strength of the North, it was hard in 1861 —and for some years after—to believe that the war could lead to the subjugation and successful reconstruction of the South; there was no precedent for a state of five million people being thus reabsorbed into a democratic unity. Thus when Lord John Russell declared in a speech at Newcastle in October 1861 that the two parties were contending not upon slavery, nor even upon free trade versus protection, but "the one side for empire and the other for independence," he was expressing what a very broad band of British opinion at that time thought about the struggle. He was also, incidentally, reflecting the irritation and suspicion which he, as foreign secretary, felt about his Unionist opposite number, William Seward, whose reputation as a truculent Anglophobe and "manifest destiny" expansionist preceded his appointment and considerably complicated the task of the North's advocates in Britain.

Thus opinion in Britain was slow to develop a firm appreciation of the issues of the war. The initial liberal view of the South as a nation struggling for free trade and self-determination yielded only slowly to the alternative liberal view of the South as a slavocracy trying to stem the tide of history in its own inhumane interests. The Palmerstonian view of the North as an aggressive, protectionist rival, in commerce, along the Canadian boundary, and on the high seas, gave way equally slowly to the middle class's conviction that they had more in common with Lincoln's kind of Union than with Jefferson Davis's kind of Confederacy. But sympathies, whether clear or confused, were only an imperfect guide to behavior. From Sumter to Appomattox it remained true, as Walter Bagehot remarked, that though the mass of Englishmen were singularly divided in their sympathies, they were also singularly united in their intentions. Those intentions were simple: they were to avoid involvement in the war and to preserve Britain's traditional rights as a maritime power. The first dictated neutrality, the second dictated a prudent insistence at every disputed point upon the principles recently enshrined in the Declaration of Paris of 1856. Though there were errors of tactics and timing, these objectives were adhered to on the whole with remarkable consistency throughout the war.

The Declaration of Paris represented the highest common factor of agreement among European powers about the rules which should govern war at sea; in particular it was a kind of codification of the principles which Britain, as the strongest naval power and, as it were, policeman of the seas, recognized as in her interest to accept and to enforce. In essence the rules provided for the abolition of privateering and for the protection of neutral goods even on enemy ships or enemy goods on neutral ships, provided they were not contraband of war. Finally, they required that blockades, in order to be binding, must be effective—i.e., sustained by a force sufficient really to prevent access to the coast of the enemy. With the exception of the ban on privateers these were all principles for which the U.S.A. had fought when she was neutral and Britain was at war and which she had vainly tried to write into the Treaty of Ghent. However, as a country with no standing navy but a large merchant marine, she did not share the British belief in the desirability of outlawing the privateer. For this reason the U.S.A. did not accede to the declaration, and in the Civil War, as a far stronger naval power than the South, she soon found some of its principles distasteful.

The war's effects were first felt in Britain in two connections. The first was Lincoln's imposition of a blockade on the South. Initially this was little more than a paper blockade, since the North had only three naval vessels with which to enforce it. Britain publicly insisted that the blockade would be recognized only to the degree to which it was effective. In fact, however, the blockade's legality was not seriously challenged, partly because it was thought, with justice, that the bolder British merchantmen would be willing to run it at their own risk, but more fundamentally because it was in Britain's long-term interests both to avoid needless conflicts with the U.S.A. and, as the greatest employer of the blockade weapon herself, to get its employment as widely recognized as possible. There was, however, a legal paradox about Lincoln's blockade: to impose a blockade was to recognize the belligerency of the South, yet Lincoln wished the Confederates to be treated as individual rebels, not collective secessionists. His blockade action therefore gave some valuable support to the British when they had to confront the second issue thrown up by the war—the status of the South.

Even before Sumter the Northern administration, through Seward and his spokesmen, was putting it about that recognition of the South by any foreign government would be regarded as a *casus belli*. Yet when even the North was unwilling to pursue to its logical conclusion the doctrine that Southerners were merely rebels, it was obvious that some sort of recognition of the Confederacy's status was essential for a state, like Britain, that had consuls in Southern ports, Southern commercial connections to protect, and a mercantile marine plying the Atlantic and the Caribbean—quite apart from the peculiar problem of the cotton trade itself. The solution adopted was to recognize Southern belligerency but not Confederate statehood. This was embodied in the Proclamation of Neutrality issued on 13 May. How serious the hazards of even this limited recognition were felt to be is shown by the virtually simultaneous reinforcement of the North American Squadron of the fleet and the dispatch to Canada of three regiments and a field battery.

To Charles Francis Adams, arriving in London as minister for the Union, this proclamation, immediately preceding his arrival, seemed a deliberately timed snub and an ugly omen (though, in fact, it involved him in less embarrassment than if it had been issued after his arrival). His unbending New England severity and his inherited Adamsite suspicion of British patrician designs were guarantees that his tenure of the London embassy would be a prickly one—for him and his hosts. In fact, given the situation, it was no bad thing that Britain had a difficult Adams to remind them how serious the consequences of a false step might be, especially since Adams's bark was generally worse than his bite and Seward's excesses were generally modified in his hands. Moreover, in Washington Britain was well served by Lord Lyons, a diplomat of experience and cool temper. Just as, by degrees, Adams unlearned most of his distrust of Palmerston and Russell, so Lyons came to learn the quality of Lincoln and to win the trust of Seward.

It was not long before diplomatic skills and national good sense were put fully to the test in both London and Washington. The South, eager for full recognition, lost no time in dispatching a commission to Eu-

rope. A. Dudley Mann, William L. Yancey, and Pierre A. Rost all arrived in London in advance of Charles Francis Adams. They were
granted interviews by Russell but their hopes that this would lead to
recognition were increasingly frustrated. In September the Confederacy,
disappointed at their failure, disbanded the commission and dispatched
instead two new representatives, James Mason and John Slidell. However, the British vessel which was carrying them from Cuba to London,
the *Trent,* was intercepted in the Bahama Channel by Captain Charles
Wilkes on the *San Jacinto* of the United States Navy. Mason and Slidell
were seized and taken prisoner to Boston and Wilkes was hailed as a
national hero. When the news reached London in November, there was
a storm of protest. There followed the well-known incident of the dispatch to Lyons of a note demanding their immediate release, softened,
however, from its original asperity by the emendations of a dying Prince
Consort. However, peace was served not only by the exercise of these
surviving shreds of monarchical authority but also by the absence of a
transatlantic telegraph[1] and the wise exercise of ambassadorial discretion. Lyons took advantage of what by now was his much improved relationship with Seward to prepare him unofficially for the ominous character of the note he had eventually to present. Meanwhile John Bright
and Richard Cobden were in touch with their old friend Charles Sumner, chairman of the Senate Foreign Relations Committee, apprising him
both of the seriousness of the incident and of Britain's basic goodwill
toward the North. Thus the gales of public feeling and the inexorable
minimum demands of national honor were both kept within bounds by
two techniques of appeasement which have been characteristic of the
Anglo-American relationship—the first, the maintenance even in moments of stress of decent personal relations between the official figures
involved, and the second, the supplementing of the official diplomatic
exchanges by unofficial communications of groups and individuals whose
friendships cut across narrow national loyalties. In consequence wiser
counsels prevailed. Mason and Slidell were released and formulas were
found to save national face. The sharpest corner of wartime diplomacy
was turned.

By now the effects of the war were being felt on the domestic front
in Britain as a result of the vicissitudes of the cotton-manufacturing industry of Lancashire. In normal times one-fifth of the British population
was estimated to be dependent directly or indirectly on the cotton indus-

try and one-tenth of the nation's wealth was invested in it. The South, which normally provided 78–84 percent of Britain's imports of raw cotton, had always seen this as her strength and hope. "King Cotton" would compel British recognition and support. To such lengths did this conviction go that the South in the autumn of 1861 actually imposed an almost total embargo on cotton exports to accelerate Britain's (and Europe's) realization of King Cotton's indispensability. There have been few more hubristic miscalculations. In 1859 and 1860 the South had produced the largest cotton crops on record and British imports had risen proportionately. When war broke out, the immediate problem in England was consequently overproduction, and stocks of raw cotton in hand in December 1861 were actually greater than in 1860. However, in 1862 the pinch began to be felt, and as the year went on, Lancashire's staple industry was on its knees. Many mills went bankrupt; all were on very short time. By the autumn 412,000 out of 500,000 cotton operatives were on relief; it has been estimated that, taking into account those who were dependent on these unfortunates, two million people in all were without means of support in December 1862. A slow recovery got under way in July 1863, as cotton supplies improved, from blockade runners making a 300 percent profit and from India, where the government stimulated production. The question remains, why did the cotton famine so little affect British policy toward the war?

Historians for whom the argument from economic causation had the same fascination as it possessed for Confederate statesmen did for a time think that they had found the conclusive reason for Britain's refusal to bow down before King Cotton. It was the superior power of King Wheat. In the years 1860–63 Britain imported abnormal quantities of wheat, her own grain harvests being abnormally poor. Most of this grain came from America, which supplied a half of Britain's total consumption. In this sense Britain was dependent on the products of the Northern prairie states for her staff of life. But only in this sense. She could as easily have bought it from eastern Europe or Russia, as indeed she did in 1864 and 1865. The main reason for buying American wheat was that it was the export by which the North could best pay for the war material which it was importing from Britain. There was nothing in this traffic which gave the North any economic trump with which to take the South's cotton trick.

There was, of course, a more general economic motive for not offend-

ing the North. The war brought profits to all those industries whose exports benefited directly, by their greatly expanded sales of all kinds, including munitions, to the North—and also indirectly, by excluding the
North Americans from many overseas markets in which they were rivals
and by virtually eliminating the American mercantile marine, Britain's
main competitor in the carrying trade. None of the commercial interests
concerned stood to gain by the British government's risking war with
the North in the protection of its cotton supply.

But it is unnecessary to seek such an exclusively economic explanation
for the comparatively acquiescent attitude of the British government
toward the cotton famine. The fundamental fact remains that none of
the national interests affected was sufficiently crucial to induce the government to run the risk of war with the North. It was one thing to com-
plain. It was another thing to put the nation at hazard. Moreover it was,
alas, true that those whom the famine hit hardest were also the most
politically impotent. The mill owners—if they did not go under in the
first wave of bankruptcies—were generally able to survive tolerably well
on higher prices and lower production. It was their workpeople, whom
the owners swiftly laid off, who carried the real losses of the industry.[2]
And they, in a Britain which was still five years away from the 1867 Reform Act, were still without votes, even though they did not lack spokesmen. It is, of course, true that the government took their plight into
account in framing its policy. Throughout 1862 the government considered, in concert with the French (who on the whole took their lead from
Britain but were erratic partners in the diplomatic waltz), whether the
time was ripe, if not for recognition of the Confederacy, at any rate for
offering mediation in the war. Individual ministers might go further—
there was Gladstone's notorious speech at Newcastle, which excited
Southern hopes and Northern fears[3]—but the cabinet always came back
to the same conclusion, that the cotton famine did not begin to constitute an adequate reason for a change of policy.

In this they were fortified by the fact that middle-class, liberal Britain, under the intellectual leadership of John Stuart Mill, Goldwin Smith,
and John E. Cairns, and under the political leadership of Bright, Cobden, and William E. Foster, was increasingly throwing its weight on the
side of the North. For such would-be Northern sympathizers, Lincoln's
preliminary emancipation proclamation of September 1862 and the operative proclamation of January 1863 were decisive. At last the war be-

gan to take on the clear lineaments of a struggle against slavery. The heart of Victorian England, home of the most bourgeois of European monarchies, began to beat in time with that of the rail splitter who was also the "Great Emancipator," and the Gettysburg speech chimed in with the rising pressure of demand for a further extension of manhood suffrage in Britain.

The collapse of King Cotton's pretensions did not end the problems which the Confederacy posed for Britain. With virtually no industrial base of its own, the South looked to Britain for much of its armament. Its purchasing agents were enterprising and skillful in evading such restrictions as British neutrality imposed. These were not as strict as the North would have wished. The British Foreign Enlistment Act forbade the fitting out of any vessel of war which was intended to serve either belligerent, but it provided no mechanism for preventing such lawbreaking, merely penalties when guilt was established. And, in accordance with the usual principles of British justice, innocence was presumed until guilt was established. This came near to saying that it was impossible to prove a breach of the law until the offending vessel was in belligerent hands. This was exactly what occurred in 1862 when, despite evidence provided by Adams that a ship under construction at Liverpool known as "No. 290" was intended for the South, the vessel was allowed to slip out to sea. She was later equipped with guns and munitions sent from England and began a two-year life as the *Alabama,* a highly successful "commerce destroyer."

The North's reaction took the form, initially, of a proposal to authorize Northern privateers that would be designed to pursue British ships which might "turn Confederate." The ominous implications of this were not lost on either side; Lyons warned Seward that it could lead to war, but in London the government took a firmer line with the next prospective Confederate craft, the *Alexandra.* She was detained, on suspicion. Public opinion supported the government; Seward adopted a much more conciliatory tone. But while the *Alexandra* case was pending in the courts, Adams presented Russell with far more alarming evidence of the construction at Laird's shipyard of two rams with great destructive potentialities and warned "it would be superfluous to point out that if they sail this is war." The rams were detained, despite their elaborate disguise as vessels which French agents were commissioning for the pasha of Egypt. The case was never pushed to a conclusion in British courts

because the government bought the rams and so evaded a possibly embarrassing decision. But it ended the use of Britain by the South as a
naval construction base. The Cotton Loan (so called because the South's
cotton crop provided its guarantee), launched in Britain while these disputes were in progress, reflected, in its melancholy decline to a 36 percent discount in the summer of 1863, the depth to which serious support
for the Confederate cause had sunk in Britain. In August the Confederacy recalled Mason from his abortive mission in London. Though in fact
he remained in Britain for a considerable time afterward, the South's
hopes of recognition never seriously revived.

The last year of the war was devoid of special diplomatic incident.
The prickly Mr. Adams mellowed with the triumph of his mission and
became, in the words of his scarcely less prickly son, "a kind of American Peer of the Realm," "a kind of leader of Her Majesty's American
Opposition." The sacrificial death of Lincoln was accorded in Britain
a tribute of grief and respect that transcended previous disagreements
between pro-Southerners and pro-Northerners. In the general election
which befell in July 1865 no M.P. who had supported the North was
defeated and several outspoken Southern sympathizers lost their seats.
But this did not mean that relations between a self-righteously triumphant North and a Britain which had presumed upon "a detached and
distant situation" would be easy. Queen Victoria noted in her diary for
12 February 1865:

Talked of America and the danger, which seems approaching,
of our having a war with her as soon as she makes peace; of the
impossibility of our being able to hold Canada, but we must struggle
for it; and far the best would be to let it go on as independent kingdom
under an English prince![4]

5

1866–1895: America and Victorian England

The Union which emerged victorious from the war against its other self, the aristocratic, slave-owning, decentralized, agrarian, backward-looking South, was a very different sovereign power from the rather irresolute entity which had eventually picked up the gage at Fort Sumter. The United States of 1865 was a *power*. By Appomattox the Union army mustered over a million men, equipped with weapons as advanced and abundant as those of any military power in previous history. At sea, the once derisory Union navy had 671 vessels of war, mounting a total of 4,610 guns; of these 39 were ironclads, of which a further 29 were building—this at a time when the United Kingdom had only 30 ironclads in the Royal Navy. On the American continent the U.S.A. was clearly invincible; at sea she equally clearly enjoyed superiority in American waters.

But there was more to the Union's strength than this. The nation which had crushed its great rebellion had revealed, to itself and to the world, an astonishing resilience and wealth of resources, human and material, in the process. Throughout the war the Union continued to attract the European immigrant—over 600,000 fresh immigrants came between 1860 and 1865. Western settlement proceeded apace and with it railroad development—railroad mileage doubled in the war years. This was of a piece with the remarkable expansion of every form of economic activity under the pressure of the war. In agriculture there was a swift response to the new opportunities provided by farm mechanization, and in industry not only the sinews of war but the consumer goods of peace were being produced in an unprecedented volume by American workmen in American factories. Though the war boosted imports and hampered exports, it stimulated domestic production as never before. Americans learned, to an unprecedented degree, to live off the products of their own hands. Economically, the war marked a shift for the United States from colonial to metropolitan status; no longer would she simply produce raw materials and exchange them for imported manufactures. Henceforward this particular cycle of the Atlantic economy was broken, never to be reconstituted. By 1874 the U.S.A. was enjoying a favorable balance of trade, exports exceeding imports overall. Similarly the U.S.A.'s heavy dependence upon the London financial market was coming to an end. The decade after the end of the war saw the emergence of a money market in New York which dealt directly with Germany and Holland as well as with the United Kingdom.

Some elements in this newly established parity of power waned as quickly as they had emerged. The Grand Army of the Republic melted away with the end of hostilities; by 30 September 1867 its total strength was down to 56,815 officers and men, a decline that continued in ensuing years. The navy was similarly cut back. By the end of 1870 there were less than 200 vessels in all, mounting a total of only 1,300 guns, and of these nearly all were obsolete or unseaworthy. The U.S.A. lost as little time as possible in reverting to what a later generation was to call "normalcy," meaning then, as later, the pursuit of economic prosperity in a world assumed to be safe for American development at home and peaceful penetration abroad.

Thus Queen Victoria's premonitions of a war with the United States in which the possession of Canada would be at the heart of the conflict were shown to be misplaced. Yet they sprang in 1865 from a combination of circumstances which certainly looked disturbing. The wise and restraining hand of Lincoln was no more; in the erratic councils of Andrew Johnson, Seward was rightly perceived to be a figure of exceptional determination and considerable aggressiveness. Victory left Northern opinion more than ever convinced of the righteousness of its cause and the impropriety of a British neutrality which was viewed as philo-Confederate. The *Alabama* claims hung in the air as a reminder of Albion's perfidy. Without doubt in such a context the situation of Canada was hazardous and, to troublemakers, all too inviting.

Troublemakers were not slow to take advantage of the opportunity. The Fenian Brotherhood, formed in the U.S.A. in 1858 to promote the independence of Ireland, enjoyed an accession of strength from the recruitment of American Irish ex-servicemen at the end of the war. In

June 1866, as a way of striking at Britain and in hopes of inspiring a
colonial revolt, 600 or so Fenians launched a raid into Canada at Niagara. The raid turned out to be wholly abortive, but though the U.S. authorities collaborated with the Canadians in quashing this particular "invasion," it was 1870 or 1871 before really vigorous American action was
taken to stop minor repetitions of such an incident along the lengthy
frontier from Vermont to the Red River Valley. Not for the first or the
last time a singular gulf of comprehension separated the U.S.A. and
Canada. At a time when the American secretary of state was telling a
Boston audience that he knew that "Nature designs that this whole continent . . . shall be, sooner or later, within the magic circle of the American Union," the deliberations within the various provinces of Canada
were culminating in the passage of the British North America Act of
July 1867, establishing the self-governing Dominion of Canada. Though
accelerated by the threats of U.S. expansionists, the federation had been
in the making since 1864 and was, of course, the product of a long historical process. In this sense the act of 1867 only put the constitutional
seal on the fact of Canadian nationhood, but its significance for Anglo-
American relations was nonetheless real. Henceforward, though "spread-
eagle" Americans would still voice dreams, or threats, of Canadian annexation, the issue lay between Washington and Ottawa, with Britain
only a highly interested bystander. Henceforward too, though Canada's
comparative weakness limited her power to stand alone, she was much
less of a hostage in North America for Britain's good behavior.

Fortunately for all concerned, the policies of Britain and the U.S.A.
quickly turned the corner of postwar hypertension into two decades of
remarkably untroubled diplomatic relations. The *Alabama* claims, which
at one stage looked like developing into an intractable wrangle—as when
Charles Sumner in the U.S. Senate asserted that they could only be met
by the cession of Canada—yielded to the good sense of the Gladstone
government which was willing to express its "regret" for the escape and
depredations of the *Alabama*[1] and to the emollient, third-party role of
the Canadians. The decision to submit the claims to arbitration was a
significant step forward in the settlement of international disputes. The
willingness of Charles Francis Adams, on his own responsibility as
American arbitrator, to drop the "indirect" claims, which would have
saddled Britain with the cost of the "prolongation" of the war, removed
the last serious obstacle to settlement, and on 14 September 1871, in

what is still the Salle d'Alabame at Geneva, the arbitrators gave their award of $15,500,000 in gold. Professor Samuel Bemis well assesses the result as "one of the most excellent investments the British Empire ever made. It bore rich dividends in international accord and in strengthening the maritime defenses of the British Empire. At a cost equal to no more than what would be then required to build a few cruisers, Great Britain had stopped forever the possibility of small naval enemies building fleets in neutral territory in future wars. During the Boer War she reaped her reward for her wise policy at Washington in 1871, just as during the World War she profited beyond measure by her far-sighted decision not to protest the blockade during the Civil War in the United States."[2] In the Britain of 1871 these advantages were hidden from public gaze. As a British historian of the period puts it, "Posterity praises the extreme wisdom [of the Gladstone government in taking] a wise but unpopular course; but what stood out at the time was its extreme unpopularity."[3]

Why was the settlement of the *Alabama* claims followed by two decades of almost complete diplomatic inactivity between Washington and London, the longest period of amicable inanition that Anglo-American relations have ever known? To some extent the answer lies in the fact that with the territorial boundaries of the U.S.A. settled, with Canada a self-governing dominion, and with neither Britain nor the U.S.A. engaged in hostilities with third parties on the high seas, all the previous familiar areas of dispute and conflict were closed. In the United States this was both a cause and a consequence of a national turning away from issues of foreign policy in favor of domestic concerns. When the most searching and disinterested of British students of America, James Bryce, subjected the "American commonwealth" to his shrewd gaze in 1888, he judged it unnecessary, in a book of over a hundred chapters, to devote more than one of them explicitly to foreign affairs. "We have hitherto found no occasion to refer to them save in describing the functions of the Senate; and I mention them now as the traveller did the snakes in Ireland, only to note their absence, and to indicate some of the results ascribable thereto."[4] The America he had before him as he wrote was the America which had turned from the conflicts and agonies of civil war and reconstruction to the vastly more agreeable and manageable tasks of internal expansion and development. The downgrading of foreign politics in the minds of both the electorate and the elected was but a special case of that downgrading of politics in general which was the hallmark of the Gilded Age. This is the period when "the best men" "do not go into politics," when the great names are not those of the incumbents of the White House and State Department, but those of the presidents of banks, railroads, and big business corporations. This America is being shaped not by the Rutherford B. Hayeses and Chester A. Arthurs, but by the Carnegies, Pierpont Morgans, and Rockefellers. And in these years the territorial confines of the United States provide for most of the time ample outlets for the ruthless energies of the magnates of business. The "giddy minds" that George Washington had once warned against "foreign quarrels" could now work off any of their surplus aggressiveness in the contests of the very aptly named "empires" of conflicting barons of industry and finance.

In Britain the situation was rather different. The imperial expansion which had been a dominant theme of so much British history pre- and post-Yorktown takes in the late nineteenth century a new course. With the establishment of a self-governing Canada, North America ceases to be an area of expansion or conflict. South of the Rio Grande there are British territorial holdings, but of secondary importance; not since Canning's time have they been regarded as beachheads for further expansion. Africa and, to a lesser extent, the Far East are now the growing points of empire, and these lie far from America's shores. Above all Britain continues to live by trade, and the North American market, for both imports and exports, loses nothing of its importance in a world in which Cobdenite aspirations for universal free trade have failed of realization and in a Europe where new considerations of economic power, like the kaiser's *Zollverein,* threaten to limit the entry of British goods. Moreover, as new power blocs build up in Europe around an aggressive Germany and a *revanchiste* France, Britain develops her recurrent insular concern both about being drawn into combinations for which she does not care and about being left isolated and friendless. The U.S.A.'s actual economic and potential military power makes her, in such a context, a state to be respected and never needlessly offended. She exists, by virtue of distance and her chosen isolationism, at a comparatively low level on Britain's strictly diplomatic horizon for most of these years, but she is never out of Britain's commercial, cultural, or social sight. She occupies a distinctive position as the inheritor of a common language and certain common traditions, with affiliations only less close than those of the white dominions, yet outside the accepted circle of power-balancing Old World governments that make up the state system within which most of Britain's official diplomatic business is done.

The public opinion which, in both countries, lies behind the overt governmental action of these years presents an interesting development when compared with that of the antebellum period. The national hypersensitiveness which was equally characteristic of the "spread-eagle" America of the *Martin Chuzzlewit* era and of the bombastic Britain of Lord Palmerston's prime gives way, in general, to a more relaxed mood. In America, the generation between 1865 and 1895 was, Henry Adams said, "mortgaged to the railways"—and, he added, to "capital, banks, mines, furnaces, shops, power-houses," etc. By comparison, politics was scarcely a serious matter, and foreign politics not serious at all. Elections were sporting contests between logically indistinguishable factions, in relation to which established Americans had established attachments, as seasoned fans have their preferred sporting allegiances. Only new Americans, the immigrants who poured in, a swiftly swelling flood, once the Civil War was out of the way, were, so to speak, "available" for recruitment to one side or the other. The pursuit of the immigrant vote became a central preoccupation of the politics of the period, to which superficially serious considerations of national policy were readily subordinated. Of this vote no component was more numerous or more demanding than the Irish-Americans, with their tenacious and ever-refreshed antipathy to Britain. This gave to the politics of the period a recurrent Anglophobic tone. It provided in the case of poor Sir Lionel Sackville-West in 1888 the classic cautionary story of what a British ambassador must not do.[5] It reached depths of self-parody, as when the U.S. Senate in 1886 refused to include "dynamiting" among the list of extradictable crimes, because of its evocative association with terrorism in Ireland. It was a sentiment always available for painless exploitation. But it had little or nothing to do with the real shaping of Anglo-American relations during the period. It did not even lead the U.S. government to interest itself seriously in the British misgovernment of Ireland.

The dominance of the business motif in American life and policies during these years was not incompatible with—indeed by action and reaction it positively stimulated—an American rediscovery of the Old World in general and of Britain in particular. It was not only that the profits of Andrew Carnegie's steel mills paid the bills for those "Carne-

gie Free Libraries" that rose, like literary citadels, in the small towns of
Scotland, England, and Wales,[6] or that George Peabody's department
stores made possible the rehousing of some of London's poor. Besides
philanthropy, the new aristocracy of New World commerce and industry reached out by a natural if clumsy instinct to their longer-established
opposite numbers in Europe. Culturally, they imported their traditional
symbols: the Renaissance palaces rose on Fifth Avenue, the French cha-
teaux above the beach at Newport, Rhode Island. Pierpont Morgan, by
a natural extension, had his castle in Hertfordshire. The landed aristocracy of Britain, whose own wealth by now was almost equally interpene-
trated by industry and finance, began to recognize an affinity which was
none the less real for being occasionally forced and artificial. The call of
wealth to wealth bridged the gulf between blue blood and red, and soon
marriage was linking the oldest names of Debrett with the richest en-
tries in the Social Register. The wedding of Lord Randolph Churchill
to Jennie Jerome in 1874 is generally considered the entering wedge, to
be followed by none more readily than other members of the same family—the eighth Duke of Marlborough to Mrs. Lilian Hammersley of
New York in 1888, the ninth Duke to Consuela Vanderbilt in 1895.
Politicians seemed to be particularly drawn to American matches—Sir
William Harcourt married the daughter of John Lothrop Motley, the
American historian; Joseph Chamberlain the daughter of William C.
Endicott, the secretary of war in Grover Cleveland's first administration;
Lord Curzon the daughter of a Chicago merchant and real estate specu-
lator. But an even more consistent pattern was that of the attachment of
dollars to title and vice versa. Less crude was the appeal which second-
generation American wealth, or merely average affluence, found in a society less overtly and intensely committed to economic pursuits and sat-
isfactions than their own. The generation which had mortgaged itself to
railways was also the generation which launched itself with unequaled
intensity and consistency upon the annual Grand Tour of Europe and
England (the two were not infrequently kept apart in American thinking and terminology), seeking in antiquity or conservatism or in mere
leisure the values it missed in Wall Street or Main Street. It found its
great memorialist and literary monument in the Henry James of the first
period, who, writing out of his direct experience, recaptured with every
nuance and subtlety young America's insistent and yet uneasy relationship with old Europe and particularly with old England.

While American wealth was reaching out to British conservatism, British radicalism was moving toward a new assessment of its relations with the U.S.A. It was in radical eyes no longer so obvious that America represented the wave of the future. In fact, of course, this simply reflected the distance that Britain had already traveled along the American road. The Reform Act of 1867 and its successor of 1884 virtually ended the anomaly of a restricted franchise, and British parties, like their American counterparts, moved to a new basis in mass organization. Though the Church of England was not disestablished nor the House of Lords abolished, neither seemed an active obstacle to religious freedom and democracy, while the road to mass education had been opened by W. E. Forster's Education Act of 1870. But it was not only that British democracy was catching up; to many radicals it seemed that American democracy was losing ground. The Gilded Age was not a good advertisement for its moral values or its party system. Could it be that mass participation in politics meant corruption and the caucus? This was a charge that the National Liberal Federation never wholly lived down.

To many an ordinary workingman the U.S.A. still beckoned as a land of opportunity, but to many its economic image began to seem as tarnished as its political one. As radicalism moved gradually into socialism, so American individualism took on the appearance of ruthless exploitation. The critics that America bred at home had their following in Britain too. The new generation of radicals was impressed and depressed by Henry George and his revelations of both progress and poverty, and by the end of the century the villainies of the trust had become as accepted an article of left-wing thinking in Britain as in the U.S.A.—both because of the muckraking exposures made in America and because by 1901 and 1902 American trusts were actually to be seen invading British industry, in areas like shipping and tobacco manufacture. British trade unionists, who in the eighties could still regard the Knights of Labor as a spearhead of working-class organization at least as strong as their own, by 1900 were contemplating the sluggish growth of the American Federation of Labor with a mixture of condescension and concern. Doctrinally, British socialists were bound to disbelieve in the workingman's prospects in such a deeply capitalist society as the U.S.A.; in observable fact, the fate of the strikers at Homestead and Pullman seemed to testify to the validity of the Marxist analysis. To those, the great majority, to whom the Marxist analysis meant little, the glow seemed nonetheless to have faded from the western sky. From such a viewpoint Anglo-American amity meant different things at different levels: it could mean the heartless calculus of international finance or the would-be revolutionary comradeship of the common man. It is an indication of the complexity and diversity of the strands that made up the connection that it could mean both and that nonetheless the political and diplomatic relationship was not determined by either.

The thirty years of post–Civil War inertia in Anglo-American relations came to a sudden end in 1895. Out of a clear sky, as it seemed to public opinion in both countries, the Venezuela dispute exploded. A long-smoldering disagreement between Britain and Venezuela over the precise boundaries of British Guiana burst into flame at American insistence that Britain should submit the dispute to arbitration. In a dispatch of 20 July 1895 Richard Olney, secretary of state in the Cleveland administration, invoked the majestic claims of the Monroe Doctrine, accused Britain of violating it, insisted that it had become "a doctrine of American public law," and concluded with a reminder that "today the United States is practically sovereign on this continent." Lord Salisbury, used to the more conventional diplomatic language of the chancelleries of Europe, replied by the traditional weapons of the calculated delay and the courteous snub. After four months he declined to accept the right of the United States "to insert into the code of international law a novel principle" and denied that the dispute had anything to do "with any of the questions dealt with by President Monroe." By the time Salisbury's dispatch was received, Cleveland had secured from Congress authority to appoint a commission on the boundary issue whose findings the U.S.A. would be committed to uphold. On both sides of the Atlantic there was talk of war.

What did it all mean? At the time men of reason and goodwill found it as incomprehensible as it was sudden. The historian, who can read it in the light of the even more explosive incident, three years later, of the sinking of the *Maine* in Havana harbor and the outbreak of the Spanish-American War, is better placed to understand it. Psychologically, what was at issue was a clash between an Old World power, oversecure in its long tenure of far-flung dominion in regions intrinsically of minor importance to it, and a newly arrived actor on the international stage, confident in its capacity to dominate neighboring areas and giving to that concept of "neighboring" an interpretation as wide as its new dynamism felt appropriate. Venezuela, like Cuba a couple of years later, was selected as the point of focus for this dynamism partly by reason of its own comparative defenselessness but also because a skillful propaganda campaign had been mounted in the U.S.A. on its behalf some time before. The question remains, over Venezuela as over Cuba, why, against a background of generally good relations with the disputing power, should that propaganda find so ready and so incendiary a response in the White House, Congress, and the nation?

Here British readers will find it helpful to draw on their historical memories as well and to recall the emotional response which the complex of issues surrounding the outbreak of the Boer War evoked in Britain scarcely four years later. The late-nineteenth-century outbreak of imperialism was an emotional infection which transcended national boundaries. (It was not indeed confined to the English-speaking peoples.) Imperialism as such was not a new phenomenon in Britain; what gave the distinctive character to its turn-of-the-century manifestations was the yoking of it to the radicalism of social reform (incarnated in such a figure as Joseph Chamberlain) and the intensification of it by a popular press, the by-product of industrial technology and mass literacy.

In the United States many of these same factors were at work. Although the leadership of American imperialism in the 1890s came mainly from distinguished figures of old American stock, such as Theodore Roosevelt and Henry Cabot Lodge, and although much of its literature, such as Alfred Mahan's *Influence of Sea Power upon History*, was directed at a sophisticated readership, there was a determined effort to enlist mass support by every agency of popular persuasion. The propaganda fell on fertile ground, not because, as in Britain, it could evoke the continuity of an imperial past—here American traditions pointed in the opposite direction, as anti-imperialists like William Jennings Bryan insisted—but because it could evoke the distinctive American continuities of manifest destiny, rivalry with the ambitions and pretensions of Old World imperialism, and the claim of a newly arrived great power to a "place in the sun." A mass public, responsive to a yellow press, habituated to a politics of crusades and demagoguery, was as ready to accept Theodore Roosevelt's mixture of imperialism and social reform as William McKinley's blend of imperialism and big business.

In all this the example of England was as potent as it was ambivalent. On the one hand, as Mahan insisted, England provided the classic demonstration of how imperialism, granted sea power, could pay off. The Victorian marriage of dominion over palm and pine with a civilizing and indeed explicitly missionary role exercised a potent fascination for an America which, in many areas and among many groups in society, was hardly less Victorian than Britain itself. The imperialism of both countries was drenched in racialism, and assumptions about the intrinsic superiority of white men in general and Anglo-Saxons in particular were normal on both sides of the Atlantic. Yet if these shared elements of inheritance and sentiment predisposed British and American imperialism to harmony, other factors put them at odds. Imperialism per se inclines to exclusiveness, and the oldest American traditions were of conflict with British imperialism. Age versus youth, the old establishment versus the newest great power, the basic assumptions of an island that lived by trade and colonization versus those of a landmass that had previously expanded by internal development and immigration—there was plenty of potential conflict here. The two related opposites were well symbolized in the personal experience of the great laureate of empire, Rudyard Kipling, read and responded to on both sides of the Atlantic. British as only an Anglo-Indian could be, Kipling nonetheless fell under the spell of an American author and publisher to the extent of collaborating with him in a bad novel and marrying his somewhat dominating sister. In 1892 the young couple settled on the family property in Vermont, but the prophet of imperialism who found a kindred spirit in Theodore Roosevelt could neither get on with his New England neighbors nor tolerate the "bounders" of the Cleveland administration, and in 1896 disgustedly shook the dust of America off his feet.

Kipling's recoil from the American variant of the "Anglo-Saxon" mission was then—and has remained since—representative of a segment of British opinion. But, as events in the nineties quickly showed, it was a minor segment. Brought up short, in the Venezuela crisis, against the choice of resisting or accepting the claims of American imperialism, British opinion, in overwhelming strength, opted in favor of collaboration even at the price of concession. The truth was that in relation to British interests and anxieties elsewhere, her concern for the boundaries of British Guiana was small. In January 1896 her romantic imperialists involved her in the discreditable imbroglio of Jameson's Raid, designed to force the annexation of the Transvaal, but provoking as its immediate consequence the rebuke and threat of the German kaiser's telegram to Kruger, which advertised to the world the antipathy that Britain's South African ambitions were provoking in Europe. This was no moment for needless alienation of Atlantic friends. By February Britain had agreed to a restricted arbitration of the Venezuela dispute, which would not involve her in the loss of any indisputably British territory. By the end of the year agreement was reached on a series of articles for setting up an arbitral board that eventually, in October 1899, produced an award that gave Britain most of what she sought.

The complex diplomacy of the ensuing few years can now be seen to be the result of certain profound changes in the relations of the great powers. Britain was becoming conscious for the first time of the perils, as well as the splendors, of isolationism. When Europe was disunited, when no emergent naval power seemed capable of threatening her home waters, much less her imperial communications, it was indeed splendid to have no commitments and no settled connections that might limit her freedom of maneuver. But with the rise of Germany and the development of the Bismarckian system of alliances this happy state of affairs was drawing to a close. Nor was Britain in any mood to adjust to it by a contraction of her ambitions. She was a leader in the "scramble for Africa" and, in the thinking of many of her statesmen, was under additional pressure to expand and develop the Empire as the consolidation of Europe into larger and more exclusive economic entities proceeded. A growing loneliness and a persistent expansionism seemed to be going hand in hand.

The United States, by contrast, had abundant grounds for satisfaction with her isolationism, so long as she stayed within the confines of the American continent. There she could with safety, as the Venezuela affair showed, energetically assert her will against all comers. Had she been content to stop there, the major developments of world diplomacy would have been largely unaffected by her existence. But she was not. Africa, the great stamping ground of conflicting European ambitions, was of no interest to her. But Asia and the Pacific were. Her interest here was partly a logical extension of the westward thrust of manifest destiny, partly a by-product, accidental almost,[1] of the Spanish-American

War. That war itself is relevant to the evolution of Anglo-American relations only incidentally, Britain being unconnected with its outbreak and at no point actively involved in its diplomacy.[2] It was on the level of public opinion, rather than of official action, that the war brought Britain and the U.S.A. closer together. Despite the surge of martial enthusiasm and near-hysteria on which the war was launched and carried through, the United States found herself, to judge from the critical reactions of most other European nations, in a somewhat lonely and exposed position. Moreover, despite the swift and easy successes of her arms, she was operating from a narrow base, in terms both of naval and of military strength. In such a situation it is always a comfort to have the support, even if it is mainly moral support, of another country. British approval, not only of America's belligerency but also of her peace demands, particularly the acquisition of the Philippines, was very welcome. Officially Britain's posture was that of a proper neutrality. But it was a friendly neutrality—particularly in Gibraltar, Suez, Singapore, and Hong Kong, those strategic points so important to far-flung navies, especially in the days of coal-fired boilers. From it readily sprang the myth of positively pro-American interposition of British naval strength between Admiral George Dewey and the German Vice-Admiral von Diederich in Manila Bay. The fact that it was a myth did not seriously limit its usefulness to the advocates of Anglo-American amity.

The Spanish-American War changed the U.S.A.'s attitude in world affairs. It left her the owner and controller of territories far beyond her shores, the ruler of peoples who were never going to become citizens of the American republic. She acquired the authority and the responsibilities of an imperialist power. With victory and with extraterritorial gains went military needs and ambitions that transcended the traditional role of the armed services, the protection merely of the homeland. The United States now saw herself as in the same diplomatic and military league as the great powers of Europe, with gains to defend and a prestige to uphold. So the war concluded with a reorganization and expansion of that standing army which had once seemed a certain menace to the liberties of the republic and a building program for the navy which, by 1907, made it second only to that of the United Kingdom. There was, of course, no formal abandonment of traditional principles. It was still a brave politician who would question the validity of isolationism, especially if that meant "entangling alliances." And of course the Monroe

Doctrine became more potent as a warning to outsiders in proportion as its self-abnegatory implications were suppressed or ignored.

For relations with Britain this changed American posture had great significance. As a partner in the white man's burden, the U.S.A. was indulgent, in a quite novel degree, to British colonial aspirations. When the Boer War earned Britain, throughout Europe, bitter denunciations both for its inception and for its conduct, the United States administration in an election year displayed the same kind of friendly neutrality that it had itself received two years before. In the Far East, whereas in March 1898 President McKinley had declined the British proposal of joint action to preserve the "open door" in China, in September 1899 John Hay, secretary of state from September 1898 to July 1905, was himself taking the initiative in proposing essentially the same thing. In this area there was, fundamentally, no conflict of interest between Britain and the U.S.A. Both wished to preserve the territorial integrity of China while maintaining her economic dependence and accessibility. Their opponents in this were the same—Russia and Germany. When the Boxer Rebellion of 1900 brought Western intervention, the Americans, like the British, participated in the rescue expedition, but both powers were concerned to restrain their partners from using the rebellion as an excuse for Chinese dismemberment.

In the Caribbean the restrictions which the Clayton-Bulwer Treaty imposed on American control of an isthmian canal became more and more out of keeping with her preponderance in all American waters, north or south, Atlantic or Pacific. Yet that same preponderance required more than ever, now that the Stars and Stripes was flying at Hawaii and Manila, swift and secure passage between the Caribbean and the Pacific. (In the Spanish-American War it had taken the cruiser *Oregon* sixty-six days to dash around the Horn.) The British desire to share the benefits of such a facility was reflected in the first Hay-Pauncefote Treaty of 1900 which, by duplicating the provisions of the Suez Convention of 1888, would have retained the principle of neutralization. The Senate would have none of it. A second treaty had to be negotiated the following year, giving the U.S.A. exclusive control and freedom to fortify. The way was now clear for Theodore Roosevelt to "take" Panama, where canal construction began in 1904, to be completed just in time for the outbreak of war in 1914.

Nearby, once more in Venezuela, America's sensitivity to any Euro-

pean intrusiveness was again demonstrated when Britain, this time in
the company of and largely at the urging of Germany, resorted in 1902
to the time-honored device of naval demonstration for the collection of
foreign bondholders' debts. When Venezuelan ships were sunk, American reaction was sharp, and Roosevelt, newly enthroned custodian of
American prestige, put pressure on both imperialist powers to moderate
their behavior. British acceptance of arbitration was swift; by contrast,
German persistence in the blockade was prolonged and was terminated
only after repeated pressures from Roosevelt on the kaiser. The incident,
not in itself of major importance, is a good illustration of the stages by
which the realignments of world power were being effected. The acceptance in Britain of America's world role and the advocacy of close
cooperation were not, in their early stages, always judged as incompatible
with an Anglo-German understanding. Indeed the racialist fantasies of
the imperialists could easily lead to such talk as that in Joseph Chamberlain's notorious Leicester speech of 30 November 1899, with its advocacy
of the "triple alliance of the Teutonic race." In America Theodore Roosevelt had his curious love-hate relationship with the kaiser, which persisted through and beyond the Venezuela incident. But gradually long-
term factors were making themselves felt. The German decision to build
an ocean navy first embodied in Admiral von Tirpitz's Navy Law of 1898
could have only one ultimate consequence in Britain. In the United
States, though it hardly affected popular opinion, it produced in naval
and strategic thinking much the same kind of reaction that it induced in
Britain. Venezuela etched the impression deeper.

But, of course, nothing in such currents and shiftings of opinion provided a basis for any diplomatic alignment of Britain and the U.S.A. on
the world stage. The abandonment of British isolationism was by other
paths and led, initially, to another destination. The Anglo-Japanese alliance of 1902 was perhaps, of all the avenues open to an anxious and
friendless Britain, the least expected in Europe. But in America it was
not unwelcomed. While it pledged neither party to more than neutrality
in a conflict with a third power, it committed its signatories to support
the "open door" and the territorial integrity of China. To the U.S.A.,
unwilling to carry any larger commitment herself, it was a welcome stiff-
ening of resistance to Russian expansionism. Nor did Roosevelt or Arthur James Balfour jib when the Japanese went the whole hog and in
1904 challenged Russia in open conflict, though it was left largely to

Roosevelt to pull the Japanese back from what America feared might be an excessively hubristic triumph. The revision of the Anglo-Japanese alliance in 1905 was effected after consultation with Roosevelt, and care was taken to emancipate Britain from an original obligation to keep a fleet in the Far East equal to that of any outside power. "Outside" was revised to read "European," a significant exclusion of any intention to let the alliance induce any Anglo-American rivalry.

In Europe the avenue out of isolationism proved to be the initially tentative Anglo-French entente of April 1904, a mere settlement of outstanding colonial claims. It was a measure of the essentially shallow quality of the U.S.A.'s new role in world affairs, even under the diplomatically adventurous Theodore Roosevelt, that it was not certain then—and remains a matter of some dispute now—what his exact intentions—or achievements—were in inserting the United States into a dispute which first put the new entente to the test. This was the Moroccan crisis, provoked by Germany in 1905. On the slender basis of America's trading interests in Morocco, Roosevelt promoted the holding of the Algeciras Conference to settle the dispute—a diplomatic gain for Germany—but he also secured from the kaiser an undertaking to accept an American plan that gave the French essentially what they wanted. The entente emerged the stronger, though whether Roosevelt realized the full long-term implications of this or merely regarded the compromise as a service to peace is far from certain. Certainly the unobtrusive process by which the Franco-British colonial understanding of 1904 hardened into the strategic commitments of 1912 passed largely unnoticed in the U.S.A., where the disposition in most quarters was to regard the early years of the century as ushering in, through such agencies as the Hague Conference of 1909, a brighter prospect for peace.

It was to the assumed momentum of this peace movement that the principal Anglo-American diplomatic activity of the last decade before World War I was devoted. Much energy, in both the Roosevelt and the Taft presidencies, was expended on the negotiation of Anglo-American treaties of arbitration. When the Anglo-Japanese Treaty again came up for renewal in 1911, care was taken to exclude from its stipulations any commitments to act against third parties with whom Britain might have general treaties of arbitration. The care, exercised of course with the U.S.A. in mind, was superfluous. None of the treaties survived the progress through both executive and legislature, the Senate's veto proving insuperable. Their fate was a timely reminder, if such were needed, of the limitations on Anglo-American alliance-building. That Britain desired the reality, if not the form, of such an alliance was by now indubitable. In 1907 it was given very personal expression by the appointment of Lord Bryce to Washington, the first British ambassador, it has been well said, "to consider himself an emissary to the entire American nation."[3] American individuals or groups might, especially if out of office, reciprocate such a desire. But the situations of the two countries were in reality very different. There was no real need for such an alliance in terms of the U.S.A.'s observable and immediate national interests. Above all there was no basis for it in the habits of thought of the overwhelming majority of the population. To a minority, notably the Irish- and German-Americans, it would have been anathema. But even to the rest there would have seemed hardly more reason in the twentieth century than in the eighteenth to abandon the advantages of George Washington's "detached and distant situation."

1914–1919: The First World War and the First World Peace

The weeks that followed the assassination of the Archduke Ferdinand at Sarajevo on 28 June 1914 saw the final resolution of the ambiguities and uncertainties in Britain's relationships with the two armed camps of continental Europe. Convinced of the dissociability of diplomatic from strategic commitments, British statesmen had not regarded the Anglo-French entente as substituting a binding alliance for Britain's traditional freedom of action; it took the German invasion of Belgium, bringing the British guarantee of 1830 into play, to bring Britain into the alignment which her long-term balance-of-power interests required.

Here there is an interesting parallelism between the British position and that of the United States. Though there was between the two countries not even the shadowy diplomatic commitment of an entente, there had been building up an increasing awareness of common interests, together with an increasing uneasiness over German intentions. In the first two years of the war the U.S.A.'s commitment to an Allied victory grew, so that it was hard to imagine that she could remain neutral indefinitely, still less side with Germany. Even so, Woodrow Wilson believed his diplomatic freedom of action to be entirely unimpaired and it took Germany's declaration of unrestricted submarine warfare—a violation of law analogous to the invasion of Belgium—to precipitate the U.S.A.'s abandonment of isolationism on 6 April 1917.

It would nevertheless have taken a singularly farsighted observer to envisage such an eventuality in August 1914. It is possible to read the *New York Times* for 4 August 1914 from cover to cover without finding the least mention of American neutrality—and that, of course, not because involvement was accepted as inevitable, but because it was regarded as inconceivable. Yet Wilson's injunction to be neutral "in thought as well as in action" was, for most Americans, impracticable from the first. A nation constructed from the human material of Europe could not remain indifferent when Europe itself was riven in two.

In this conflict of sympathies the Allies in general, and Britain in particular,[1] enjoyed a clear advantage, derived from the preponderance of their national stocks in the makeup of American society and from the shock which the violation of Belgian neutrality administered to American sensibilities. This advantage was intensified by certain largely adventitious factors that worked in Britain's favor. In London the U.S.A. was represented by an ambassador, Walter Hines Page, as consistently—one might almost say extravagantly—pro-British as his colleague in Berlin, James Gerard, was anti-German. Colonel House, the president's diplomatic *alter ego,* was early convinced of the basic righteousness of the Allied cause, and Robert Lansing, when he became secretary of state in succession to Williams Jennings Bryan, was convinced that an Allied victory was essential for America. However, Wilson was not a president who allowed his ambassadors, or even his intimate colleagues, to shape his thinking for him and he remained tenaciously loyal to his own injunctions of impartiality. What swayed him more, in the long run, was the pervasive awareness in London of the nature and grounds of American susceptibilities and the need for respecting them. A hundred years and more of Anglo-American relationship, in peace and especially in war, had not failed to leave their mark on the British official memory.

From the beginning it was apparent that World War I, even more than the previous great conflict with Napoleon, would be a war of attrition, with blockade as a major weapon. Here Britain's command of the seas gave her an overwhelming advantage, but it brought of course an almost commensurate hazard in the clashes it involved with the U.S.A. as the world's greatest neutral trader. For the Allies it was fortunate that at the outset their trade with the U.S.A. exceeded that of the Central Powers by about ten to one; it was nevertheless characteristic of Britain's concern to avoid needlessly painful disruption of American trading patterns that cotton was not put on the contraband list until August 1915,[2] although 1.75 million bales went to Germany in the first six months of the war.

But, of course, with America so potent, to aid or harm, any belligerent's violation of her neutral rights might have dangerous consequences. In September 1914 Woodrow Wilson pointed out to House that he and

Madison were the only Princeton men who had become president: "The circumstances of the War of 1812 and now run parallel. I sincerely hope they will not go further." There was one reason, which Wilson overlooked, why they did not go further—the fact that in 1861–65, during the Civil War, the United States had herself established precedents for naval blockades which had won general acceptance.[3] The Allies built on these, and pressed them hard; they extended the contraband list, interfered with mails, exercised sweeping powers of search and detention, intercepted shipments to neutral ports, and confiscated neutral cargoes. Such acts provoked a stream of American diplomatic protests, but neither side pushed the issues involved *à outrance*. For Lord Grey, the British foreign secretary, it was a guiding principle that no Allied action must be allowed that would provoke a rupture with the U.S.A., while from the American point of view Allied infringements of neutral rights were overshadowed by those attributable to Germany and her chosen naval instrument, the submarine.

The submarine was a technological innovation born too late to be easily accommodated to the existing rules and practices of international law. In any case its full employment had one inexcusable consequence in American eyes: it threatened (and indeed took) American lives.[4] This could only be avoided if Americans were to forgo their right to travel on belligerent vessels—i.e., substitute noninvolvement for neutrality. Wilson and his fellow countrymen were in no mood to contemplate such a derogation of sovereignty, especially in deference to a practice which they felt crossed the line that separated "civilized" from "barbarous" warfare. Hence Wilson's sharp response to the first German declaration of unrestricted submarine warfare in February 1915, that Germany would be held to "strict accountability." It may· have been illogical, since the *Lusitania* was carrying munitions, that her sinking three months later should have brought America within even sighting distance of war, but with 128 American lives lost, and granted the known sentiments of the period, it was predictable. The incident simmered down with the German pledge not to sink liners without warning. But the *Lusitania* episode nevertheless marks a turning point in Wilson's attitude toward the war; henceforward "mere" neutrality seems less possible and less adequate and his thoughts turn more and more to stopping the war and to American mediation.

The *Lusitania* affair had another consequence. Its handling lost Wil-

son his secretary of state, William Jennings Bryan. Bryan was a mud-
dled, woolly-minded rhetorician, but he represented a tradition as old as
the republic itself of an America which, to preserve the purity of its
ideals, should have as little to do with Europe as possible and should
prefer to pay whatever price isolation demanded rather than run the risks
involvement imposed. It was in this tradition that Bryan in August 1914
found loans by American bankers to belligerents "inconsistent with the
true spirit of neutrality." However in October Wilson overruled him,
declaring that loans were in order provided they did not involve floating
bond issues for public sale. This meant a great deal to the Allies as the
volume of their American purchases of supplies and arms in the United
States grew. The bulk of these purchases was paid for by the sizable balance which the U.S.A. owed Britain at the outbreak of war, by wartime
exports from Britain, and by the sale of British-owned American securities. But this left a significant gap which was bridged by loans—the
first in October 1915, floated by the House of Morgan for the British
and French governments, and others later. Their American justification
was found by the secretary of the treasury to lie in the contribution that
the Allied purchases made to the American economy and the hardship
that their cessation would involve. For obvious reasons there was no
German counterpart to this and there can be no doubt that the effect was
to create at every level in American economic life, from banking house
to shop floor, a substantial interest in Allied and particularly British survival. Between 1914 and 1917 the Atlantic economy was restored in
all, or more, of its previous vitality, but depending not on the normal
processes of free trade, or even of peacetime mercantilism, but on the
forced and extravagant demands of war. It has subsequently seemed a
short step to argue that this economic stake in an Allied victory explains
America's 1917 involvement, but the step is longer in fact than in logic.
Not only was American thinking at the time surprisingly reluctant to
translate economic interest into military intervention, but in Woodrow
Wilson it had a leader who regarded the conduct of the nation's diplomacy as a responsibility which he could not delegate and moreover as
something over which it was inconceivable that the nation's bookkeep-
ing should cast so much as a shadow. Indeed the considerations determining Wilson's diplomacy during these crucial two years were very
different.

At the end of 1915 Wilson sent House on a mission to the warring

European powers to investigate the possibilities of peace negotiations being begun. House got little encouragement in Paris or Berlin, but in London he had long talks and established a close relationship with Grey. The product of these talks was the secret House-Grey Memorandum which envisaged the calling of a conference to end the war. If the Allies accepted such a proposal and the Germans rejected it, the U.S.A. would (probably) enter the war—on the Allies' side. The "probably" was a deliberate insertion of Wilson's. While the House-Grey talks were in progress, the waters were muddied by Lansing, Bryan's successor as secretary of state, proposing a "modus vivendi" (arising out of the *Lusitania* controversy) by which armed merchantmen would be treated as warships, though German U-boats would abide by "cruiser rules"— i.e., would not sink unarmed merchantmen except after surfacing and warning. This ill-judged proposal to change the existing law of the sea to the Allies' disadvantage was, of course, unacceptable in London and was soon dropped by Lansing. Wilson returned to his previous posture on submarine sinkings and indeed, after the sinking of the unarmed *Sussex,* extorted from Germany a pledge to observe cruiser rules before sinking merchant vessels. Meanwhile the House-Grey proposals hung fire, the Allies being too hopeful of victory to judge the moment propitious to take them up. The result was a softening of American attitudes toward Germany and a hardening toward Britain. In part this was due to the tightening screws of British economic warfare and in part to the harmful effects on America of events in Ireland—the Easter Rising of the Irish Republican Brotherhood and its suppression. But basically it was a reflection of Wilson's disappointment at the Allies' refusal to talk peace—which in turn reflected a hubristic confidence in military victory and a reasonably well-grounded doubt of Wilson's ability to bring the United States in if his mediation failed.

For Wilson 1916 was an election year and the failure to have tangible peacemaking successes to offer the electorate must have chafed. The emphasis of his campaign shifted increasingly to pacifism—"he kept us out of war"—and less and less was heard of American responsibilities, as either a neutral or a world power. The election once over, and won, Wilson became, however, increasingly obsessed with the need to take positive action for peace. If the Allies would not respond, the U.S.A. must force the pace. As a preliminary twist of the screw Wilson actually went so far as to let it be known that he was opposed to the sale of British treasury bills designed to meet Britain's crucial shortage of dollars—this at a time when Britain and her Allies were dependent on the U.S.A. for 40 percent of their war supplies. On 18 December he dispatched his peace appeal to both belligerents. Outwardly it just called on them to define their war aims, but it was intended as the entering wedge for an American mediation which, if Germany accepted and the Allies declined, could result, Wilson admitted to House, in America's finding herself at Germany's side.

Dis aliter visum. Though both sides returned answers to Wilson which, as might have been expected, were more in the nature of forcing bids than pacific overtures, the really decisive action was taken in the German Admiralty which, on 31 January 1917, announced the resumption of unrestricted submarine warfare—a gamble on a quick victory. Though this left Wilson with no choice but to sever diplomatic relations with Germany, he still hoped in the absence of "overt acts" that peace might be preserved. On 25 February Wilson received from the British a telegram which they had intercepted from Arthur Zimmermann, the German foreign secretary, to his minister in Mexico; if war broke out, the minister was to try to secure a Mexican alliance by offers of territorial gains from the U.S.A. Wilson took the next step, the arming of American merchantmen. As the total of Allied ship losses mounted alarmingly, the "overt acts" occurred—the sinking, with heavy loss of life, of three American merchant vessels. On 6 April Congress passed a resolution "recognizing" that Germany was at war with the United States.

The American entry so eagerly welcomed in Britain was thus not the result of a gradual process of alignment in the two countries' policies. If Wilson's war message emphasized the idealistic grounds for entry— "to make the world safe for democracy," etc.—it was American, not Allied, ideals for which he was asking his fellow countrymen to crusade. This was made clear by the statement he had issued in January, accompanying his war aims negotiations; while both Germany and the Allies in their replies were blending idealistic professions with material and territorial demands, Wilson was adumbrating the objectives which later took shape as the Fourteen Points. It was in line with this distinction that when he went to war, Wilson did not bring America into the Alliance; she remained an "associated power." She alone was truly disinterested in her war aims; her war was wholly idealistic. That Wilson was sincere in thinking this cannot be doubted, but the consequences for

America were serious. When the high goals of 1917 were not realized in the peacemaking of 1919, disillusionment was needlessly pervasive. The idealism had obscured the strategic realities which would have retained their validity whatever the outcome of Versailles. Here again the analogy with Britain is strong. Whether Belgian neutrality had been violated or not, Britain could not have afforded to see the further shores of the English Channel dominated by a hostile and expanding naval power. Similarly, whether submarine warfare violated American requirements or not, the U.S.A. could not have afforded to see the further shores of the North Atlantic dominated by a Germany which had defeated France and Britain and assumed the sea power which had been theirs.

It is no accident that Anglo-American wartime cooperation was closest in that service which for over a generation had been developing a growing realization of the strategic interdependence of Britain and the United States. At sea there was a joint command under a British admiral who flew his flag indifferently in the ships of either nation. The two navies cooperated closely in convoy duty, the blockade, and the war against the U-boat. Elsewhere things were different. John Pershing, the American commander in chief, rejected the Allies' initial proposal that American battalions should be brigaded with British troops until full American divisions were ready to absorb them. Instead from the first he insisted on maintaining the separate identity and unity of his forces, two million of them overseas by the war's end, and indeed the Allies' reluctance, until April 1918, to establish an Allied commander in chief set him a poor example. But the American refusal to be represented on the Supreme War Council, except by "listeners," meant that the political and diplomatic planning of the war proceeded in two distinct and largely unconnected compartments. Britain did establish a kind of beachhead on Wilson's lonely shore with the Balfour, Northcliffe, and Reading missions to Washington in 1917. But though Balfour won a personal success and though the missions facilitated cooperation in a number of important areas, especially of procurement and supply, no enduring intimacy was established at the top, despite basic similarities in British and American thinking about the war and the peace that was to follow. This was well illustrated by the fact that Lloyd George and Wilson each made wholly separate and yet strikingly similar announcements of peace aims within three days of each other in January 1918. Wilson's was his Fourteen Points—and these were issued without consultation not only with his cobelligerents but also with Congress. He was determined to retain his political and moral autonomy, no matter what the price. Two of the Fourteen Points bothered the British, the first as members of an alliance, the second as the leading sea power. The first was the seeming exclusion of reparations, by which the French set understandable, if mistaken, store. The second was the ambiguous pledge to the freedom of the seas. Did this mean a denial of the blockade weapon? To Britain this was unthinkable. The ghosts of 1812 began to walk again. The gap between American and British objectives seemed dangerously wide. When a mutually acceptable reply had to be found to Germany's request for an armistice on the basis of the Fourteen Points, the United States was even threatening to make a separate peace. Eventually a compromise was patched up, leaving the freedom of the seas open for subsequent interpretation and making clear the Allied insistence on reparations. On this basis Germany surrendered and the process of peacemaking was begun.

Through the diplomatic and political wranglings and maneuvers at Paris there runs a surprisingly consistent thread of Anglo-American agreement—surprising, because the superficial indications pointed the other way. The two leaders, Wilson and Lloyd George, who had never met throughout the war they fought together, remained at the end of the Paris negotiations as mutually distrustful as they had been at the beginning—Wilson blind to the genuine streak of humanitarianism in Lloyd George's makeup, Lloyd George convinced of Wilson's essential hypocrisy. Wilson's relative (not, of course, as he imagined, absolute) disinterestedness did enable him to reach out to British liberal opinion and in some measure to take the place that Lloyd George had forfeited by his conduct of the Khaki Election of 1918. But, as Wilson's tour of Britain, undertaken en route to Paris, quickly showed, his inability to enter fully into the experience of a country wracked by four years of devastating warfare limited his effectiveness as an advocate of supranational ideals.

But beneath these clashes of personality and national moods lay deeper long-range similarities of outlook and interests. This was most apparent in the shaping of the Covenant of the League of Nations, the task which above all others at Paris engaged Wilson's mind and heart. The League was, in its conception, as much British as American. What in the U.S.A. had evolved from the ideas of former President Taft's "League to En-

force Peace" in Britain emerged from the complementary thinking of
the Fabians and a group around Lord Bryce. At Paris the two streams of
national planning emerged in the form of a joint draft, the work of David Hunter Miller for the U.S.A. and of Cecil Hurst for Britain. Already
at this stage the main outlines of the Covenant were agreed between
Britain and the U.S.A., with its emphasis on the voluntaristic character
of a league which would employ compulsion only as a last resort, as
opposed to the French conception of a military league with rigidly de-
fined powers of enforcement. The voluntary concept was adhered to
throughout and, of course, won the day. Such differences as there were
between the British and the American draftsmen reflected, surprisingly,
a greater American belief in the desirability of using the League as an
agency of collective security. It was Wilson who insisted on Article 10
(the mutual guarantee of member states against territorial aggression)
as "the backbone of the League."

There was less similarity of view over the actual peacemaking provisions of Versailles, but even here the agreements were major, the disagreements minor. Both victorious naval powers favored the elimination
of German naval might, though they differed over some details of the
arrangements for effecting it. Both victorious but "overseas" powers
wished to preserve the territorial integrity of Germany as against the
annexational designs of the continental and security-minded French. The
occupation of the Rhineland and the League administration of the Saar
were made temporary, while Germany's eastern frontiers, like those of
Eastern and Central Europe generally, owed more to Wilsonian and British liberal ideas of self-determination than to strategic considerations.

To anyone with any sense of history the mere idea of an American
president sitting down with European colleagues to fashion the frontiers
of states not even abutting on the Atlantic would have seemed inconceivable a mere two years before Versailles. Yet here was Wilson, not
only playing the decisive role in this but, in order to clinch his concept
of what was just in peacemaking, committing his country to a guarantee
of indefinite duration of the most disputed frontier of all, that between
France and Germany. There have been many theories to explain Wilson's astonishing departure from a tenacious American tradition of no
entangling alliances—that it was merely a device to circumvent Clemen-
ceau which he fully expected the Senate to reject, that he expected it to
be strictly temporary until the League guarantees took over, that he was

the victim of mental derangement brought on by a cerebral thrombosis. But in terms of Anglo-American relations the significant thing about the guarantee is the way in which it yoked America and Britain in Europe. The treaties, which were made separately between France and the United States and between France and Great Britain, were at Lloyd George's insistence to go into effect only if each was ratified by the signatories according to their own constitutional procedures. Britain and the U.S.A., like Alpinists crossing a crevasse, were roped together by an agreement that each would go into Europe as far as the other, but no farther. Thus the central security provisions of Versailles depended upon the U.S.A. and Britain making identical commitments toward a country which was three thousand miles away from the first and only twenty-one miles away from the second. Viewed either as an abandonment of isolationism by the first or as a return to it by the second, it was an equally remarkable linchpin for a reconstructed Europe. Ratified by the French and the British and rejected by the U.S. Senate, the treaties lapsed within the year. It is an indication of the strength of British insularity that, when the news of the Senate's rejection reached Britain, the predominant reaction was one of relief.

There was rather less agreement between the Anglo-Saxon powers on the issue of reparations. Here again the main pressure came from France, the most directly injured of the major combatants. Here the U.S.A. asked nothing for herself and considered that the pre-armistice agreement put a strict limit on Allied demands. Lloyd George found himself the victim both of his reckless pledges to the British electorate and of the need for placating his French allies on an issue which he thought relatively unimportant for Britain. The result was a British vacillation that on nearly every major point ended in support for the French position against the American. But of course the reparations issue, as was quickly to become apparent, could not be seen in isolation. It was one element in the larger theme of the costs of the war. Here, though it was not directly at issue, the Americans took a line which was consonant with the belief in the autonomy of economics, the self-sufficiency of laissez faire, which was a central part of Wilson's creed. American loans to the belligerents were no different from any other commercial transaction, due to be repaid on the terms laid down at the time of borrowing. Though the Allies did not dispute this at Paris, one can detect here and elsewhere the ground swell of feeling that a nation which in the grim calculus of war had contributed only some 100,000 dead to victory compared with Brit-

ain's 700,000 and France's 1,300,000 had not earned an equal voice in
the disposition of the fruits of victory.

Such a line of calculation was unlikely to yield constructive results.
There was another meeting point of economics and diplomacy where the
British sought American support with more reason but with no more
success. Despite all its inadequacies of rational planning, the war had
thrown up certain agencies of international control, in areas like food
and shipping, in which the U.S.A. had played a substantial part. In the
stricken Europe of 1919 it seemed little more than common sense to
keep these agencies in being until "normal" economic life got going
again. The British took the lead in urging such a course, but it failed to
capture Wilson's interest; the apostle of political world order was willing to argue with his wartime economic "czar," Bernard Baruch, that in
economic matters "the salvation of the world must rest upon the initiative of individuals."

There was another area in which Wilson showed himself a prisoner of
prejudice rather than a prophet of the future. But here he was no more
than accomplice of the British Empire. The Japanese asked for a declaration of racial equality to be inserted in the League covenant; William
Morris Hughes, prime minister of Australia, took the lead in refusing it.
Britain supported her Dominion. Wilson, not unmindful of the color
prejudice that persisted in the Pacific states over the issue of Japanese
power and Chinese immigration, supported the United Kingdom. The
Japanese were denied their request. This left the Anglo-Saxon powers in
poor moral shape to resist the other Japanese demand, for the transfer
to them of German rights over Kiaochow and Shantung. The British
had pledged themselves to this as a reward for Japan's support in the
war. The Americans had no such commitment, but Wilson was convinced that the concession was necessary if Japan was to be brought into
the League. By one of history's more blatant ironies, the American out-
cry over the transfer of Shantung was one of the strongest arguments
used by Wilson's opponents for the rejection of the treaty by the U.S.
Senate.

One issue remained at Paris of direct, passionate, and, in retrospect,
wholly unnecessary Anglo-American controversy. It stemmed from the
earlier discussion over the "freedom of the seas" item in the Fourteen
Points. Behind Britain's continuing anxiety on this issue lay an irrational
concern over America's naval building program. If existing plans were
carried out, the U.S.A. would have, in three years' time, the greatest fleet

in the world. British pride quivered at the prospect of Britannia's demo-
tion to second place; more reasonably, when the pacific Wilson used
language implying that the construction of such an armada could be a
club to coerce Britain on the "freedom of the seas" issue, Lloyd George
and his colleagues were indignant and alarmed. In March 1919 their
opportunity to retaliate arrived. Wilson, returning to Paris after a visit
home, pressed his peacemaking colleagues for a concession necessary to
get the League covenant past the Senate. This was an amendment to
safeguard the sacred Doctrine of President Monroe. It was in everyone's
interest to make this ritual obeisance to American ancestor-worship if it
would assist in securing America's adhesion to the League, but Lloyd
George saw in it his long-awaited opportunity. He fixed the price of his
consent as an agreement on naval armaments. On 10 April he got it.
Wilson agreed to withdraw the administration's support for the naval
building bill still pending and to consult Great Britain on any future
American naval plans. It was a barren bargain. The amendment safeguarding the Monroe Doctrine did not save the treaty in the Senate; a
congressional economy drive would have curtailed the naval building
program anyway. More fundamentally, national pride had blinded both
sides to realities. Though Britain as an island empire and the U.S.A. as
a two-ocean landmass had different naval requirements, the fear that
either side's naval power constituted a threat to the other's security was
wholly illusory—the result of the tenacious survival of ancient rivalries
combined with a complete misreading of the history of the previous hundred years.

In the summer of 1919 the product of the Paris peacemaking went to
the U.S. Senate, to be thrown out on its first presentation in November
by thirty-nine votes to fifty-five, and on its second in March 1920 by
forty-nine votes to thirty-five. Into the complex of forces that resulted
in its rejection many factors entered that had nothing to do with Anglo-
American relations. Indeed it is arguable that nothing Britain did or did
not do at Paris could have made the outcome essentially different. Certain Anglo-American issues did, however, enter the debates and indeed
persisted afterward in the unhappy days of alienation that followed.
One, of course, was Ireland, then at the height of the bitter postwar
struggle with England which was to lead to the establishment of the Irish
Free State in 1921. At Paris the pressure of the Irish-American lobby to
have an endorsement of Ireland's claims inserted in the treaty had been

so crude as to be counterproductive. Unable to satisfy their demands, Wilson decided to ignore them rather than provoke an outright clash with Britain. In the Senate they had their revenge; they joined hands with other disaffected immigrant groups like the Italians and Germans. To the fifteen original "reservations" to the treaty was added a sixteenth, affirming sympathy with Ireland's struggle for independence. Such sentiment found wider support in America's even older anti-imperial tradition. This fastened on the provision in the Covenant which gave separate votes to the six British Dominions, a recognition, of course, of the transformation of this element in the old Empire into the new self-governing Commonwealth. But again memory and suspicion proved stronger than intelligence and trust. What could it mean but that Britain would have six votes to the U.S.A.'s one? Grey, in the U.S.A. on a mission "to deal especially with questions arising out of the peace," urged on his government a declaration of self-denial—that in a dispute involving Britain or the Dominions none of the members of the Empire would cast a vote. Sir Robert Borden, for Canada, welcomed this, but neither Jan C. Smuts of South Africa nor William M. Hughes of Australia would entertain such an idea. It is hard to believe that it could have affected the outcome; what was involved was not a constitutional disagreement but a gap, unbridgeable at that moment, of comprehension and confidence.

However, not all the weapons that slew Versailles were manufactured in America. One, and not the least potent, was forged and sharpened in Britain, by the pamphleteer and economist John Maynard Keynes. His *Economic Consequences of the Peace* was to Versailles what Tom Paine's *Common Sense* was to American Independence; no doubt the course of history would have been ultimately the same without it, but it certainly ran much smoother after it. Keynes's caustic exposure appeared in Britain in December 1919 and within a month was published in the U.S.A. Its significance was that it provided the liberals with their reasons for rejecting the treaty—opposite to, but if anything even more potent than, those deployed by the conservatives. For use against the compromised brainchild of Wilson it provided a corrosive liberalism perfectly attuned to a postwar mood no longer receptive to Wilson's own moralistic idealism. But to any real understanding between Britain and America it contributed nothing at all—merely a set of criticisms and excuses for a generation on both sides of the Atlantic that had a conscience but no faith.

The return to peace set both Britain and the United States adrift, in relation to the rest of the world and, in consequence, to each other. It took two decades for them to plot a decisive course, a delay that cost them and the rest of the world dear. Part of the reason for this lay in the persistent belief that the war had been some sort of irrational disruption of an orderly progress and that the aim of national policy should be to get back to prewar conditions as soon as possible. Part of it lay in a quickened rate of change in the world outside their borders, change which they were reluctant to recognize and to which they reacted, wherever possible, by withdrawing within themselves.

The roles that Britain and the United States played in the war carried very different implications for each of them. To organize a coalition against a dominating European power and to fight in Europe, and indeed around the world—this Britain had done before; whereas for the United States to join, even only de facto, such a coalition and to send two million men to Europe—this was not merely going beyond, it was going positively counter to the precedents of American history. The fact that the United Kingdom was her prime accomplice in this enterprise did nothing to reduce the enormity of its innovation. Yet the impact of the war had been vastly greater on Britain than on the U.S.A. It transposed their relative significance in the world. In 1914 the pound sterling was the universal currency, the Royal Navy the guardian of the seas, the British Empire truly an extension of British power and prestige. By 1919 the dollar had displaced the pound as the dominant world currency, the U.S. Navy challenged her ancient rival, and the Empire was in process of a transition which, among other things, paid tribute to the gravitational pull of American power across the world. And of course the im-

mediate toll of the war—in lives lost, in physical damage, in disruption
and diversion of the national economy—had been prodigious in Britain,
whereas it could even be argued that, save for a modest loss of life, the
war had actually increased the well-being and enhanced the productivity
of the United States. Yet since national awareness always lags behind
national realities, revulsion against the war, and especially against the
consequences of it, the peace settlements and their burden, was more
swift and savage in the U.S.A. than in Britain. American participation
was quickly and widely judged to have been at best misplaced idealism,
at worst gratuitous folly. The revulsion stimulated the search for a
scapegoat. It was often found in an entity called "Europe," which sometimes took the more precise form of "Britain." The British, fighting obviously for survival, had expected less from victory and were proportionately less disillusioned. But as the privations and follies of the peace
were felt, cynicism set in with them, and in the ensuing reassessment of
the warmaking and peacemaking, Britain's allies became a target of national resentment. Nor did the fact that the United States had been
careful not to become an ally diminish her share of criticism and recrimination.

The war left Britain in an uncertain posture in relation to the world
which, before 1914, she had half dominated, half ignored. No return to
isolation was really practicable. But full realization of this obvious fact
was obscured by the elimination, through defeat, of her major opponents
and by the opportunities afforded by the League of Nations to substitute
an international order for a system of alliances. It was insufficiently ap-
preciated that opponents do not stay eliminated unless measures are
maintained to keep them so and that an international order requires for
its operation at least as much effort and devotion as an alliance. In fact
Britain gave little serious thought to the problem of security in Europe,
once her joint guarantee with America to France collapsed, and only
intermittent support to the League as an agency for maintaining a worldwide substitute for the nineteenth-century Pax Britannica. Another factor is relevant here. The transformation of the Empire into the Commonwealth, for which the war was not responsible, but which it certainly
accelerated, left Britain in the twenties and thirties uncertain what this
worldwide association meant for her. Did it offer an alternative to European entanglements? Many thought so, exaggerating its possibilities as
a closed trading and joint defense system. Some even believed it could

relieve Britain of any dependence on the U.S.A., though these were a minority. Others speculated, since it imposed peculiar burdens, of defense and finance, upon the mother country, whether it was not a distraction and an encumbrance of which Britain should relieve herself as soon as possible. Few believed this, but certainly the need to keep at least the dominions, if not the colonies, in accord with British policy often acted as a brake and a deterrence.

The United States had no such overseas appendages (save Puerto Rico and the Philippines) to complicate her assessment of her role in the postwar world, and to this extent she was free, once she had decided to pull out of Europe and the League, to determine her own course of action. But the war had left her as well in a different world from that of 1914. It was hard to wish away power. She tried valiantly in the twenties and thirties to impose self-denying limitations on her political and military might, but the result was merely to postpone the day when her strength would have to be deployed across the world and to aggravate the eventual conditions of such deployment. Her economic might she was less willing to forgo, but here she showed herself sadly unaware of the responsibilities that go with power. She carried the mentality of a debtor and a satellite into a world in which she was the principal creditor and the center of the financial and trading system.

In political ideology the war had turned Britain and the U.S.A. in opposite directions. In Britain it had produced many of the consequences of a social revolution: it greatly narrowed the gulf between the classes, in manners, incomes, and expectations. The final stages of manhood suffrage reached in 1918 (to be followed by the women's vote in 1926) marked a climax of political democratization (which, of course, outside the South, America had reached long before). More importantly, the two-party system had taken a leftward lurch, with Labour ousting the Liberals and committed, after 1918, to a dual reliance on the trade unions and socialism. By contrast the U.S.A. retained its nonideological two-party system and its capitalist-oriented trade union movement, which after 1918 became increasingly alienated from its British opposite number. And from 1920 to 1928 a Republican party deeply devoted to the ethos of big business dominated the American scene. Neither country's leadership, of course, gave any countenance to the ideological appeal and menace of communism, but whereas in Britain it was viewed in general as a remote and external threat, in the U.S.A. it was a far more lively bogey available for use against liberals as well as reds. Consensus in Britain cracked in 1926 in the General Strike and was threatened again in the economic crisis of 1931. In America it lasted longer in the twenties, only to crack more severely, but, as it turned out, by no means irretrievably, in the Great Depression. On public opinion in each country these trends produced divergent effects. British Labour, estranged from American trade unionism and ostensibly wholly anticapitalist, abandoned what remained of radicalism's traditional belief in the American experiment and committed itself, especially in its intellectual leadership, to an anti-Americanism which became almost a hallmark of the British Left between the wars. The New Deal moderated but did not eliminate this ideological commitment. British conservatism, nervous for the country's place and power in an uneasy world, oscillated between two views of the United States: sometimes the U.S.A. was seen as a rival—particularly in trade, but also in the insidious appeals of a vulgarizing and plutocratic culture; sometimes it appeared as the natural ally against communism from Russia or resurgent nationalism in Germany, but, after the experience of Versailles, always as an uncertain ally, an undependable quantity.

In America the wartime connection with Britain had been close enough to create friction without promoting understanding. The two countries shared a sense of betrayed ideals, but none of common suffering. The conservative elements in the British tradition seemed further than ever from the business ethos of the American twenties, while the innovative tendencies of British socialism found little echo even among American liberals. The Empire was a standing rebuke, a kind of moral proving ground, in which what was proved was the hollowness of the other man's moral professions.

At a nonpolitical, extra-economic level the intercourse between the two countries was more extensive than ever before. Travel was easier and cheaper, especially for Americans, financed by a strong dollar. And Europe, however politically rebarbative, had lost none of its cultural appeal. Britain shared less in this than France but there was still the steady undertow of academic, literary, theatrical associations. In the area of popular culture, however, these are the decades of American exports. In the new and potent medium of film Hollywood bestrode the world. It had begun its conquest of the British screen before 1914, and the war completed its triumph. The surest tribute to this triumph was the cultural protectionism it evoked in the British Films Act of 1927, which obliged ex-

hibitors to show a quota of British films; the act did not sensibly diminish the gigantic, if superficial, penetration of British entertainment by
the United States. The U.S.A.'s other great cultural export was of course
in light music, popularly termed *jazz,* in which the American Negro led
the world. The postwar generation in Britain just as much as in the
United States found its restless rhythms uniquely matched to their emotional mood.

Significant though the cultural impact of these potent American exports was, the image of America which they left in the public mind bore
little or no relation to reality. Any real understanding between the two
nations had to be hammered out of the hard facts of their political and
economic relationships. In the immediate aftermath of war it probably
helped Britain and the U.S.A.—whatever it may have done to the rest
of the world—that, in varying degrees, they both wanted their "boys
back home," with all that that evocative phrase implied for strategic and
diplomatic policy. At the armistice Britain was perhaps the most powerfully armed nation in the world, with an army of over 3,000,000 men,
a navy of over 4,000 ships, and an air force with a first-line strength of
3,000 aircraft and a backup of over 20,000. The U.S.A. had an army
of 3,600,000 men, but her navy was still inferior—some 16 battleships
to Britain's 33 and a total tonnage substantially less—while her air force
constituted only about 10 percent of the total Allied strength at the end
of the war. But such figures were doubly misleading. With the return
of peace the soldiery of both nations melted away, the Americans particularly fast.[1] But equally obviously the American potential for military
might was vastly greater than Britain's. This was most apparent in the
service on which the two "island" powers principally relied in both
peace and war, the navy. Here, if ships under construction were brought
into the calculation of comparative strength, America was clearly going
to overshadow Britain in the near future. But fortunately for British
pride, Congress was even more anxious to cut taxes than the admirals
were to expand their fleets. To this financial justification for avoiding
competition strong diplomatic arguments were added.

Versailles had left Japanese-American relations badly frayed. On most
of the points at issue Britain had sided with the United States. What did
this imply for the Anglo-Japanese alliance, due to expire in the summer
of 1921? Britain was concerned, in the first place, to delimit its applica-
bility. In July 1920 she persuaded Japan to agree to a joint statement

making it clear that the alliance, if renewed, must be in a form compatible with the League covenant. But this was not enough for Canada, who, at the Imperial Conference of June 1921, pressed for the alliance's termination. She shared the U.S.A.'s exaggerated concern over the issue of Pacific immigration and, in her newfound dominion independence (of Britain) and dependence (on the U.S.A.), shuddered at the thought of any British commitment which might conceivably bring her two closest associates into conflict. Britain yielded to the pressure. But if the Anglo-Japanese alliance was to be allowed to lapse, there would be need for some alternative settlement for the Far East, an area where Britain's economic and commercial stake was still larger than that of the U.S.A.

Out of these dual necessities, for economies at sea and a new modus vivendi in the Far East, the Washington Naval Conference of 1921–22 was born. It was fortunate in its symbolism and its substance. By calling the conferees to Washington the Harding administration was able to play the role of America the World Power, while the actual objective of the conference was entirely in line with the worldwide contraction of responsibilities which America had begun when she rejected the Treaty of Versailles. At Washington, agreement was reached simultaneously on naval disarmament and a Far East settlement which involved the United States in neither an alliance nor a commitment to any guarantees. In place of the Anglo-Japanese alliance the Four-Power Treaty emerged in December 1921. By its terms the U.S.A., the United Kingdom, France, and Japan gave a ten-year undertaking to respect each other's Pacific rights, to confer in the event of a dispute arising on any Pacific question, and to consult if one of them were threatened by the aggressive action of any other power on a Pacific issue. On the back of this, as it were, was erected the Nine-Power Treaty, which brought in Italy, Portugal, Belgium, the Netherlands, and China as well. It constituted in effect a multilateral endorsement of the "open door," pledging respect for China's territorial and administrative integrity and abstention from the seeking or granting of special rights or privileges at each other's expense. In immediate furtherance of this Britain joined the U.S.A. in putting pressure on Japan to abandon her 1919 gains from China. While Britain gave up the lease of her naval base at Weihaiwei, Japan gave up Kiaochow.

This was the diplomatic framework into which the Five-Power Naval Treaty was fitted. Signed on 6 February 1922, it provided that after scrapping and completion of ships then on the stocks, the principal naval

powers of the world would retain capital ships in the approximate ratio
of 5:5:3:1.7:1.7, roughly giving the U.S.A. and Britain 500,000 tons
each, Japan 300,000 tons, and France and Italy 175,000 tons each. There
would be a ten-year holiday in capital ship construction. To this was
appended an important set of strategic agreements: the U.S.A. was not
to establish any new fortifications west of Hawaii, nor Japan in the
Kuril, Ryukyu, or Pescadores islands or in Formosa, nor Britain east of
Singapore.

Thus in place of a harmful armaments race and an embarrassing alliance with Japan Britain secured—what? An amicable naval settlement
with the U.S.A., creating parity in a context of agreed attitudes toward
the other principal naval powers. What did the U.S.A. secure that made
the U.S. Senate approve all three treaties? A recognition from Britain
of her claim to equality at sea and an amicable acceptance by her Pacific
rival of her superiority—at a distance. The bases she agreed not to build
would in any case have been too expensive in the cost-accounting mood
of the 1920s. But the strategic disabilities which the agreement imposed
on her could only have been offset by an Anglo-American alliance in
the Pacific. As it was, the principles for which she won acceptance in
the Four- and Nine-Power Treaties (and which Britain equally welcomed) were, if Japan chose to flout them, virtually unenforceable. Thus,
at Washington, Britain and the United States realigned themselves, to
sail, almost literally, on parallel courses, but they achieved their realignment in large measure by closing their eyes to the longer-term implications of their decisions.

The Washington disarmament agreements applied only to capital
ships. They did not extend to cruisers or submarines, in which the strategic requirements of Britain and the U.S.A. were very different. Britain
with imperial lines of communication to protect felt the need of more
numerous, but lighter, armed vessels; the U.S. Navy operating from
home bases could do with fewer provided they were heavier. In 1927 at
Geneva these contrarieties prevented agreement, but in 1929 President
Herbert Hoover and Ramsay MacDonald (the first British prime minister to visit the U.S.A. while in office) found a basis for accord. This was
embodied in the London Naval Treaty of 1930 in the form of a compromise that gave Britain an advantage in lighter cruisers within a total
of 339,000 tons and America an advantage in heavier vessels. This made
possible an extension of the 5:5:3 formula of 1922 to noncapital ships,

as far as the U.S.A., Britain, and Japan were concerned (France and
Italy could not agree), and this in turn made possible the postponement
until 1936 of the 1931 replacements in capital ships allowable by the
Washington treaty. The London treaty in fact represented the high point
of naval (or any other) disarmament between the wars. When the signatories remet in 1935 to discuss the extension, the climate had completely changed. Japan would have nothing less than total parity, and
Britain, the U.S.A., and France merely agreed on an "exchange of information" about building intentions. But by this time, of course, the
old worries about Anglo-American naval rivalry were taking second
place to a common concern about the menace of Germany and Japan.

The decade that witnessed the winding down of Anglo-American
naval rivalry saw a much less happy outcome to the other controversial
Anglo-American legacy of World War I, the war debts. In February
1922 Congress passed the Debt Funding Act, to determine the basis on
which the loans extended to the Allies during and after the war should
be repaid to the United States. This opened a Pandora's box of mutual
misunderstanding and recrimination. Even at this distance of time it is
impossible to follow the course of the so-called war debts controversy
without a feeling of disgust and irritation at the stupidity, insensitivity,
small-mindedness, and demagoguery displayed by almost all the participants. Some of the dissension was perhaps inescapable given the whole
grisly enterprise of trying to incorporate in one agreed balance-sheet the
incommensurable costs of war—financial, material, human. How many
lives equal how many dollars? When is a war a common war? How far
is it merely a temporary and limited conjunction of separate national interests? On none of these questions was there any prospect of agreement
among the victorious powers. Nor was this all. Two great illusions hung
over the debate. The first was the one common to all the Allies, though
in varying degrees; this was the illusion of reparations, that Germany
could be made to pay the cost of the war. The other was the illusion of
the United States, that it is possible to pursue simultaneously the policies
of a creditor and a debtor country.

In the controversy that followed, Britain was caught in the middle.
Her world financial leadership at the outbreak of war had enabled her
to sustain the coalition against Germany, as a hundred years before she
had sustained that against France, by making loans to her necessitous
cobelligerents. When funds ran low in the U.S.A. for the necessary pur-

chases of foodstuffs and munitions, she had assumed the role of money raiser on the American market; even after America entered the war, this relationship continued, with Britain borrowing in the U.S.A. with one hand, to lend in Europe with the other. The result was that by 1920, when these transactions drew to a close, Britain was owed approximately $8,000 million (some £1,825 million) and owed to the United States approximately $4,000 million (some £850 million).

When therefore the United States, in the wake of the Debt Funding Act, invited her debtors to make proposals for settling their obligations to her, it was natural for Britain to make the first response. This she did in the Balfour note of 1 August 1922, addressed also to all her debtor countries. The optimum solution, the note stated, would be an all-round cancellation of all inter-Allied debts and of reparations as well. (By now, Britain was a good deal less optimistic about the working of reparations than she had been earlier.) Had such a proposal been accepted, Britain would, of course, have done well; though a heavy net loser, she would, as the great trading nation, have gained from having the whole international slate wiped clean. But of course there was no chance in 1922 that the French would abandon reparations or the Americans repayment, and the note was content to settle for the principle that Britain would pay the U.S.A. whatever her allies and Germany paid her and that her allies' payments need not rise above the level of Britain's American debt.

But in fact there was never any chance of the United States accepting this professed link between war debts and reparations or even that between Britain's debts and Britain's loans. Instead, anticipating Calvin Coolidge's crisp conclusion—"They hired the money, didn't they?"— the administration insisted upon each debtor state negotiating separate agreements for repayment. Britain was the first to settle and, as it subsequently turned out, secured the hardest terms—full repayment over sixty-two years and an annual interest rate of 3.3 percent. Although these terms were generous within the limits of the accounting principles on which the U.S.A. was working, their relative severity compared with those granted to other debtors made them unpopular in Britain, and the settlement during the years in which it was in operation was a source of persistent ill feeling in both countries. In fact the total sum was never paid. By 1931 Great Britain had paid $1,911 million, a sum approximately $200 million more than she had received from reparations and

her own debtors and one reflecting a considerably higher percentage of
her American debt than any other large debtor nation had paid. Britain's
payments, nevertheless, were broadly dependent on her receipts—i.e., in
effect, on reparations. Thus the connection which the United States would
not recognize was in fact present—and present in the peculiarly prepos-
terous form that such payments as Germany made of reparations were
made possible only by the loans which private American capital made to
Germany throughout the twenties. The basic reasons for these loans, in
their turn, lay in the desire of American business and agriculture to sell
abroad to customers unable, by reason of American tariffs, to export to
America in turn. The new economic giant of the Western world, with
a huge surplus for export—producing in the late twenties 46 percent
of world manufactures—celebrated her newfound potency at the war's
end by an immediate rise in import duties, followed by the Fordney-
McCumber Tariff of 1922, which imposed the highest average rates in
American history. Thus, throughout the twenties, the U.S.A., while fi-
nancially a creditor nation, was making it progressively more difficult for
her debtors to pay what they owed her.

   On the main diplomatic front the twenties saw Britain drift purpose-
lessly around the central problem of European security, unable to find
any reassuring substitute for the American presence which was lacking
at Geneva, and indeed at most other places. In place of the lapsed Anglo-
American guarantees of 1919 she gave to France her signature on the
Locarno Agreements in 1924. This treaty of mutual guarantee between
Britain, Belgium, France, Germany, and Italy did not extend beyond the
territorial status quo in Western Europe, and it was only in response to
a flagrant violation of its provisions that an obligation to lend immediate
aid existed. As the thirties were to show, Locarno was a commitment of
a very limited degree. It did not even lead on to the Anglo-French staff
talks which had followed on the prewar entente. Much more widely acceptable in Britain was the Kellogg pact of 1928, not because of its potency, but because of its auspices. A sop to American pacifist sentiment,
the Pact of Paris, to give it its official name, committed no one to anything, for all its high-sounding "renunciation of war." But there were
many who hailed it as the thin entering wedge of a revived American
responsibility for the world beyond her shores. It was at least equally
arguable that it was the first manifestation of the recurrent illusion that
peace could be had by incantation.

The patched-up world order of the 1920s began to come apart first at its economic seams. Although Herbert Hoover loved to trace back the blame for the worldwide economic depression to Europe (a theory which gave comfort to American isolationism), it was the American stock market crash of 1929 that first shook the world from its belief in the makeshift relationships of the 1920s. Britain and the U.S.A. reacted—as indeed most countries did—in an essentially identical, defensive retreat into economic and political nationalism. There was one act of bold statesmanship, Hoover's 1931 announcement of America's willingness to waive all debt payments for a year, provided other nations did the same. But it was not enough. The Hawley-Smoot Tariff of 1930 had raised even higher the walls of American protectionism. Britain's "National" government, though it had the good sense to abandon the gold standard which it had been formed to protect, embarked on a deflationary course which encouraged the myth so dear to the British Left of the period that American bankers had forced the workers' government to its knees. Within months of its formation the "national" government introduced protection, substituting in the homeland of Adam Smith and Cobden the mercantilist expectations of the Ottawa Agreements for the free trade that had made Britain the workshop of the world. Small wonder that in such a context there was less than no rapport on economic crisis measures between the governments of Ramsay MacDonald and Stanley Baldwin and the new administration of Franklin Roosevelt. The World Economic Conference planned by Hoover and MacDonald to stabilize international currencies was bound in these circumstances to be fruitless. It met in London in 1933 only to have its basis kicked from under it by Roosevelt's determination not to give up any of the competitive advantage opened to him by the American devaluation of the dollar. With Anglo-American trade cut by a half to a third, and with each country almost exclusively preoccupied with its internal recovery, economic relations between the two nations could hardly be at a lower ebb.

On the political front it was the Far East which first brought Anglo-American statesmanship to an impasse. In choosing September 1931 for launching her attack on Manchuria, Japan chose well. Britain, in the throes of the 1931 economic crisis, was in poor shape for prompt, strong action, while the thought of imposing economic sanctions on one of her strongest trading partners was especially unattractive at a time when one of her chief anxieties was for her balance of payments. This was even

more true for the U.S.A., similarly crisis-ridden and with an even greater
trading stake in Japan than in China. By comparison with these considerations and the fundamental facts of geography, the unhappy accident that
the British foreign secretary, Sir John Simon, and the American secretary
of state, Mr. Henry Stimson, were mutually incompatible was of minor
consequence. Both powers temporized in the face of Japan's aggression;
from Washington, and subsequently from Geneva, the invasion of Manchuria brought forth only the moral reproof of the Stimson Doctrine—
that the United States would not recognize changes, territorial or otherwise, brought about by force. The Japanese attack on Shanghai in the
early months of 1932 did not even produce any invocation of the Nine-
Power Treaty. The common Anglo-American front in the Pacific lay in
ruins, and in its place there existed only a tangle of mutual recriminations.

Roosevelt's first term in the White House, which saw that remarkable
reinvigoration of American life which went by the name of the New
Deal, witnessed no corresponding revitalization of American foreign
policy. The years which were marked in Europe by the tyranny of Hitler, his alliance with Mussolini, the collapse of the Versailles settlements,
and the outbreak of the civil war in Spain were conspicuous in the United
States for a rise in isolationism, a reassessment and repudiation of Woodrow Wilson and all his works, and a rather pathetic determination to
avoid involvement in future "foreign wars" by enacting American neutrality in advance. That Roosevelt's own aspirations and convictions in
foreign policy should even today be a matter for historical debate is the
surest indication of his failure at the time to present a clear challenge to
the prevalent mood of his country. We cannot even be sure that he did
not share it. Yet the affirmative character, the dynamism of his administration could not indefinitely be arrested at its own shores, now that the
United States, willy-nilly, was a world power. The dictators sensed as
much, and those European democrats who were not mesmerized by the
menace of fascism and communism pinned many of their hopes—sometimes too many—on the American giant awakening from his isolationist
slumbers before it was too late.

The isolationism of America had its counterpart in Britain. By the
1930s the United Kingdom was being ruled by a generation which, after
seeing its contemporaries slaughtered en masse in Flanders and Gallipoli,
felt deeply committed emotionally and morally to avoiding a like catas-
trophe. There was, all the same, little unity beneath the pervasive vague

pacifism and nervelessness that animated the bulk of the electorate. Some placed a quasi-mystical faith in the League, with a remarkably poor awareness of the limitations and obligations of Geneva. Some thought Britain could ignore Europe and live off or with the Empire. Some thought communism a greater menace than fascism and were willing to tolerate the one in the hope of thwarting the other. All, or almost all, took it as axiomatic that Britain and the United States could never be found ranged against each other, but they differed as to how far, or in what ways, the two countries' policies could be aligned.

The thirties were indeed a curious time in Britain for relations with the United States. The New Deal struck responsive chords among the public at large, a natural inclination to vicarious liberalism being further stimulated by the comparative timidity with which Britain seemed to be tackling similar problems at home. At certain levels—journalism, the stage, fashionable society—these were years of easy and reciprocal inter-course and understanding. For the last time in the century the dollar and the pound could look each other in the face, and the comfortably-off in each country could, on a basis of equality, enjoy the pleasures of each other's company. Bertie Wooster was to be seen as often in Long Island as in Mayfair, and his creator was justly credited with being the last writer to have an equal command of both the British and the American languages. But outside the limited circle of the "talking classes" there was in Britain little real awareness or understanding of the United States. The same held true in reverse. Indeed even among American politicians few knew much of the realities of British and European politics; their British opposite numbers, especially those in power in the thirties, had no sure comprehension of the springs of American behavior. It was al-most unthinkable that the rulers of the two countries should actually meet and get to know each other. Indeed in the U.S.A. there was a per-vasive concern not to be seen in foreigners' company, lest this provide a handle for isolationist criticism. Instead there was a pathetic reliance, especially on the American side, on ill-chosen and unrepresentative go-betweens.

Thus it came about that even in an area like the Far East where inter-ests and policies ran in common, especial care was taken by the U.S.A. to avoid joint action. Japan's attacks on China, in clear violation of all the agreements of the twenties, were met by repeated rejections by the State Department of all proposals from the Foreign Office for a common front. The uncertain feeler that Roosevelt put out in his Chicago "quarantine speech" of 5 October 1937 was almost immediately withdrawn. When the signatories of the Nine-Power Treaty met in Brussels in November, the meeting took no decisions and merely adjourned. In December Britain and the U.S.A. found themselves simultaneous victims of the random character of Japanese aggression in China when the H.M.S. *Ladybird* and the U.S. gunboat *Panay* were attacked in Chinese waters; the *Panay* was sunk with heavy casualties. Even so, the U.S.A. would entertain no joint protest, only separate, parallel notes.

However, at Sumner Welles's instigation, Roosevelt did seem to be contemplating some American response to the rising level of dictators' threats and misbehavior in Europe as well as in Asia. In December, as a necessary preliminary to any joint Anglo-American confrontation with Japan, Roosevelt proposed secret naval staff talks, and in the New Year the head of the U.S. Navy's war plans division, Captain Royal E. Ingersoll, visited London. Roosevelt also proposed calling a conference of heads of missions in Washington to reach agreement—it was not *quite* clear on what—but on some sort of measures to arrest the slide toward war. This proposal has been the subject of much controversy then and since. Its immediate fate was to be turned down by Prime Minister Neville Chamberlain, while Anthony Eden, his foreign secretary, was on holiday, on the grounds that it would cut across Chamberlain's own plans for opposing Germany and Italy, plans which included the de jure recognition of Italy's Ethiopian conquests. Though Eden, on his return, got the rejection modified to postponement, Cordell Hull was deeply hostile to the de jure recognition (he had in 1935 imposed a "moral embargo" on oil shipments to Italy), and the proposed conference was further postponed until Hitler's annexation of Austria killed the idea. It was Eden's conviction that in rejecting Roosevelt's proposal Chamberlain had missed a heaven-sent opportunity to draw the U.S.A. into closer cooperation, and Eden's resignation, a month or so later, was due as much to this as to Chamberlain's policy toward Italy. Winston Churchill later described Chamberlain's action as "the loss of the last frail chance to save the world from tyranny otherwise than by war."[2] If the epithet "frail" be stressed, so much can be agreed. Chamberlain, in effect, decided to accord appeasement a higher priority than Anglo-American cooperation. But it would be a mistake to conclude that he was also making a choice between appeasement and "standing up to the dictators." There is nothing either

in the terms of Roosevelt's proposal or elsewhere to suggest that, particularly in relation to Germany, he was much less of an appeaser at the
time than Chamberlain. To quote Langer and Gleason's judicious ap-
praisal: "It is plain that the President's project . . . was intended to but-
tress the attempt of Britain to reach agreement with Germany. Though
involving no approval of British appeasement, it certainly implied acceptance of it."[3] That appeasement did not get woven into the fabric of
Anglo-American relations is principally due to Chamberlain's vanity and
insularity, his determination to pursue his own brand of appeasement
on his own. Nevertheless, though in the Munich crisis Roosevelt was
careful to stress America's noninvolvement, he used what influence he
had, e.g., with Mussolini, to promote a peaceful settlement, encouraged
Chamberlain to go to Munich, and endorsed Chamberlain's belief after
the Munich agreements that "there exists today the greatest opportunity
in years for the establishment of a new order based on justice and law."

Roosevelt awoke more rapidly than Chamberlain from the euphoria
of Munich, but even when the British disillusionment was complete and
the March 1939 guarantee to Poland (which led to war in September)
had been given, there was very little cooperation in the formulation of
any joint Anglo-American policies. Roosevelt embarked on an American
rearmament program and struggled, without success, to extricate himself
from the cramping restrictions of the Neutrality Act, with its ban on
the export of arms to belligerents. He facilitated British and French
arms purchases, but there was no joint contingency planning, no coordi-
nating of diplomatic action. The two democracies lay under a kind of
spell, having essentially the same interests and ideals in relation to the
international society that was crumbling before their eyes but unable to
concert the most elementary measures for their preservation. The British
switch from appeasement to "thus far and no farther" won sweeping
acceptance in the U.S.A., and both Britain and France were able to take
for granted the administration's approval of a course of action which
could have only one result when Hitler chose to make his next strike.
The King and Queen symbolized this ideological solidarity by paying, in
June 1939, the first visit of any reigning British sovereign to American
shores. But this was all set in a framework of American noninvolvement.
If war came, it would be Europe's war, the isolationists insisted. And in
the summer of 1939 the isolationists, by all the criteria of congressional
votes, public opinion polls, and that intangible something which politi-

cians scent as "the mood of the country," were as strong as at any time in the decade. So Roosevelt was refused his revision of the Neutrality Act, the Allies made their fumbling and unsuccessful attempts to enlist Soviet Russia against the Axis, and the initiative remained with Hitler. On 1 September Germany invaded Poland. On 3 September Britain and France declared war on Germany.

In 1914 the United States had been able to view the war that broke out in August as a truly European war. Americans had sympathies, some with one side, some with the other, but few felt their basic ideals and interests at stake and few envisaged their ultimate involvement in the conflict. In 1939 the U.S.A., even before the outbreak of hostilities, was a partisan in thought and feeling. The Axis powers by their whole course of conduct, from anti-Semitism at home to brutal aggression abroad, had alienated all but a lunatic fringe of American opinion. Consequently, in striking contrast to the period 1914–17, the years 1939–41 are, in the diplomatic and political record, marked principally not by the deterioration of America's relations with the eventual enemy—they were already so bad they could hardly get worse—but by the unevenly developing intimacy with her allies, Britain in particular. The story of the U.S.A.'s approach to war is very largely the story of Anglo-American relations in 1940 and 1941. Thanks to radio, the experiences and reactions of Britain in the blitz reached directly into the ears of Americans in their own homes and elicited a deeply sympathetic response. But the national will remained suspended like a compass needle subjected to two competing magnetic pulls. At a deep level in the national consciousness there was an ineradicable, almost fatalistic conviction that, do what she might, America must sooner or later be drawn in. Of equal strength was a reluctance to abandon, of her own will, her peace and independence and to join a conflict being fought far from her shores but so devastating in character that, were America involved, the consequences would be incalculable.

Small wonder if, placed at the head of a nation so deeply impaled in an agony of indecision, Franklin Roosevelt himself often found it hard to know what he should do, quite apart from what he could do. In Britain between 1939 and Pearl Harbor the general image of FDR was that of an eager foe of the Axis restrained from leading his country into battle only by the need to carry with him the less enlightened or courageous of his fellow countrymen. It meant indeed a great deal for British morale to see their FDR in such a light. We now know, however, that the contrast was not so stark. The farseeing and courageous man in the White House shared many of the hesitations and misgivings of the man in the street. His resolution often lagged behind his convictions; more than once he allowed his decision to depend upon events. Much of this was the shrewd calculation of a master of timing, ever conscious of the need to carry his people with him at every step of the way. But much of it was not. "It is a fearful thing to lead this great peaceful people into war," said Woodrow Wilson in 1917—a sentiment that Franklin Roosevelt might often have echoed between 1939 and 1941. It was not the least of his good fortune that at Pearl Harbor the Japanese relieved him of that final fearful decision.

By September 1939 the British had been through all the agonies of indecision, of letting their instinctive convictions wait upon their fears, and found themselves in the settled frame of mind of people who know the die has been cast. There were few illusions. A long war was taken for granted, and while its course could not be foreseen, it was known to be painful and costly. There was not, from the first, very much confidence placed in France. Nothing in the course of interwar diplomacy, least of all in the last year or two before the outbreak, had created in Britain any intimate rapport with her ally across the Channel. For the long run Britain's hopes were pinned far more on the United States. Not that anyone hoped for an early American entry. By 1939 there was a very realistic awareness in Britain of the state of American public opinion and a widely diffused understanding of how it should and should not be handled. In large part this was because, having been through an isolationist phase of their own, Britons had themselves already undergone something of the American experience, even retained some residual sympathy for the timidities and illusions upon which it rested. At official levels the assurance of American sympathy and cooperation within the limits set by popular feeling meant a great deal, not only practically, but also in the maintenance of morale and the capacity to take the cool gamble on the long term. And of course the reliance on American materials and supplies was basic to the whole Allied strategy. On the American side similarly the desire to escape direct involvement led to an enhanced willingness to believe that the British could, if given "the tools," "finish the job."

When war broke out in 1914, American neutrality had been a real thing, resting not upon legislation but on a genuine belief that America was not obliged, by self-interest or moral commitment, to side with either party. In 1939 neutrality was a towering legal structure drawing little or no support from any intellectually or morally convincing concept of America's interests or duties. It depended for its appeal upon a deep-seated aversion to war. Thus when Roosevelt, in November 1939, at last secured from Congress a lifting of the arms embargo and a substitution of a cash-and-carry provision, he did not pretend that this made America any more neutral, merely that, taken together with the ban on U.S. ships entering danger zones, it gave America greater protection against the contagion of the European conflict. It was in keeping with this that the Declaration of Panama in October lined up the Pan-American republics behind the proclamation of a 300- to 1,000-mile neutral zone or "safety belt" in the Atlantic—a multilateral extension of the Monroe Doctrine. But it was also significant that, like the Monroe Doctrine, it depended in its first formulation on the support of the British fleet; when they violated it, as in the Battle of the River Plate, there was nothing the Latin Americans could or would do about it. At the same time the U.S. naval patrols of the "safety belt" scarcely made a pretense of neutral behavior, informally and freely exchanging information with the British on the movements of German naval vessels.

In line with this, the defense of neutral rights, the oldest American tradition in the North Atlantic, shriveled to token protests purely "for the record." From the outset the administration was determined to take an indulgent attitude toward the British blockade, which indeed, in its definition of contraband and blacklisting, was carefully based on American practice in 1917 and after. When disputed points arose, they were handled whenever possible by friendly discussion rather than by public protest.

For all its friendliness the U.S. government was still, in important aspects of its behavior, little more than a detached observer of the Allied struggle. "Cash-and-carry" left the prohibition on loans to belligerents fully in force. This derived from the Johnson Act of 1934, which im-

posed a ban even on private loans to governments in default on their
war debts. Thus Britain had to husband her dollar holdings and even
adapt her strategy to keep crucial dollar-earning exports going. The
"phony war" inspired many Americans to believe that appeasement was
not really dead. Neville Chamberlain was congenitally incapable of establishing a real rapport with Roosevelt, though fortunately for Britain
Lord Lothian, ambassador in Washington from August 1939 to his death
in December 1940, proved to be an ideal spokesman for the British
cause. By contrast Roosevelt was served in London by an outright appeaser and defeatist, Joseph Kennedy, while William Bullitt, his ambassador in Paris, was as suspicious of the British as he was devoted to the
French. For these and other reasons illusions persisted in Washington
that peace might yet be restored. This led in February and March of 1940
to Sumner Welles, the under-secretary of state, doing a Colonel House–
like tour of the belligerents. The best that can be said of the venture is
that it served to destroy the illusions that provoked it.

In May came the German hammer blows on Scandinavia, the Low
Countries, and France. Suddenly the scene was transformed. The realities of the world conflict were laid bare and its implications for America
could no longer be denied. The revelation of the power of the blitzkrieg
produced what were arguably exaggerated reactions in the U.S.A. Yet
the vista it opened up of a possibly lonely America in a world dominated
by an Axis that had overrun Europe was more realistic than the previous
illusory world-view of the isolationists. As France fell, Britain was more
and more clearly seen as the last remaining outer bastion of the U.S.A.'s
defenses. A movement sprang up under the leadership of William Allen
White, Republican, Midwesterner, and editor of the *Emporia Gazette,*
to "Defend America by Aiding the Allies"—a title which perfectly ex-
pressed the belief or hope that the war could still be won 3,000 miles
away by American arms but in Allied hands. Those more realistic or less
politic, who recognized the Allies' cause as more directly America's own,
formed themselves into a ginger group within the larger movement, the
Century Group, and for the first time openly advocated that the U.S.A.
should declare that a state of war with the Axis already existed.

In Britain the German breakthrough brought to the premiership Winston Churchill, the embodiment for the next five years of the national
resolution and will to win. This put Britain's affairs in the hands of a
leader who placed the highest priority upon relations with the United

States and who by his own exuberant Anglo-American personality guaranteed that the British case would never go by default in American councils. With Roosevelt he enjoyed a rapport which came as near to truly personal intimacy as the relations between two heads of state can ever be. Some record remains of it in the remarkable wartime exchange of correspondence between the two leaders,[1] but even more remarkable is the sequence of personal meetings à *deux* or in the company of other national leaders which, to a degree unprecedented in history, kept the diplomacy and the ground strategy of the conflict under continuous personal review.

In 1940, to the single-minded urgings of Churchill, concerned only with the overthrow of the Axis, Roosevelt had to respond with the less heroic and necessarily more complex considerations of a president concerned to preserve the unity of his people and to develop a policy which would protect their national interests, their pride, and their principles. If in an election year and in the face of desperate isolationist criticism and pressure this resulted in lapses from decisive action and plain, honest speaking, the critic must remain mindful, as Franklin Roosevelt ever was, of the fate of Woodrow Wilson who (not indeed in 1916, but in 1918) had pursued a bolder course to a more disastrous end.

Immediately, in face of the French debacle, there was little Roosevelt could do. In June he ordered the army to turn over any surplus weapons to make good some of the British losses at Dunkirk. Of enormous value, in terms of morale, was his Charlottesville speech of 10 June, on the morrow of Italy's entry into the war, which extended "to the opponents of force the material resources" of the U.S.A. With justice it could be argued that this really committed the U.S.A. to the Allied cause almost as much as a declaration of cobelligerency. Certainly if the Axis leaders had chosen to regard it as a hostile act they would, by any standard of traditional diplomacy, have been within their rights. Yet for all its boldness it was not followed by the really vigorous program of war production which was its logical corollary. The president would not even allow publication of his "Fight On" message to poor Paul Reynaud, prime minister of a tottering France. He declined to send a U.S. squadron, as Churchill urged, to Eire, to stiffen Irish hostility to Hitler. Above all, he was slow to respond to Churchill's desperate, reiterated pleas for fifty over-age destroyers to ease the strain in the Atlantic war against the U-boats. It would seem as if FDR was either infected by the doubts of

his military advisers about Britain's survival or intimidated by isolationists like Senator Thomas J. Walsh who raised a storm about the transfer
of even a few motor torpedo boats. Churchill for his part had no shame
about playing what might be called the weak man's ace and reminding
the president that a defeated Britain would not necessarily be able to
keep its fleet out of the clutches of the Axis. But poor men's aces seldom
avail against rich men's trumps and Roosevelt was able to gamble on the
British holding out and then to secure for the fifty over-age destroyers a
quid pro quo almost as profitable as the Louisiana Purchase. This was
the "destroyer-bases" deal, negotiated at the height of the Battle of Britain, by which the U.S.A. obtained ninety-nine-year leases of eight air
and naval bases in Newfoundland and the British West Indies. Thus a
century and a half after Yorktown the territories that Britain still retained in North America acquired a new significance for the security of
the United States—and also for the unity of the North Atlantic. For in
making the deal the U.S.A. was certainly being induced to take a long
step away from neutrality. More valuable to Churchill than fifty over-
age destroyers was the ability to say to the House of Commons: "This
process means that . . . the British Empire and the United States will
have to be somewhat mixed up together. . . . I do not view the process
with any misgivings. I could not stop it if I wished: no one can stop it.
Like the Mississippi it just keeps rolling along."[2]

Roosevelt, with an election campaign on his hands, could hardly express it so. Indeed at one moment, hard pressed as he was by the continuing isolationist sentiment, he gave one pledge which he was to live
to regret: "Your boys are not going to be sent into any foreign wars."[3]
However, the election once secure, the "mixing-up" process resumed its
inexorable way. By the end of 1940 American munitions of war were
reaching Britain in a steady flow, though the cash to buy them was running out. The law and still worse the folk memories and legends of the
war debts stood in the way of allied loans. With a bravura touch, by-
passing controversy with a metaphor, Roosevelt launched the idea of
lend-lease—of supplying Britain with what she needed and postponing
settlement until after the war, to be effected then by repayment in kind
or otherwise. True, even the loan of a garden hose has been known to
cause friction between neighbors, and sovereign states have clashes of
interest that metaphors cannot wholly resolve. Even so, lend-lease was a
brilliant invention that served the interests of both parties at a crucial

moment, a proof, if ever there was one, that nations *can* learn from history. Despite strong opposition, it cleared Congress by majorities of 317 to 71 in the House and 60 to 31 in the Senate, to become law in March 1941. American neutrality was now a transparent fiction.

While lend-lease was going through Congress, secret staff talks with representatives of the British chiefs of staff went on in Washington designed to prepare a common strategy in the eventuality of America's becoming a belligerent. Their report—"ABC-1"—was typical of the many more such strategical plans that were hammered out by Americans and Britons over the next five years, in its form—of free argument and give-and-take—in its broad concept of an Atlantic First strategy, and in its allocation of specific tasks and responsibilities for each fighting front. Also, slightly more ominously, is the fact that it was in relation to the Far East that its recommendations were least harmonious and precise.

It was not long before the rate of shipping losses in the North Atlantic forced Roosevelt, despite a suspicious public opinion, to take the next steps to guarantee that there would be a Britain to lend-lease to. At the navy's urgings he extended the patrols beyond the 300-mile limit into the mid-Atlantic, agreed with the Danes to take Greenland under U.S. protection, and declared an "unlimited national emergency." In June Hitler unleashed his attack upon the USSR. It may have counted for a good deal that Britain's response through Churchill was swift and unequivocal: "Any man or state who fights on against Nazidom will have our aid." For the U.S.A., not actually at war and acutely apprehensive of the Communist infection, Britain's action may well have tipped the balance in Russia's favor. Roosevelt declined to invoke the Neutrality Act in relation to the conflict and pledged aid to the USSR. To the isolationists this was a new challenge. "Are we going to fight to make Europe safe for Communism?" The continuing vitality of their appeal was strikingly demonstrated in August when the limited conscription measure, the Selective Service Act, passed a year before, came up for renewal. Congress refused to give Roosevelt power to keep the draftees in service for the duration of the present emergency or to send them outside the Western hemisphere. Instead their service was extended for only eighteen months and the measure only squeaked through the House of Representatives by one vote. The fact was that the shock and stimulus administered by the fall of France and the Battle of Britain had abated and the war had once more assumed the remote, slightly unreal quality of something being fought "over there."

This helps to explain the paradox of the much dramatized Roosevelt-Churchill meeting, the Atlantic Conference held at sea in Placentia Bay, Newfoundland, on 9–12 August. Here were two statesmen producing an agreed set of principles—a kind of updated Fourteen Points—to govern the peace settlement of a war not yet won, in which indeed the more powerful of the two partners was not even as yet a combatant. The Atlantic Charter was a valuable reminder at home and abroad of the bonds of interest and principle that united Britain and America. The meeting demonstrated solidarity, boosted British morale, and enabled a great deal of useful coordination to take place between the military and diplomatic officials of the two sides. It also papered over the fact that Roosevelt was reluctant to take any further steps into belligerency, even the convoying of supplies, or to commit the United States any further toward deterring Japan in the Far East.

Here indeed some reversal of attitudes had occurred. In the summer of 1940 Japan had maximized her opportunities and put pressure on a beleaguered Britain to close the Burma Road, the main avenue for Western supplies to reach Chiang Kai-shek's China. Britain's reluctant acquiescence in a three-month closing had exposed her to much criticism in the U.S.A. But American policy was torn between a desire to check Japan's expansionism and a consciousness that war with Japan would overstrain her resources and endanger her Atlantic First strategy. So although she gradually applied economic pressures, embargoing sales of aviation fuel (July 1940), scrap iron (September 1940), and iron ore (December 1940), she remained anxious to play for time in the Far East. Hence the dilatory and inconclusive Hull-Nomura talks in 1941. To a degree this matched the requirements of British policy as well, but when in July 1941 the Japanese began to move into southern Indochina, the British began to have serious concern for their base in Singapore. At Placentia Bay they pleaded, in vain, for a firm American commitment to deter Japan. Instead there was the rather fumbling handling of Prince Konoye's overtures, with Roosevelt responding more warmly and Cordell Hull more coldly, and the steady slide, once Tojo had taken over, into the abyss. Yet as late as early December Roosevelt would give no public assurance that a Japanese attack on British or Dutch possessions would be regarded as an act of war.

Meanwhile, in the North Atlantic the process of American involvement seemed as slow as it was inexorable, with the movement of American policy seemingly dependent on Nazi behavior. In September the alleged attack on the destroyer *Greer* elicited from Roosevelt the response that American ships might shoot at sight and would help to convoy. In October it took the attack on the destroyer *Kearney* to effect the repeal of the Neutrality Act's ban on the arming of merchant ships. In November similarly the sinking of the *Reuben James* induced the Senate to agree that U.S. merchantmen should be allowed to enter combat zones. The U.S.A. had moved from being the arsenal of democracy to being almost the supply corps of the British and Russian forces. Yet "the overt act" was still awaited. In Britain it was being anxiously asked how much longer she would have to hold out before American aid experienced that transformation which only open war could bring. On 7 December the answer came, but not from the direction expected. Indeed had Hitler not gratuitously honored his pledge to his partner in the Tripartite Pact and declared war on 11 December, the United States might still have lacked an adequate justification for proceeding to a "shooting war" in Europe and the Atlantic. As it was, the die was cast and the long period of letting the national will be shaped by events was over. In Britain the relief was undisguised. In a celebrated passage in his war memoirs Winston Churchill gives expression to the sentiments that not only he, but the nation also, felt. "So we had won after all! . . . Once again in our long island history we should emerge, however mauled and mutilated, safe and victorious. . . . Many disasters, immeasurable cost and tribulation lay ahead, but there was no more doubt about the end."[4] Roosevelt put it more succinctly to "the Former Naval Person, London": "Today all of us are in the same boat with you and the people of the Empire and it is a ship which will not and cannot be sunk."

The "boat" or "ship" or indeed ark into which Pearl Harbor precipitated the United States was one which had no parallel in the history of the United States or indeed of Western civilization. Of all the "United Nations" combatants the United States was the most powerful, yet in striking contrast to her behavior in 1917–18, she threw in her lot with her allies, helping to devise and operate a unified and intimate set of arrangements for the conduct of the war which represented a fusion of national identities, if not of sovereignties, hitherto unprecedented. Why such self-abnegation in the context of such power? The explanation without doubt is to be found in the Anglo-American relationship. The years of undeclared war, of what Robert Sherwood called the "common-law alliance," had paved the way for the peculiarly close interlocking of their efforts when they came to fight openly at each other's side. Though essentially the weaker power, the United Kingdom brought to the partnership on 7 December 1941 a greater strength in all active departments, save perhaps the navy, and—what was of crucial importance—two and a quarter years' experience in fighting the Axis not only in Europe but all over the globe. The contribution which she could make to the joint enterprise was therefore out of proportion to her share of the combined potential. The years of "common-law alliance" had, moreover, demonstrated how on essentials the American and the British views of the job to be done and the way to do it were, if not identical, at any rate remarkably compatible. The structure of cooperation which seemingly sprang up overnight after Pearl Harbor had thus its origins in a gradual and tested evolution of policies and procedures.

To the fused effort of Britain and the United States it was not difficult to add the smaller contributions of the minor members of the United Nations—though one of them, Canada, by virtue of scale, location, and relationships, had an especially important contribution to make. There were, however, two signatories of the United Nations Declaration of 1 January 1942[5] which, for all their magnitude and potency, did not accept the Anglo-American model of what a wartime association should be. These were Russia and China. Russia, with an ideology detaching her from, if not opposing her to, the democracies, was governed by a bureaucratic despotism incapable of genuine cooperation save at the highest levels. This had the effect of confining Russia's partnership to the broadest issues of strategical planning and, even there, of making it dependent on personal relationships to a degree that Roosevelt and Churchill's never was. If this, in certain contexts, threw the British and the Americans closer together, in others it drove them apart. The cruciality of Russia's role, both in war and in peacemaking, led to a certain competition for Stalin's favors. Paradoxically, while the British electorate, fighting a war of austerity, found more common ground with its Russian allies than did the Americans, it was Roosevelt who was willing to drive closer to the limits of what was democratically tolerable in his pursuit of Stalin's cooperation.

Where China was concerned, the case was different. Her remote position and detached interests made any real fusion of her war effort with that of her allies impossible. Where America and Britain differed was in the value to be attached to her symbolic role. To the U.S.A. this was considerable; there was a sustained pretense that she could be a member of the Big Four, even that Chiang's regime could be treated as democratic. On the conduct of the war these illusions did not have a great effect, but they fostered problems for the peace. More worrying, in day-to-day terms, were the British and American differences over France. Here immediate circumstances played some part—the British commitment to Charles de Gaulle, the American experiment with Vichy. Personalities entered into it too, particularly the abrasive personality of de Gaulle. But there was a longer-range divergence: the British believed that after the war they might need a vigorous France to help control Germany, while the Americans had less immediate fears about the shape of postwar Europe.

Behind the military and diplomatic conduct of the war, and basic to it, was a great production effort. The main instruments of Anglo-American cooperation in this vital field were the Combined Boards.[6] These were bodies on which sat representatives of both the American and the British governments. Their job was to bring their respective policies into harmony. Sometimes the boards had power to command, but essentially they were agencies of persuasion. If they encountered resistance or disagreement, they appealed to the informal combination of Roosevelt and Churchill, who, as Admiral Leahy, Roosevelt's chief of staff, put it, "really ran the war." The Combined Munitions Assignment Board was peculiar in that it functioned in two parts, one in London headed by Lord Beaverbrook (later by Lord Lyttelton) to arrange the distribution of munitions produced in Britain, and one in Washington headed by Harry Hopkins, Roosevelt's "man Friday," to distribute those produced in the U.S.A. The Combined Raw Materials Board administered the resources of the whole Commonwealth as well as those of the U.S.A., and as such was as important for the U.S. war effort as for the British. A link between these two boards was provided by the Combined Production and Resources Board. This might have been the "super-czar" of war production, had the American economy ever become as tightly organized for war as the British was. In fact, the U.S.A. achieved its gigantic production effort not by substituting guns for butter but largely by superimposing the one on the other. Rationing, controls, and governmental integration were always much less than in Britain. Thus there was never a single American production department which could be equated and combined with the British Ministry of Production. Perhaps indeed the

principal value of this board was to make British experience in organiz-
ing for war available to the U.S.A. in those areas where she needed to
draw on it. Finally, in two sectors, shipping and food, the U.S.A. disposed of so much larger resources that their Combined Boards were a
good deal less than fully integrative in their operations; they mainly
provided a kind of machinery by which British claims could be handled.

All this blending of national administrations required the presence in
Washington of a small army of British officials—some 9,000 at its peak
—and the creation, around the British Embassy, of a miniature Whitehall. As the U.S.A. got deeper into the war and its presence in Europe
expanded, something similar happened in London, where Grosvenor
Square became known as "Eisenhower Platz," the center of a complex
American administrative network. The result of this elaborate interlocking machinery was, despite inevitable friction and slippage, a much
higher degree of cooperation and unforced fusion than had ever before
existed between two sovereign nation states. As William McNeill in his
classic study of wartime relations well says:

The pooling of industrial and raw material resources between the United
States and Great Britain raised the war potential of the two nations far
above what could have been achieved by each working alone; and the
reality of economic interdependence facilitated and indeed required
the continuance of close strategic co-operation. After 1942 it would have
been almost beyond the power of either nation to disentangle itself from
the alliance with the other, even had anyone considered such a step
desirable.[7]

It is not true, as some have claimed,[8] that the two countries' economies
were completely integrated. Their differences were too great for that—in
scale and diversity, and also in the kind of war they were fighting: for
Britain a really total war, with every aspect of the nation's life directed
to victory; for the U.S.A. a struggle that called forth great effort but
which, given her resources of time, space, and riches, she could win with
a good margin to spare. Nonetheless, while the war lasted, new entities
were created over many areas of decision making, in both countries, in
which narrowly national interests were subordinated to a common dedi-
cation to victory.

If this was true on the home front, it was even more true for the military. The early months of 1942 saw the evolution of the Combined Chiefs

of Staff as the effective day-to-day directorate for running the Anglo-American war. Of course the British chiefs of staff could only meet their American opposite numbers in person at infrequent intervals; ordinarily they were represented at Washington, where the combined chiefs had their headquarters, by a team of deputies in constant telegraphic communication with London. The British deputies were headed by Sir John Dill. Between him and General George C. Marshall, chief of staff of the U.S. Army, there developed a relationship of remarkable intimacy that had a lot to do with the smooth working of the alliance. Below the Combined Chiefs of Staff came the commanders in the field, and here Marshall's insistence on unity of command led to another remarkable cooperative experiment. In each theater there was a supreme commander of one nationality and a deputy of the opposite. Below them came the service commanders in chief, of whom the supreme commander might or might not act as one. But at every level in the staff there was a balancing and fusion of national identities to create a genuinely unified structure. The classic example of this was in SHAEF (Supreme Headquarters of the Allied Expeditionary Forces), the command which launched the invasion of Europe. There Dwight D. Eisenhower as Supreme Commander had the British Air Chief Marshall Tedder as his deputy, with the British Leigh Mallory as air commander, the British Admiral Bertram Ramsay in charge of naval operations, and successively the British Bernard Montgomery and the American Omar Bradley as army commanders as the proportion of British and American soldiers in active engagement changed.

The Eisenhower integration was due as much to his own warm yet diplomatic personality as to the particular circumstances of the invasion. During the year preceding the invasion hundreds of thousands of U.S. servicemen had been living in Britain (in addition to those, mainly in the air force, who were there throughout the war). This, in a myriad ways and in purely personal terms, constituted an experience in Anglo-American relations just as significant as the intermeshing of officialdom. What might have been a gigantic problem of national incompatibilities under stress turned out, in personal terms, to be an extraordinary success. This in turn undoubtedly made its own contribution to the remarkable triumph of Anglo-American arms that followed. The European theater was of course exceptional in this, though something of the same objective was generally realized elsewhere. The Pacific, however, was different. Here was a peculiarly American war, in its inception, in the heavy dependence on one arm, the navy, in which the U.S.A. had overwhelming local preponderance, and in the vastly greater and more direct American interest in the area. The Pacific war was also in the hands of three remarkably autocratic American commanders, Generals Joseph Stilwell and Douglas MacArthur and Admiral Ernest King, with whom cooperation was seldom easy, even for some of their fellow countrymen. For all these reasons the British share in strategy and execution was low and both the commands and the forces were almost exclusively American.

The main outlines of this structure of Anglo-American partnership were worked out with surprising smoothness in Washington at the Churchill-Roosevelt "Arcadia" Conference in January 1942. The same meeting agreed on a basic strategy. "ABC-1" was adhered to with striking tenacity. The Atlantic First principle was maintained, and despite the provocation of Pearl Harbor the flow of American supplies to Britain was not diverted. This harmony of basic purpose persisted throughout the war against Italy and Germany. Disagreements were mainly about timing and execution. They reflected the contrast between an impatient and optimistic U.S.A., concerned almost exclusively with getting there "fustest with mostest," and a cautious Britain, determined to avoid the huge bloodletting of World War I and more conscious of the problems that a triumphant Russian presence in Eastern Europe would create. The delay in mounting a second front in Europe, so much resented by Stalin, was at bottom due not to any differences between Roosevelt and Churchill but to brute facts of logistics and the slow progress achieved in North Africa and Italy. Roosevelt's consistency, in the face of these disappointments, in adhering to an Atlantic First and "second front" strategy, despite heavy pressure from his Pacific commanders and congressional Pacific Firsters, is not the least remarkable feature of his wartime leadership. It paid off in the year between June 1944, which saw the Normandy landings, and May 1945, when the German Wehrmacht surrendered. With consummate generalship and a surprisingly low rate of casualties, a combined effort which was more than a partnership in arms, which was indeed a fusion of national wills and talents, carried Anglo-American arms to victory in Europe.

It was Churchill's intention, both for the preservation of Britain's role in the alliance and in defense of Commonwealth interests, to switch British arms, after victory in Europe, to the fight against Japan. America's

Pacific strategists made little secret of their indifference to this. They were confident of their naval competence. What worried them was the probable costliness of the final assault on the Japanese homeland, and here they entertained greater hopes of Russia, with its huge manpower and close proximity. It was this, no doubt, that motivated a good deal of the rapprochement which Roosevelt carefully cultivated with Stalin even at Churchill's expense in the Big Three conferences at Teheran in November 1943 and Yalta in February 1945. Political factors also played their part. Roosevelt's suspicions of Britain's imperial designs were as sincere as Churchill's devotion to empire was profound. Roosevelt tried without success to adduce the parallels of 1776 as guidelines for British policy in India, only to receive one of Churchill's sharpest rebuffs. In the State Department there was concern lest Churchill's determination to keep the Communists from gaining control in liberated Italy and Greece should result in the establishment of reactionary regimes there. At the same time the U.S.A. turned a deaf ear to Churchill's pleadings to drive as far and as fast into Europe as possible in order to keep Russia at arm's length. Nor at Yalta would Roosevelt take up the cause of the non-Communist Poles with the vigor that Churchill desired. Instead his top priority was to secure by concessions, some at China's expense, a Russian commitment to enter the war against Japan. Thus the pressures of the Pacific war combined with the emerging problems of peace in Europe to loosen the intimacy and harmony of the Anglo-American alliance. "I hope," cabled Churchill, a month after Yalta, "that the rather numerous telegrams I have had to send you on so many of our difficult and intertwined affairs are not becoming a bore to you. Our friendship is the rock on which I build for the future of the world so long as I am one of the builders."[9] Less than a month later Roosevelt was dead. On 26 July Churchill, defeated in the British general election, resigned the premiership. On 8 August the Russians declared war on Japan, and on the ninth the second atomic bomb was dropped, on Nagasaki. On 14 August the Japanese surrendered.

The end of World War II left the United States in a position of unparalleled power. Her arms were triumphant across the world, in every theater in which they had been deployed. Her enemies, Italy, Germany, and Japan, were not merely prostrate; they were positively anxious to have their new master come in and take full control. For the enforcement of her will there were six million men under arms on land, over three and a half million at sea, and over two million in the air. They were all equipped with the most up-to-date weapons, in unparalleled abundance, and maintained, behind the fighting lines, at a level of comfort and efficiency unique in the annals of warfare. Finally, in the atomic bomb the United States had at her exclusive disposal an instrument which, in its appalling destructiveness, well deserved the appellation of the ultimate weapon. Supporting this panoply of military power, safe behind two oceans and distributed over a vast landmass, lay a productive capacity which was also unparalleled in history. The equipment and maintenance of the vast American military machine had been achieved without the imposition of any severe stringencies on America's civilian population. Indeed the overwhelming majority of Americans enjoyed a higher standard of living during the war than ever before. Moreover their labors supplied not only the U.S.A.'s war effort but also much of the requirements of her allies, both for arms and for food, as well as the basic necessities of life for many of the former enemy countries. This extraordinary productive capacity, industrial and agricultural, deployed for the first time at full throttle, meant that the United States, alone among the combatant powers, was ending the war richer than when she began it. Her territory was unravaged by bombardment or invasion, her casualties in conflict had been vastly less than those of any other major belligerent, her forces had shown the flag triumphantly in most parts of the world, and her products, from Spam to Jeeps, had penetrated in the service of war markets which her exporters had never tapped in time of peace.

By comparison, the United Kingdom, whose arms were also triumphant across the globe, had purchased survival and, in 1945, victory at a price heavier than any in her national experience. She escaped invasion, but not bombardment. The physical destruction wreaked by the Luftwaffe was estimated at £1,500 million, while at sea a third of her vital merchant marine had been sunk. She lost 60,000 civilians from air raids, and 265,000 of her fighting men were killed in action. This still left her in 1945 with an army of almost 3,000,000, an air force of almost 1,000,000, and a navy of 790,000. But this formidable fighting force was desperately needed at home to relieve the strain on a civilian population which had been mobilized to the last man and woman to maintain the war effort at its final pitch. The British economy had been strained to its limit and beyond to keep this fighting machine in operation. Civilian consumption had been slashed to a minimum, capital resources had been squandered, huge debts had been incurred. A small, densely populated island, dependent on overseas trade and investments for its living, had seen its overseas investments sold to a total of £1,117 million, its gold and dollar reserves halved by over £400 million, and its overseas indebtedness rise to £3,355 million. The best estimates suggested that about one-quarter (£7,300 million) of Britain's national wealth had been lost in the war. It was as if all the resources and treasures which in the days of her preeminence had been built up by Victorian thrift and enterprise had now been flung, with a kind of calculated prodigality, upon the pyre of total war. Moreover, by a harsh paradox, even the American aid which was indispensable in the struggle created at the end certain additional handicaps. It had been a mutually agreed condition of American lend-lease that the United Kingdom should switch her export industries to war production and abstain from using lend-lease materials for manufacturing export goods. Thus there was for Britain a desperate necessity to restore her export trade, now down to 30 percent of its prewar level—this, moreover, in a world where the cost of imports had risen by 50 percent. Alone of the allied combatants she had fought the war from the beginning to the end. It had brought her the one reward without which all others would have been worthless—victory. But it had left her impoverished, overstrained (it was 1954 before the rationing of consumer goods ended), and, vis-à-vis America, dependent in a way she had never known before the summer of 1940.

It was thus from very different situations that the two Atlantic allies contemplated victory. Yet by a paradox it was America, the rich and powerful, which was the more impatient for a quick transition from the postures and disciplines of war to the "normalities" of peace, and Britain which retained the keener awareness that the end of the fighting did not of itself assure a termination of the conditions of war. The explanation of these different attitudes was rooted deep in history, as well as in the circumstances of the moment. Despite Pearl Harbor, World War II resembled all America's foreign wars since Yorktown in being a war which she had gone to—in this case across two oceans—while for Britain, despite her decision to declare war on Hitler, it was a war which had come to her—literally, across twenty miles of channel, thanks to the invasion threat and the bombing plane. It was natural, therefore, for America to think that with victory went disengagement: one went to war, one conquered the enemy, one returned home. But Britons in this sense had never returned home. Even in peacetime they knew that the maintenance of home depended upon British ships sailing the seven seas and British flags flying in remote corners of the world. After wars, the restoration of a world in which Britons could trade and live involved in all their experience a positive effort of peacemaking and of superintending the transition from war to peace. To them it was obvious that World War II, which had wreaked greater damage over wider areas than any of its predecessors, would require a comparably greater effort of superintendence and reconstruction. Moreover, as Europeans, however detached their posture, the British knew that they could not return to national health before the continent of Europe was even convalescent.

Related to these differences was a rather complex set of disagreements about the structure and ordering of world power. American optimism and idealism, well exemplified in Franklin Roosevelt, envisaged a continuance of the wartime relationship of the Allies, in which Soviet Russia, her rightful claims respected by her capitalist rivals, would be content to compete in the arts of peace rather than in those of subversion and war. British empiricism was equally anxious to reach an accommodation with the Russians but was considerably more skeptical about the possibility of doing so without the ability to oppose, as and where necessary, force with counterforce. It is not possible to dogmatize about the details of Roosevelt's grand design for the postwar world, because he left behind no political testament and was himself struck down, so to speak, at the keyboard while playing his relationship with the Russians by ear. But we do know that, like Woodrow Wilson before him, he placed great reliance on a world organization, of which both Russia and the U.S.A. would be members, and that, more explicitly than Wilson, he envisaged this organization as endowed with coercive powers—essentially indeed a continuance into peace of the wartime coalition. To the British there was nothing intrinsically unacceptable about such a conception. But whereas its appeal to most Americans lay in the prospect it offered of lightening America's burden and devolving the responsibilities for world peace upon an international consortium, its main attraction to Britain was as an agency by which America's involvement in affairs outside her borders might be caught and held. In the hammering out of the United Nations structure which took place during the war and immediately after, there was a very high level of agreement between Americans and Britons, but it was significant that in denominating the permanent members of the Security Council the British were as keen to include France, despite her temporarily low estate, as the Americans were to include China, despite the hollowness of Chiang Kai-shek's pretensions. In relation to the area of most acute British concern, Europe, the British wanted France as a counterpoise to the USSR, while in relation to an area more important for American aspirations than vital interests, Asia, the Americans were principally concerned to nourish a protégé, however unreliable. At the San Francisco Conference in the spring of 1945, at which the final provisions of the United Nations Charter were hammered out, it was not, however, any such Anglo-American differences of emphasis that caused the major disagreements; it was the divergences that existed between the Anglo-Americans and their supporters on one side and the USSR on the other. Even so, looking back at the San Francisco debates in the light of the subsequent history of the U.N., one is primarily struck by the irrelevance of most of the disagreements. No permanent member of the Security Council was really prepared to envisage abandoning his veto where any enforcement action was involved. The Russians, admittedly, were primarily responsible for the subsequent failure of the Military Staff Committee to agree on the standby forces which were to be the Security Council's policemen, but the more one considers the essential nature of the U.N., the less likely it seems that its evolution could ever have proceeded along these coercive lines. Indeed the most striking things about San Francisco were the universal acceptance of the Anglo-American determination that an international organization should be created and the concern of all the wartime allies to make it truly inclusive. The Americans were no less desirous of Russian membership than the Russians were of theirs. The British finally formed a common front with the Russians in voting for an American location of the headquarters of the organization, so anxious were they both to retain American interest and involvement.

Behind America's attachment to the U.N. and Britain's concern to preserve that attachment lay the common problem of Germany. As America saw it, it was the problem of disengagement. How soon could her occupation troops be brought home? Roosevelt had already given Churchill sleepless nights by warning him[1] that American forces would not remain in Europe more than two years after the last shot was fired. To the British, concerned with the vast vacuum of power that a defeated Germany—and also a divided France, a shaky Italy, and a guerrilla-menaced Greece and Balkans—presented, this seemed a wholly insufficient period, especially since the Russian presence had been legally sanctioned as far east as the Elbe. The full implications of the German vacuum took a little time to display themselves, but the economic strains it imposed were felt almost at once. To Britain, as an occupying power, they presented themselves as an aspect of her own grievous economic plight. How, politically, could she neglect any of her victor's responsibilities without endangering her future security? How, economically, could she possibly discharge them without placing an insupportable burden on herself? The answer seemed to lie in persuading the Americans that war had not ended with V-E Day, nor even with V-J Day, but was in fact still present in all but name. This would provide the breathing space necessary to adjust the British economy to her changed role in a changed world.

In the United States a very different style of thinking predominated. To Harry Truman, the brisk decision maker, the facts and the law were equally plain. Within a week of V-J Day he announced the ending of lend-lease. And just as he swiftly dismantled domestic wartime controls and relied upon the vitality of the market mechanism to carry the U.S.A. by its own momentum over the bumpy road from war to peace, so he also wound up the whole structure of Anglo-American economic "pooling."[2] Only the Combined Food Board led a tenuous existence until December 1946. The shock wave that ran through Britain and especially through the newly elected Labour government of Clement Attlee was all the more traumatic for coming on the heels of victory. Fortunately, as often with Truman's presidential announcements, there was a time lag between words and deeds. The goods in the lend-lease pipeline provided some breathing space in the months before any alternative relief could be devised.

The U.S.A. was not acting with the total indifference which her impoverished British ally was sometimes tempted to imagine. In economics as in politics, Truman was the inheritor of an American grand world design. Basically, it was the brainchild of Cordell Hull, inheriting the classic concepts of Adam Smith. After a century and a half of protectionism the U.S.A., so Hull believed, had now a duty and an opportunity to embrace and inculcate the liberal doctrines of free trade. To the British, free traders for a century, this fervor of a late convert was both a challenge and an embarrassment. In the contracting world economy of the 1930s the British had turned their own backs on pure free trade and adopted the modified form of protectionism which went by the name of imperial preference—i.e., a generally low tariff with special advantages to (and, in return, from) Empire countries. For a country that lived by trade it was an inadequate solution, but in a world of rising tariffs it provided some shelter from the harshest economic winds. Should it be dismantled, now that America, Britain's largest potential market, was talking free trade? British opinion was divided. The cautious counseled a wait-and-see posture. In negotiating the Atlantic Charter Churchill had been careful to insert the clause "with due respect for their existing obligations" into the article which spoke of "the enjoyment by all states . . . of access on equal terms to the trade[3] . . . of the world." The U.S.A., however, had in the weapon of lend-lease a lever which could prize the door open a little further. The agreements which all lend-lease recipients had to sign contained an Article VII that committed them to "the elimination of all forms of discriminatory treatment in international commerce" and "the reduction of tariffs and other trade barriers." To further the objectives of multilateralism the United States at the Bretton Woods Conference of July 1944 set up the International Monetary Fund and the International Bank, which were to be the institutions that would provide the adjustment mechanism needed for a world economy of free trade and free convertibility. In this the British acquiesced, partly perforce, since a stronger partner called the tune, but also because under the leadership of John Maynard Keynes they recognized that, with all the immediate hazards of letting a vibrant United States economy call the tune for weaker brethren, Britain stood to gain more by a world directed along these lines than by any other. But a gap between American and British thinking still remained. The British, desperately conscious of their immediate weakness, conceived of a fairly extensive transitional period before the full apparatus of multilateralism came into operation and during which American aid in one form or another would be available. The Americans, confident in their own strength and their new convictions—and aware too, no doubt, of how often the temporary becomes the permanent—were all for striking while the iron was hot, in the malleable moment of armistice, before bad prewar habits reasserted themselves. A dash for freedom, they insisted, would pay off and the new institutions of international fund and bank would be adequate, of themselves, to take care of any transitional problems.

Against this background the final settlements of lend-lease were worked out in late 1945. The essence of these was that "no financial obligation was created on the part of either country in respect of the goods furnished under Lend-Lease, or Reverse Lend-Lease, which were lost, destroyed or consumed in defeating our enemies." Thus some $26,000 million to $27,000 million of lend-lease and some $6,000 million of reverse lend-lease were wiped off the slate, leaving only a total of $650 million still to be paid for, mostly a markdown of material still in Britain at the end of the war and originally valued at $6,000 million. From the United States point of view this was very generous. In relation to the total provided, the residual debt was trifling. The basic good sense of the settlement is demonstrated most eloquently by the fact that there has been no lingering post-lend-lease acrimony or controversy such as the war debts occasioned in the twenties and thirties. The British, however, at that moment of victory and penury, could not resist the disposition to view it otherwise. They had believed themselves to be allies in a war governed by the principles of equality of sacrifice and mutual aid. This would have implied writing off lend-lease in toto. It would also have implied some generous arrangement to handle the return to peace, if only as a kind of terminal offset to those years when Britain "stood alone." It was in this mood that British negotiators, led by Keynes, approached Washington for that transitional aid which, distasteful as it was to seek, they could not possibly do without.

The British began the three hard months of negotiations with an illusory expectation of securing an outright American grant-in-aid of $6,000 million, the minimum which they thought adequate to equip Britain for her part in the bracing new world of multilateralism. The American negotiators thought differently. They were, as Keynes subsequently told the House of Commons, "interested not in our wounds, though incurred in the common cause, but in our convalescence." Moreover, with Britain only the first of a potentially long line of crippled allies, they were necessarily conscious of the limits which Congress would impose on any generosity which the executive arm might be tempted to extend.

In retrospect it is easy to see how both sides were right. The terms agreed proved insufficient to realize the objectives which both sides were seeking. The loan of $3,750 million at 2 percent interest payable over fifty years, though generous by any commercial standards, was inadequate, despite stringent British economizing, to bridge the needs of the transitional period. Moreover, the strings attached to it—particularly the obligation to make sterling freely convertible within a year—were to prove impracticable as well. Yet, as the six-month-long debate in Congress showed, it is very doubtful whether any better terms could have been approved by the legislative branch. Where the clash between national attitudes, rooted in different sets of experiences and directed to different sets of expectations, is subject to the open debate of national legislatures, a fair amount of animosity and mutual criticism is sure to result. The Anglo-American Loan Agreements were no exception. Indeed many recalled the months of their ratification as the lowest point in Anglo-American relations since the Depression. In the House of Commons they were attacked on the grounds already mentioned, but also, in an alliance of imperial tories and newly Commonwealth-conscious socialists, as a sellout of Britain's imperial assets and obligations to a United States anxious to substitute a new American dollar imperialism for the old British variety. Outside such doctrinaire quarters there was a widespread anxiety about the commitment imposed on Britain, in line with the lend-lease settlement, to enter into negotiations for the elimination of preferences, while the U.S.A. was only committed to "substantial reductions of tariffs." There was skepticism about the sincerity of the U.S.A.'s conversion to the new faith. The negotiating executive might be genuine, but what about the Congress which would ultimately dispose? A Republican Congress frustrated by more than three terms of Democratic presidents was not necessarily going to follow through on the bold schemes of the multilateralists. Already in the spring of 1945 it had refused Truman a renewal of the Reciprocal Trade Agreements Act until he gave assurances that he would respect the claims of any American industry "in danger" from foreign competition. What if the British lowered their defenses without any adequate American quid pro quo? Beyond these economic arguments there was a profound aversion at having to seek aid at all. Was it for this that Britain had stood alone, that London and Coventry had burned, that the nation had, as Churchill said, "worn austerity like a garment"? This was, of course, no fault of the U.S.A.'s, but it was perhaps of all the objections to the loan the one that rankled most deeply in the national consciousness.

But to all these arguments and sentiments there was one conclusive answer. Britain simply had to have the dollars if she was to survive in any tolerable and recognizable shape. So on 13 December the House of Commons approved the agreements by a vote of 343 to 100, with 169 M.P.'s abstaining, including the new leader of the Opposition, Winston Churchill. There followed what for many Britons was the even more painful phase of the scrutiny by the United States Congress of these same agreements. The debate was long, the objections often even more violent than those raised in Parliament. Many of them derived from a familiar deep-rooted economic nationalism. Many proceeded from an equally deep-rooted and recurrent congressional fear that America was being played for a sucker—a relic of the days of postcolonial hypersensitivity persisting into a world in which America was the prime mover, not the inert victim. Both schools of criticism drew considerable strength from the complaints already aired in Britain. "If the British don't like the loan, why should we give it to them?" To all this the multilateralists made much the same answer as they had been making all along. Yet at the end of the day it was not the economic arguments from multilateralism that carried the day, but a simpler, bilateral, and political one. Sam Rayburn, the Speaker of the House, left the chair to make a decisive personal intervention: "I do not want Western Europe, England, and all the rest pushed toward an ideology that I despise. I fear that if we do not co-operate with this great natural ally of ours that is what will happen. . . . If we are not allied with the British democracy I fear someone

will be and God pity us when we have no ally across the Atlantic Ocean
and God pity them too." On 10 May 1946 the Senate passed the agreements by 46 votes to 34. On 12 July the House, by 219 votes to 155, followed suit. The agreements became law out of the need to preserve the
alliance of the war years—but against a new threat, the threat, not of
Germany, but of Russia.

The process by which Russia passed from being an ally into being an
opponent of both the United States and the United Kingdom is not our
primary concern. The evolution of the cold war can be read elsewhere in
interpretations to suit every ideological taste. It is rather the effect which
this development had upon the course of Anglo-American relations that
is important here. In the U.S.A. the Rooseveltian optimism about Russia's peacetime intentions did not long survive the president's death, at
least in administrative circles. Truman, lacking both the charm and the
accompanying vanity of his predecessor, did not inherit his illusion that
personal relations could be made into a substitute for a genuine harmony
of policies. His was a more direct approach, a franker recognition of
real differences. And steadily the evidence of these differences accumu-
lated—over Poland, indeed over all of Eastern Europe, over Turkey, as
the gateway to the Mediterranean, and over Greece, despite its agreed
inclusion in a British sphere of influence. By January 1946 Truman was
telling James F. Byrnes, his secretary of state, that he was tired of "baby-
ing the Soviets." Even so, it was one thing to desist from concessions to
the Russians, another thing to regard them as a threat, the new enemy.
It took Churchill's speech at Fulton, Missouri, to bring into the open
the thesis that the USSR was an expansionist power, that it wanted, not
indeed war, but the fruits of war, that the dreams of Big Three unity
must give way before the realities of the iron curtain and the balance of
power, and that an alliance of the English-speaking peoples was a pre-
requisite for peace. The call came from a voice which was, from an
American point of view, singularly authoritative and informed—that of
the greatest remaining war leader, the trusted messenger of hard tidings,
the repository of those British virtues of solidity, realism, and determination which shone the more brightly because he spoke now as a private
individual, not as the head of a government seeking favors or advantages.

Even so there was a deep reluctance in administration circles to accept
Churchill's analysis, if only because its implications were so clearly painful. Already by this date the processes of American demobilization were

far advanced. In place of the twelve million men under arms at V-E Day, there was less than half that number by the end of 1945. By mid-1946 the army was down to one and a half million and the navy and marine corps to little more than a million. And the rapidity of this disintegration meant that in certain theaters, such as Europe, their military effectiveness was practically nil. To reverse or arrest this process after four years of war was something which no American president could be very eager to propose, least of all a Truman with no personal electoral mandate and a critical Congress with the opposition party in the majority. The disposition was strong, especially in the State Department, to keep outright confrontation with Russia to the minimum. It was significant that in the early meetings of the United Nations in 1946 it was Ernest Bevin, the British Labour Foreign Secretary, who battled with V. M. Molotov over the contentious issues of Iran, Indonesia, Greece, Lebanon, and Syria, the probing points of Russian imperialism, and James Byrnes, the American Secretary of State, who sought to play the role of mediator between these acrimonious contestants. Yet Bevin's own attitude had to take account of two strong strands of feeling in Britain, especially in his own party. Proceeding from the assumption that Britain had a distinctive world role to play, the one faction contended that "Left could talk to Left" and that a Labour government could speak to Russians in a language they would understand, while the other, not so clearly confined to Labour circles, saw in America's new discovery of her world role a potential American imperialism, less menacing no doubt than the Russian but potentially antagonistic nonetheless. The influence of such sentiments can be traced in Bevin's speech of as late a date as 22 December 1946, when he told the House of Commons that Britain was "midway" between the U.S.A. and the USSR, "not tying herself to anyone." And when Stalin alleged that this meant that Britain was welshing on the Anglo-Soviet Treaty of 1942, Bevin agreed to "reaffirm" the treaty a month later.

It is hard, however, to resist the conviction that circumstances had already aligned the U.S.A. and the U.K. in an anti-Soviet posture well before 1946 ran out. The key issue here, predictably, was Germany, where humanitarian and economic considerations combined to make the Western allies resist the Soviet policy of treating the country merely as a treasure house to be looted as some compensation for Russia's own sufferings at Hitler's hands. In May 1946, in face of the Russians' refusal to cooperate in the treatment of Germany as an economic unit and their insistence on stripping their own zone not merely of capital goods but also of goods currently produced, Lucius Clay, the general in command of the U.S. zone, halted reparation deliveries to the USSR from his territory and the British followed suit in respect of theirs. The economic absurdity of running each zone separately led the Americans in July to propose the economic merger of their zone with the others. The Russians and French declined the proposal; the British accepted it. "Bizonia" came into existence and with it the de facto division of Germany. Thus the breakdown of any agreed treatment of the vanquished by the victors became explicit and the community of British and American policies unmistakable. In August Britain and the U.S.A. acted together in resisting Russia's proposed revision of the Montreux Convention of 1936 which kept her navies from passing through Turkish waters into the Mediterranean. In September the U.S.A. announced that she would be maintaining her naval units in the Mediterranean, and Byrnes in a speech in Stuttgart gave a pledge that American troops would stay in Germany "for a long period." In November 1946 the British reduced the tempo of their demobilization (already much slower than the American), so as to leave them at the end of the year with 1,427,000 men under arms instead of 1,200,000. This, in relation to her population, represented twice as many men under arms as the U.S.A. had.

Then in 1947 events suddenly escalated. A winter of phenomenal severity brought the still highly delicate British economy almost to a standstill, halting coal deliveries, crippling exports. It suddenly became glaringly obvious that Britain could no longer afford to expend her precious foreign exchange on the economically unremunerative burdens of postwar peacekeeping—at least not at the rate previously maintained. Something had to be cut, as critics pointed out that the £300 million spent on British civilian and military operations mostly in Germany and the Middle East was exactly equivalent to the gap in her balance of payments. The countries selected for the ax were Greece and Turkey, where British financial and military support for their hard-pressed anti-Communist governments was costing her $250 million a year. On 21 February Britain gave notice to the United States that she could no longer continue to provide this support and, in effect, put it up to the U.S.A. to pick up the discarded burden or to let it go by default. Truman, with characteristic decisiveness, accepted the challenge. Indeed his 12 March address to Congress took Britain by surprise. She had expected no "Truman Doctrine," just a willingness to extend the line of American responsibilities a little further.

Truman's decision to dramatize the occasion and to generalize the response—"It must be the policy of the United States to support free peoples who are resisting attempted subjugation by armed minorities or outside pressure"—derived in part no doubt from his assessment of the national psychology and of the political situation. But of course it tore aside the last pretense that a compromise solution could be found to East-West differences; it committed America to holding the line for keeps, in a far more active sense than mere membership of the United Nations implied; and, incidentally, since the occasion was the assumption of a British burden, it placed America unequivocally at Britain's side. Yet it also illustrated only too clearly the gap between words and action imposed by American habits and the American constitution. The Congress which applauded Truman's stand was about to allow the Selective Service Act to expire on 31 March 1947 and would not replace it by another measure of conscription until June 1948. The president did indeed secure a vote of funds—$400 million for military and economic aid—but the military and naval missions it provided were to be of an advisory nature. There was no immediate provision for the dispatch of troops. During the summer of mounting pressure from Yugoslavia, Bulgaria, and Albania, the Greeks had to hold out as best they could with the help which Britain, at repeated American urgings, managed to give them. The first shiploads of American material did not arrive until August. With great reluctance, Britain maintained 5,000 men in Greece until 1948; the last of them did not leave until 1950. The Pax Britannica and the Pax Americana were thus seen, not as alternatives, but as complements.

In one adjacent area, however, there was to be no such Anglo-American complementing. When the British carried their retrenchment a logical step further and announced that they would wind up the costly and thankless Palestine mandate, they got no such response from President Truman. More than once the U.S.A. had declined, despite—or because of—the strong interest of American Jewry in the establishment of a national home in Palestine, to accept any joint responsibility with Britain. In 1947, when the United Nations voted for partition, the U.S.A. voted for it but would take no part in enforcing it. Now, faced as it was with the actuality of British withdrawal, the U.S.A. reversed its stand and favored a United Nations trusteeship in place of partition. But by then it was too late. The mandate ended, as planned, on 15 May 1948, and on 30 June the last British troops left.

On the economic front meanwhile the strain had increased for Britain. It had become apparent that "the transitional period" of adjustment to multilateralism was proving much more like the pessimistic British forecasts than the optimistic American assumptions. Neither the International Bank nor the International Monetary Fund had been able to fill their expected roles and the American loan had proved to be inadequate for its purpose. Years later Dean Acheson, a Treasury official at the time, sadly commented, "We vastly underestimated the extent of British and European economic and financial exhaustion."[4]

Initially the omens were not so bad. By the end of 1946 British exports were up 111 percent above their prewar levels, while strict rationing kept imports down to 72.2 percent. The resulting deficit on the balance of payments was less than half the £750 million that had been estimated in the Washington talks. But with 1947 the picture changed —in part because of severe conditions in Britain, but also because of a rise in United States prices, equivalent to a 28 percent drop in the value of the U.S. loan, and a deterioration of 10 percent in the terms of trade. Thus by the middle of 1947 over $2,000 million of the $3,750 million loan had been used, considerably more than was expected. When full convertibility of dollars and pounds was permitted, as arranged, on 15 July, a severe run on the pound developed. By 16 August the loan was evaporating so fast that it would only last a month. In place of the hoped-for emergence into the bright sunshine of multilateralism there had to be negotiated, with precipitate haste, a set of supplementary agreements between London and Washington, permitting Britain to suspend convertibility and to exercise discrimination against the U.S.A. by switching her purchases wherever possible from scarce dollar items to those which could be bought in sterling. And of course there had to be cuts in British spending on commitments overseas, of which the suspension of aid to Greece and Turkey in March 1947 had been only the first. A speedup in demobilization was ordered; first the army was to be cut to 1,007,000 by 31 March 1948, then to 937,000 by the same date. A further 220,000 were due to be trimmed by the end of 1948 and a two-ninths cut in the defense budget was imposed. How far would this obligatory retreat from Britain's share of her responsibilities in the postwar world take her? Would the retreat turn into a rout? What would this imply for the United States? As 1947 wore on, these questions were asked almost as insistently in America as in Britain. Fundamentally they were questions not of economics but of politics, and they found their answer, in Europe and in America, in a revitalizing impulse to common action against a common threat.

It is, alas, by no means always true that the crisis calls forth the man. But in the critically formative years of 1947 to 1949 both Britain and the U.S.A. were fortunate in being able to command the services of an exceptional group of leaders—exceptional in their individual talents but even more exceptional in their capacity to work together as a group. Deeply patriotic, their vision nonetheless transcended parochial nationalism and served the interests of a wider community, sometimes of the North Atlantic, often of a yet wider world.

At the apex, in Harry S. Truman and Clement Attlee, the two democracies were led by figures who almost ostentatiously disavowed the romantic, flamboyant, heroic leadership to which Roosevelt and Churchill had accustomed their wartime electorates. But below the matter-of-fact, low-toned "ordinariness" of both Truman and Attlee there were a firmness and a courage which made an excellent basis for mutual respect and trust. Truman, coming out of the blue, as it were, to his great responsibilities, displayed a decisiveness and capacity to learn which more than compensated for his previous inexperience and occasional insensitivities. Attlee, well trained as Labour's leader in the wartime cabinets, guaranteed a consistency in essentials along with a wholly unsentimental responsiveness to change. At the subordinate levels Attlee was served superbly by Ernest Bevin, a Labour Churchill, who as foreign secretary displayed a ready grasp of a craft which he had first learned in the hard school of trade union politics. With the appointment of General George C. Marshall, in January 1947, to succeed James F. Byrnes as secretary of state, Truman brought into civilian and diplomatic service talents that had been developed in wartime soldiering, but also a character which in its straightforward integrity and republican virtue re-

minded his countrymen of no one so much as George Washington himself. When his subordinate in the Department of State, Dean Acheson,
succeeded Marshall in January 1949, not only was continuity preserved
but a remarkable rapport developed between the ex-lawyer who in appearance might have been a British Guardsman and the ex-haberdasher
who was the president of the United States. In the embassy at St. James's
during these years, first Averell Harriman and then Lewis Douglas represented the United States, while in Washington Lord Inverchapel and
Sir Oliver Franks represented Great Britain.

But these headline figures were by no means the whole cast. They
were supported by a remarkable team of diplomats, departmental heads,
and service chiefs who in the United States came to bear the label of
"the East Coast establishment," a label accurately descriptive not so much
of their origins, which were far more diverse and scattered than it implied, but of a certain community of outlook. Many had served wartime
apprenticeships in Washington or the armed services which had given
them firsthand experience of alliance politics. Most shared the experience
of having battled against parochialism and isolationism at home. Most
—though not all—had been Atlantic Firsters. In Britain a longer commitment to world participation meant that there was no exactly equivalent group of self-conscious advocates, but in Whitehall and in Westminster there was a common bond among those, a very large number,
who had served either in Washington or with Americans in London or
the services during the war, men for whom the keystone of British policy had been and would remain the alliance with the U.S.A.

In Britain there was an easy interpenetration of view between the executive and the legislature, and even if, under Attlee's Labour government, "Little Englandism" was occasionally vocal in Parliament, in general there was no serious gap between Whitehall and Westminster in
their approaches to world problems. In the U.S.A. this was less true.
The isolationism which had been virtually routed in the executive branch
had retired, sometimes in very good order, although seldom command-
ing a majority in either party, to Congress. Moreover, what was more
serious in many ways, a time lag existed between executive and legislature—a time lag in awareness and in response. This sometimes prevented
the executive from speaking in unequivocal terms and sometimes meant
that the good intentions of the executive emerged watered down or muddied at the end of their congressional processing. Some of this was due

to the separation of powers, some to the predominance of a rival party in Congress; some of it was merely the necessary expression of the diversity and scale of a continental country. But to the British at the other end of the seesaw, used to the tight, responsive government of their own island, this could often introduce a disturbing and incalculable factor into the relationship.

Down to the proclamation of the Truman Doctrine, Western Europe was to all intents and purposes a passive object of British and American diplomacy—a casualty of war too sick to fend for itself, in need of the relief, rehabilitation, and protection which only North America and Britain could supply. But gradually the embers of national self-assertion quickened into life and the patient began to demand a voice in his own convalescence. For Britain this first took a form familiar from the aftermath of World War I, a French demand for insurance against the recurrent threat from across the Rhine. In 1919 this had been met by the abortive Anglo-American Assistance Treaty with France which collapsed when the Senate declined to ratify the Versailles settlement. Now in 1947 with the U.S.A., Britain, and France all permanent members of the Security Council, an American and British commitment at least as good as that of 1919 existed through the United Nations. However, the French seemed to need something more, and on 4 March 1947 Bevin gave it to them, in the form of the symbolically named Treaty of Dunkirk which pledged Britain and France for a period of fifty years to give each other full support in the event of either being involved in hostilities with Germany.

Basically, however, the reassurance that France and the rest of Western Europe wanted most in the spring of 1947 was not military but economic, and such as only the U.S.A. could provide. Not only was Britain's economic plight reduplicated on the Continent, but there it was also accompanied by serious signs of possible social and political disintegration. It was in these circumstances that the Truman administration, after courageous initiatives by Acheson and Marshall, launched the Marshall Plan upon a Congress which was still quivering under the impact of the Truman Doctrine. Such a Congress was in no mood to acquiesce in a further installment of mere "aid," however inadequate its previous provision could be shown to be. Nor indeed could any British government have found it easy to get Parliament to accept another American loan couched in terms similar to the last. The emphasis from everyone's point of view had to shift from one-sided aid to multilateral endeavor. Thus the idea, not merely of a series of recovery schemes, but of the European Recovery Program ("ERP," as it was quickly known) began to develop.

If Acheson and Marshall sowed the seed in the U.S.A., it was Bevin who next watered it. On hearing of Marshall's 5 June speech at the Harvard commencement with its expression of American willingness to cooperate with those nations which would coordinate their efforts for recovery, Bevin did not wait to ask the Washington administration what it had in mind. He got together with Georges Bidault, the French foreign minister, and persuaded him to invite Molotov to a joint meeting in Paris—a reminder of how little, at this stage, the East-West split was accepted as obviously irremediable—and there they considered how they could best respond to Marshall's overture. What would or could have happened if Russia had cooperated remains one of the great "ifs" of postwar history. In fact Molotov would have nothing to do with a cooperative effort, but insisted on individual approaches to the U.S.A. On 2 July he ended his participation with a warning to the British and French against a course of action which "could lead to no good." Bevin replied: "My country has faced grave consequences and threats before, and it is not the sort of prospect which will deter us from doing what we consider to be our duty." The invitations went out from him and Bidault to twenty-two countries to meet as the Committee for European Economic Cooperation (CEEC). The Soviet satellites declined. The rest, sixteen of them, met under Bevin's chairmanship to hammer out an outline joint recovery plan by 22 September.

Thus the imaginative and generous concept of the Marshall Plan was embraced by Britain and France and became simultaneously an instrument for uniting and dividing Europe. To those who accepted it, it became the embryo of a new kind of Western European unity; to those who rejected it, it became a new and especially subtle tool of American economic imperialism. When the time came, as it quickly did, for Congress to make up its mind about the plan, it cannot be denied that each opposite set of reactions contributed to congressional willingness to accept it. It promoted Western European unity—that was judged to be a good thing. It would construct a shield against communist subversion—that was even better. In the first function in particular Britain played a key role. In the working out of the first set of CEEC estimates Sir Oliver Franks, who took over the chairmanship from Bevin, played a major part, especially as a link with those influential American consultants, such as William Clayton, who were on hand to advise the committee how best to shape their program so as to win congressional compliance.

Congressional compliance came with commendable speed, thanks partly to Acheson and Marshall's careful preparation but also to the role of the Republican leadership under Senator Arthur H. Vandenberg, who in his abandonment of a lifetime's isolationism displayed all the zeal of a convert. In the autumn of 1947 Congress passed an interim aid bill and then on 31 March 1948 passed the first of its annual (for four years) foreign assistance acts, authorizing $5,300 million for the first twelve months of the program. It was, for all parties concerned, a courageous action in a presidential election year. For Europe it made the difference between recovery and collapse, and its effects are to be seen on the face of the Continent to this day. For Britain it arrived just in the nick of time, just as the last carefully husbanded dollars of the original American loan were being expended. For the first year the United Kingdom received $1,263 million, of which $312 million was conditional upon her making equivalent grants to other beneficiaries of the plan. Unlike the loan, Marshall aid was a free grant or gift and it had no ideological strings attached, although recipients undertook to stabilize their currencies and try to balance their budgets. Its clauses said nothing about nondiscrimination or multilateralism. In this the U.S.A. had learned and applied the lessons of the loan agreements, abandoning the hopes of instant and global multilateralism and accepting instead a cooperative effort toward a regional multilateralism even though this involved transitional paradoxes, such as initial discrimination within the Marshall Plan countries against dollar goods. The United Kingdom in particular made it a settled policy to restrict dollar imports whenever her balance of trade with dollar areas was too unfavorable. As a consequence, between 1947 and 1950 imports to Britain from the dollar area fell by 40 percent, while total imports rose by 12 percent. Thus the U.S.A. accepted her role and responsibilities as a creditor nation at the same time as she provided the sine qua non for restoring a European economy which could be both a rival and a counterpart to her own.

By the time the recovery program had taken shape, it was becoming apparent that, if Western Europe was to survive, its collective defense would have to be organized as well. Here again, for obvious reasons, Britain's role was crucial. At first Bevin seemed to think in terms of applying the bilateral model of the Treaty of Dunkirk and having similar arrangements with the countries of the newly formed Benelux customs union (Belgium, the Netherlands, and Luxembourg). But by January 1948 he was talking, in rather general terms, about the time being ripe "for a consolidation of Western Europe." In February the Russians sharply quickened the tempo of crisis by contriving the coup in Prague which overthrew the last traces of democracy in Czechoslovakia. On 17 March the Brussels Treaty was signed, providing mutual security arrangements for Britain, France, and the Benelux powers. On the very same day President Truman acclaimed the treaty as "deserving our full support" and called on Congress to pass legislation providing for universal military training and selective service.

In their pattern of European initiative accompanied by American encouragement and support, the Marshall Plan and the Brussels Treaty were the models for the even larger commitment of the North Atlantic Treaty. For the United States this was a historic innovation of tremendous significance. Never before in her history had she committed herself in peacetime to a binding alliance with a power outside the American hemisphere. Membership in the United Nations, despite all the commitments it involved, left American freedom of action still protected by her veto in the Security Council. Moreover there was a real, if not legally definable, sense in which a commitment to all was less binding than a commitment to a specific few. The North Atlantic Treaty established a specific commitment, a truly "entangling alliance." By the terms of the treaty the United States agreed with the United Kingdom, Canada, France, Belgium, Holland, Luxembourg, Iceland, Denmark, Norway, Portugal, and Italy[1] that "an armed attack against one of them should be considered an attack on all" and that in such an event each would assist the victim "by taking forthwith, individually, and in concert with the other Parties, such action as it deems necessary, including the use of armed force." Nor was such action left to be improvised, as in the United Nations, at the moment of aggression. To make this mutual defense realistic a comprehensive allied structure was erected, the North Atlantic Treaty Organization (NATO), with interlocking roles and responsibilities for the principal signatories at every level.

Such a sweeping departure from national tradition would never have been achieved had the United States not been deeply impressed with the menace of the USSR and, also, with the significance for her own security of Western Europe. It was in relation to the second of these factors that the British role was crucial. Twice, in face of a threatened "takeover" of Western Europe by a power which the U.S.A. regarded as hostile, the United Kingdom had held the ring until the United States was ready, psychologically and otherwise, to come in. In the changed circumstances of modern war, it was obvious that no such breathing space could be expected in the future. Britain and Western Europe could only discharge their traditional roles as outer bastions of American defense if they were organized in advance and united with the U.S.A. before hostilities commenced. Thus indeed, it was hoped, not only would the aggressor be repulsed; almost as important, he would be deterred.

From the British point of view the alliance was less of a novelty but even more of a necessity. With varying degrees of explicitness she had committed herself in advance on previous occasions to Continental allies and the British tradition of island independence did not necessarily exclude "entangling alliances." Nonetheless she had always been reluctant to accept commitments in Europe that were both solitary and automatic. The lessons of 1917 and 1940 were deeply engraved on the national consciousness; unless America was with her she could not hope to save Europe, even if she were able to survive herself. And in the age of nuclear weapons it was imperative for a small, densely packed island not merely to "win" a war (whatever that might mean) but to prevent it. It was not even enough to have Britain's frontier on the Rhine, or the Elbe, or even the Vistula. She must deter the ruin that rained from the skies.

The Dunkirk and Brussels treaties showed that even in the dangerously overextended condition in which Britain then found herself, she was willing to give the Continent such assurances as she could. But it did not need second sight to realize that these commitments acquired their value as earnests of Britain's willingness to do all she could by herself before overtly involving the United States. Of themselves they were not enough, but they were a demonstration that Europe, under Britain's stimulus, was ready to play an active, not a merely passive, role in the organization of collective defense. Thus it was that in March 1948, immediately after the Communist coup in Prague, Bevin made what seems to have been the first explicit proposal for a North Atlantic pact, building around the core of the Brussels Treaty.[2] Throughout the spring and summer of 1948 the dual operation proceeded, the Europeans (the British Joint Chiefs of Staff in particular) persuading the Americans of the seriousness of their commitment and the United States administration working upon and through the United States Congress to secure the necessary legislation for this unprecedented and profound realignment of the nation's thinking and behavior.

Events in Europe demonstrated both the urgency and, paradoxically, the inadequacy of NATO. In June, while the United States Congress was just on the point of reintroducing conscription, in the form of a twenty-one-month selective service, the Russians imposed a blockade on Berlin as a protest against the Western powers' decision to establish a federal government for their zones in Germany. It was a situation pregnant with the risk of war, and significantly the immediate response to it was found in two Anglo-American decisions that relied for their execution upon the arm which had proved itself the most potent in the war just concluded—the air force. (It was also perhaps significant that the USAF and the RAF had never wholly gone back on their wartime intimacy and at the end of 1946 had agreed to continue their cooperation in such areas as the standardization of training and equipment.) The first decision was to maintain the Allied position in Berlin by operating a gigantic airlift that would fly in all the city's supplies. In the eleven months that ensued before the Russians abandoned their abortive blockade, 1.5 million tons of food, fuel, and other materials were flown in by nearly 200,000 flights, of which two-thirds were flown by the Americans, and one-third by the British—one of the most remarkable feats of supply in the history of aviation. The airlift reduced, but did not eliminate, the risk of a clash which could lead to war. To provide a swift deterrent to that, the second decision was taken—to station "temporarily" in Britain, and of course with British agreement, two squadrons of American B-29s, the aircraft designed to carry the atom bomb. This employment of the United Kingdom as "an unsinkable aircraft carrier" had, of course, profound significance for both countries. In August 1948 the temporary became even more permanent, with the arrival of another B-29 squadron and an increase in the number of USAF personnel in Britain to 6,000. When Sir Stafford Cripps, chancellor of the exchequer, visited Washington in October, he told Secretary of Defense James Forrestal that "Britain must be regarded as the main base for the deployment of American power and the chief offensive against Russia must be by air."[3] Thus, in advance of NATO, there was a de facto commitment by Britain to an American alliance, with Britain assuming a rather advanced and exposed role. At the same time, the U.S.A. was accepting a moral commitment to defend the United Kingdom that was hardly less far-reaching. And all this was done without any formal treaty provisions on either side.

NATO, of course, soon provided the written and ratified agreements. Signed on 4 April 1949, to come into effect on 24 August, the North Atlantic Treaty cleared the Senate on 21 July by eighty-two votes to thirteen. Its signature by Truman on 25 July was accompanied by a message to Congress seeking expenditure of $1,450 million on military aid for its first year. (Some $1,000 million was later voted.) The machinery set up by the treaty provided for a highly integrated alliance organization. At the apex was the Council, on which all member states were represented and which was served by an international secretariat. The strictly military direction was in the hands of two committees: the Military Committee, which held representatives of the chiefs of staff of all members, and the Standing Group, consisting only of representatives of the U.S.A., Britain, and France, which met at Washington. Below these came the various regional commands, of which that of the supreme allied commander in Europe (SACEUR) was the chief.

The predominant role of the U.S.A. in the alliance was reflected, in its initial stages, by the appointment in December 1950 of General Eisenhower as SACEUR, in effect to re-create that brotherhood in arms which he had both established and symbolized in World War II. Indeed the very resonance of his H.Q.'s acronym—SHAPE—echoed that of its wartime predecessor—SHAEF. In British eyes no appointment could have been more welcome.[4] Continuity with wartime leadership was also demonstrated in 1952 by the appointment of Lord Ismay, chief of staff of Britain's wartime Ministry of Defence, as secretary-general of the NATO secretariat.

There was indeed some disagreement between London and Washington about the essential character of the new alliance. The British saw it as a near-fusion of the democracies of the North Atlantic, linked by similar ideologies as well as mutual interest. The Americans were more strategic in their thinking—concerned from the first to bring in an ex-enemy, Italy, for her position on the flanks of the alliance; early advocates of the inclusion of Greece and Turkey, however remote their "Atlanticism," because of their value for Mediterranean defense; and would-be incor-

porators of Spain, had her ideological offensiveness not been too much
for the European democracies to accept.

There was, however, one aspect of NATO which, though formally
perhaps its greatest fault, yet recommended it most strongly both to the
U.S.A. and to Britain. This was, paradoxically, that NATO never disposed of the full power needed to realize its objectives. NATO was indeed the West's shield, but it was never the West's sword, even a
defensive sword. Behind NATO, but also outside it, lay the ultimate
striking power of the atomic deterrent, and this was retained in the hands
of the U.S.A. and the U.K. and not put at the disposal of the supreme
NATO commander or anyone else. The principal vehicle of this deterrent
was the U.S. Strategic Air Command (SAC), an arm exclusively and
directly under U.S. control. But Britain had a share in the atomic deterrent
partly by virtue of her own atomic weaponry and her own delivery systems
(initially by B-29s provided by the U.S.A., later by the V-bomber force
of British construction), but also by her role as an advance bombing base
for SAC, a base initially almost indispensable and even subsequently more
dependable than any other of those available. That Britain attached great
importance to her voice and role in relation to the ultimate deterrent in
North Atlantic strategy is demonstrated by the effort she made, at a time
of great financial stringency and when she was denied any technical aid
from her wartime ally, to develop and maintain a nuclear capability. This
made sense in the circumstances of the time. Not only could NATO never
have obtained, from any or all of its members, the number of ground
troops needed for a fully convincing strategy of ground defense; but it
could reasonably be argued also that from a strictly European point of
view it was a good thing to have a European power sharing in the disposition and strategy of the atomic deterrent. Moreover, from the British
point of view this assisted her in building and maintaining the unwritten
Anglo-American alliance within the formal structure of Western European security. Finally, it put her on an equality with the United States in
respect of an issue on which she was peculiarly sensitive—her degree of
commitment to Europe. As a world power and head of the Commonwealth she could not, she felt, put all her eggs in the European basket;
instead she formulated the principle that, an island herself, she would go
into Europe and the defense of Europe as far as her main ally, that quasi
island the U.S.A., would go—thus far and no farther.

Nonetheless the British deterrent was not the product of her partnership in arms with the U.S.A. Quite the contrary. The field of atomic weapons and atomic energy represented the most conspicuous failure of the so-called special relationship. During the war all work on atomic weapons—"the U-bomb," as it was then known—was concentrated, for reasons of security and economy of resources, in the U.S.A. British research, initially in the lead, was pooled in 1942 with American to produce, thanks also to the work of other, mainly émigré, physicists of the free world, the truly international discoveries that resulted in 1945 in the first atomic explosion. A 1943 Quebec agreement between Churchill and Roosevelt provided for mutual exchange of information and joint control of the use of the bomb. The agreement was, however, somewhat loosely worded. It was also kept so secret that Truman and Attlee learned of it for the first time when they assumed their respective "summit" positions in 1945. There was also an even more secret 1944 Roosevelt-Churchill "aide-mémoire" which provided for a continuance into peacetime of full collaboration on atomic research and development "for military and commercial purposes . . . unless terminated by joint agreement."

The end of the war which the atomic bomb so signally accelerated created a new situation. In the U.S.A. there was a powerful conviction of possessing "the secrets" of the bomb. Opinion was divided as to whether these "secrets" should be preserved as an American monopoly or put under some form of international control. For Britain, anxious both to develop the peaceful potentialities of atomic energy and to have atomic weapons of her own, neither attitude was promising. The monopolists were opposed to any sharing, the internationalists were opposed to singling out any one country for partnership. Truman's announcement in October 1945 that the United States would not share the "know-how" of the bomb's manufacture with its allies precipitated a meeting in November at Washington (at which Mr. Mackenzie King was also present, for Canada) from which emerged an "agreed declaration," which, while advocating international control and inspection, provided for "full and effective cooperation" between the United States, the United Kingdom, and Canada. But at the operational level this agreement went awry, British requests for information encountering a blank refusal. While Attlee was still trying to secure from Truman what he regarded as fair implementation of a tripartite agreement, Congress on 1 August 1946 passed the McMahon Act, which in effect slammed the door on the disclosure or exchange of information in the atomic field. There was thus no alternative for Britain but to go it alone.

In 1947 Congress heard for the first time of the Anglo-American wartime agreements. Its reaction was to protest against the partnership they
implied and to demand their "re-vamping" as a condition of support for
the Marshall Plan, to quote the sentiments of Senator Vandenberg.[5] As
a result, in January 1948 a two-year "modus-vivendi" was agreed upon,
in which Britain formally abandoned her claim to be consulted on the use
of the bomb (though it appears that Truman gave a personal assurance
that he would continue to act in the spirit of Quebec) and also agreed to
supply the U.S.A. with increased quantities of uranium ore, to which it
had access in the Commonwealth and elsewhere. In return the U.S.A. was
to make available nuclear information "in nine specific areas . . . not
related in any way to military weapons." Meanwhile in the American
executive branch the desire to collaborate with Britain was growing: it
was felt that she had a moral case; what was more, she might soon have a
bomb of her own. So in December 1949 Truman proposed what would
have been something like a revival of the wartime arrangements—full
exchange of information but actual production to be centered in the
U.S.A. The project broke down because what would have been acceptable
to Britain was unacceptable to Congress, and vice versa. At the end of
1949 the modus vivendi ran out (though ore supplies to the U.S.A. continued) and nothing took its place. Early in 1950 the case of the British
"atomic spy," Klaus Fuchs, raised the further complication of security.
This dovetailed with the rise in the U.S.A. of Senator Joseph McCarthy's
"red scare" and so effectively ended all hope of restoring Anglo-American cooperation in this field. When in October 1952 the British exploded
their first atomic bomb, they could fairly claim that it was at least as
much their own as the American ones had been. When they exploded a
hydrogen bomb in 1957, it was still a British-made weapon.

Practical considerations of economy combined with deep-seated resentment at what was felt to be unfair treatment impelled Churchill
when he took over from Attlee to press Britain's claims again, especially
when Eisenhower became president. In December 1953 at their Bermuda
meeting Churchill, armed with a photostat of the 1944 "aide-mémoire,"
pressed his case. It was a good moment. Eisenhower was personally sympathetic. The Russians had just broken the West's monopoly by an explosion of their own atomic bomb in August 1953, and a generally less
paranoiac atmosphere surrounded the whole subject, as evidenced by
Eisenhower's "atoms for peace" proposal made to the United Nations
immediately before the Bermuda meeting. Moreover the continued short-

age in NATO of conventional forces was driving the U.S.A. to favor training her allies in the use of tactical nuclear weapons. This could be facilitated by more sharing of information. As a result the logjam was broken and in August 1954 the McMahon Act was amended to permit the sharing of information on the external characteristics of nuclear weapons. Such sharing, on a "to him that hath shall be given" principle, was restricted to powers who already had atomic weapons—i.e., the United Kingdom. Britain was thus in some degree restored to her partnership status, while she could still claim, with some justice, to have available, for her own and NATO defense, her own "independent nuclear deterrent."

Whereas in Europe American and British postwar policies were, if not identical, at any rate complementary, in Asia the war created and the peace stimulated two quite different sets of attitudes, interests, and expectations. The circumstances under which the Far Eastern war broke over the heads of the two allies were significant. It was the U.S.A., not Britain, that first felt, at Pearl Harbor, the weight of the Japanese onslaught; the bombs that fell on the U.S. Pacific Fleet fell also in American waters. The Philippines saw the first bloodying of American troops, under the leadership of a commander, Douglas MacArthur, who was a master of histrionic gesture. At Hong Kong and British Borneo small British garrisons quickly succumbed, but the fall of Singapore and the sinking of two capital ships, the *Prince of Wales* and the *Repulse,* were not merely damaging losses in themselves but also humiliating disasters which greatly lowered British standing in the Far East. The subsequent course of the Far Eastern war lay largely in America's hands; it constituted, particularly in its later stages, not merely a triumphant progress for American arms but also, in significant degree, a kind of vindication of the national spirit after the humiliation of Pearl Harbor. Indeed it is not too much to say that the price that was paid for the adoption by the Allies of an Atlantic First strategy—a strategy crucial for Britain—was the virtual substitution of an American for an Allied strategy in the Far East. This meant for Britain that the destiny of the Pacific parts of the Commonwealth, conspicuously New Zealand and Australia, passed temporarily into American hands. Even the recovery of Britain's lost possessions in Southeast Asia, though a result of highly creditable achievements under the commands of Lord Wavell and Lord Louis Mountbatten, was, by comparison with the great task of liberating Europe, of minor concern to the British public and even less to the American. Moreover, in relation to China, the area where their commands made closest contact, the British and American strategies meshed very poorly, basically because Chiang Kai-shek was in British eyes little more than a provincial warlord, whereas the Americans viewed him as the fourth member of a grand alliance.

There was another factor present in the Far East situation which was not operative in Europe. Roosevelt in particular was critical of what he saw as British imperialism throughout the area. Although more than once made aware of Churchill's combative response, he never gave up pressing for Indian independence with analogies drawn from 1776 (though seldom from 1861). There was a frank disinclination to see American arms assisting in the restoration of European colonial rule in any part of Asia. Churchill, on the other hand, not only was unrepentant in his imperialism but was also concerned to accelerate French and Dutch postwar recovery in Europe by securing the restoration to them of their Far Eastern possessions. By contrast we now know that Roosevelt saw Western imperialism as more of a threat than Stalinist communism. He advocated the return of Hong Kong to China, while at Yalta agreeing that Stalin should recover Port Arthur, which had not been Russian since 1905, as well as the southern part of Sakhalin and the huge industrial complex of the Manchurian railway.

In fairness, of course, this has to be set in the context of that deep-seated concern for Russian aid in the closing stages of the war against Japan which Hiroshima and Nagasaki showed to have been so misplaced. But it must also be seen in relation to the aversion which the U.S.A. entertained at this time to any larger British participation in the onslaught on Japan such as Churchill never ceased to proffer. The fact was that the war powerfully stimulated and at the same time gave opportunity for that American sense of mission in relation to both China and Japan which, if not imperialist, bore strong resemblances to the self-conceived role of the British raj in India. This was evident in the exclusive character of MacArthur's occupation policy in Japan. It was as if manifest destiny after its long halt at the shores of the Pacific (or at least of Hawaii) had now resumed its westward course and reached the offshore island outpost of Asia.[1] Thus though a Far Eastern commission of eleven nations with interests in the Pacific area was set up in Washington in 1945 in response to complaints by Britain and the USSR of

being ignored, it was expressly forbidden any say in military or territorial questions and could only communicate with the authorities in Japan
through the United States government. Similarly, though there was an
Allied Council for Japan, sitting in Tokyo and set up at the same time,
on which there was one seat for a joint representative of Britain, India,
Australia, and New Zealand, its powers were purely advisory and in fact
none of its members had any more effective say in what went on than
the Allies had in relation to any of the Soviet zones of occupation in
Europe. A token body of Australian–New Zealand and British-Indian
troops participated, under MacArthur, in the occupation.

Behind this near-monopoly on the ground there existed in the U.S.A.
a rather special body of politically active opinion in relation to the Far
East. Inferior in number, brains, and influence to that dominant element
in American society which had shaped and led an Atlantic First war, the
"Pacific Firsters," to give them a convenient but not quite accurate label,
were nonetheless widely diffused throughout America. Geographically,
they tended naturally to be stronger on the West Coast than the East,
with some following in the Midwest. Politically, they were more often
found in the Republican than the Democratic party for reasons partly
of tradition—going back to Theodore Roosevelt and McKinley—but
more significantly of very recent history, their exclusion from power during the years of the New Deal. Administratively, they had their best-
informed members in the territorially relevant units of the Navy, War,
and State Departments. America's lack of large, coherent economic interests in the Far East, which was almost as true after the war as before
it, denied them any strong occupational or interest group base. But perhaps this very fact made it easier for them to attract the frustrated and
disaffected, the adventurers and the also-rans of every kind. Thus isolationism, denied its traditional role by the inexorable march of history
and technology, found a substitute existence for itself in a concern for
America's place in the Pacific and in Asia, an area where the tentacles
of Europe did not reach and the demands of allies were less vocal or
persistent. Later, a paranoiac obsession with communists found a comparably ready nourishment in the misfortunes of America's Far Eastern
policies, and the "China lobby" and McCarthyism became for many purposes interfused.

The immediate postwar years saw little active disagreement between
the U.S.A. and Britain over policies in the Far East or Southeast Asia.

The very exclusiveness of MacArthur's shogunate meant that the most active area of American assertion was isolated from interference by the British or anyone else. Moreover the potential clash between the old British and the new American imperialist attitudes was largely averted by the change of government in Britain that replaced Churchill's toryism by Attlee's socialism. The British presence had indeed been restored throughout all her Asiatic possessions but only to resume in most of them, with accelerated tempo, the process toward self-government which had already got under way well before the war. In 1947, in the most spectacular act of imperial disengagement in history, the British, working to a strict timetable, terminated their rule throughout the whole Indian subcontinent, leaving in their place the independent states of India, Pakistan, Burma, and Ceylon. Whatever the consequences of this swift surgical operation were for the countries concerned, it removed at one stroke one of the oldest debating issues in the long Anglo-American dialogue about freedom and democracy. Just as slave emancipation had robbed nineteenth-century British critics of their broadest target in the American scene, so now their American counterparts would have to get along without the anomalous British raj. Not, of course, that British interest in the area ended with independence. Indeed British Labour, in particular, in the glow of its great emancipating achievement, was inclined to develop a proprietary attitude toward its former protégés which contrasted strongly at times with the sense of irritation that Americans often felt when confronted with some of the more impassive and self-righteous manifestations of the Hindu mentality. In Malaya at the same time the British found progress toward self-government impeded by a menace of Communist subversion and guerrilla warfare which was a reminder to them and to the Americans that the removal of imperial rule was not an automatic guarantee of peace and freedom.

It was, of course, in China that the Communist menace presented itself most forcibly to American diplomacy. Here the long attachment to Chiang Kai-shek undoubtedly made it more difficult to arrive at a realistic assessment of the forces involved and to formulate a policy which would best safeguard American interests. The British wore no such rose-tinted spectacles where Chiang was concerned, but the Labour government in particular was prone to fall into the opposite illusion, of seeing in Chinese communism only a movement of oppressed peasants and high-minded intellectuals intent on a process of national redemption and modernization. This difference of attitudes surfaced in a contradiction of policies when, in 1949, the Chinese Communists expelled the Kuomintang from mainland China. The Truman administration now found itself faced with a storm of criticism over the "loss of China" (a phrase whose proprietary overtones were indicative of the way in which many Americans had viewed the country). Huge sums of money had obviously been wasted; worse, American prestige had received a severe blow. Whether one clung to the relics of Chiang Kai-shek's regime (now confined to the island of Taiwan) or regarded him as a deflated creation of American wishful thinking, it was equally undeniable in the light of American experience that the Communist regime which replaced him was the enemy.

For Britain this was not so. For practical reasons, as lessees of Hong Kong (until 1997) and as a trading nation which in 1949 could ill afford the loss of any export market, the British were eager to recognize the new government of China. The Americans were not. Acheson said he required proof not only that the government controlled the country but also that it would carry out its international obligations and rule with the acquiescence of the ruled. There were echoes here of the moral criteria that Stimson had invoked over Manchukuo in 1932, when the doctrine of nonrecognition of territories acquired by force was the only weapon left to American diplomacy in the days of omnipotent isolationism. The British had generally been much more matter-of-fact over issues of recognition. (They had been eight years ahead of the Americans in their recognition of Soviet Russia.) They also indulged hopes (premature rather than illusory) that Mao Tse-tung might become the Tito of the Far East (Tito's Yugoslavia had broken with Russia in July 1948). In this they were encouraged by India. Indeed the pressure from their newly emancipated Asiatic Commonwealth partners was a strong factor. India accorded recognition on 30 December 1949, Pakistan on 4 January 1950, Ceylon on 6 January.[2] Under these pressures, Britain and the U.S.A. parted step. Soon, when the issue of Chinese representation came up at the United Nations, the disaccord between the two Atlantic allies was spelled out before the world. It was a tribute to the basically good relations between the governments, and especially between the foreign secretaries, Bevin and Acheson, that they disagreed so amicably, especially since the Truman administration was under savage fire from the "China lobby" for the failure of its policies. Possibly, had the Korean War not broken out when it did, the British action might before too long have brought the Americans around and saved the needlessly long lapse of contact, which was terminated only in 1972. But it is also true that the British had little immediately to show for their prompt decision. Acheson indeed avers that Bevin in May 1950 confessed doubts about the wisdom of Britain's action and saw little profit in it.[3] Partly this was because Britain illogically continued to recognize Chiang's claims to Taiwan and to China's seat in the United Nations. From a longer perspective, however, it is plausible to argue that British recognition did serve a purpose, and was even profitable to the U.S.A., in preserving a channel of communication between East and West and preventing the total insulation of the new regime.

All this, however, was quickly overlaid in June 1950 by the outbreak of the Korean War. That "police action," to use Truman's misleading understatement for it, severely taxed American strength and morale, occurring in a faraway country with which the average American had no ties of history or culture, involving an enemy who enjoyed all the advantages of fighting on home ground and from an adjacent protected base, and, above all, denying the possibility of that clean-cut military solution which Americans felt their power and their tradition entitled them to expect. The United Nations auspices under which the war was fought encouraged the belief that at least the non-Communist members of the organization would feel an obligation to assist. But in fact the exclusive character of the United States role in the Far East pretty well determined that the U.S.A. would have to bear most of the burden herself. Britain, quite apart from her United Nations obligations, had long been used to fighting colonial wars in faraway countries amid alien cultures and often to indeterminate conclusions, and to this extent the Korean War was a less painful novelty to her than to the U.S.A. On the other hand, Korea was, of all countries on the globe, almost the farthest from Britain by geography or, in 1950, by interest, and she had played virtually no part in the arrangements whose breakdown preceded the war. The hostilities came at a time when Western Europe, though for the moment rescued from collapse by NATO, was still in a fragile condition and when the British economy, though similarly rescued by the Marshall Plan, was ill placed to stand the strain of another war. Moreover Britain was already carrying on a taxing and not wholly dissimilar contest with the Communists in Malaya, where over 20,000 British troops were tied down until 1954. Finally, there was lacking that basic confidence in American policy and leadership in the Far East which was the bedrock of NATO. MacArthur's Napoleonic complex and his right-wing affiliations were profoundly distrusted in Britain; the persisting American attachment to Chiang Kai-shek was regarded as a standing invitation to imprudent adventures; and the rise of McCarthyism in the United States which began in February 1950 with the senator's denunciation of "communists in the State Department" seriously impaired British confidence in the reliability of the American governmental and military machine.

For all these reasons there was little or no real enthusiasm in Britain for the Korean War. Nonetheless the validity of Truman's prompt decision and his invocation of the United Nations were fully recognized in Britain and fully supported, both in the United Nations and outside. Britain supplied the equivalent of two regimental combat teams of ground troops, substantially the largest non-American contribution, save for that of Turkey, and their record, measured by conduct or by casualties, was highly creditable. The British naval units in the Far East were also put under the United Nations Command. At the end of 1950, indeed, the only foreign units assisting the Americans were those from the United Kingdom, other Commonwealth countries, and Turkey. Moreover, not only did the Korean War in itself demand fresh armaments; by heightening tension between the Communists and the West it also raised the requirements for a realistic defense of Western Europe. In August a revised British defense program was drawn up for the next three years, involving an increase in the proportion of the national income spent on defense from 8 percent to 10 percent, and in early 1951 the total figure of defense expenditure was raised still further. There was much less enthusiasm for another form of Western European reinforcement which the United States now began to advocate, the rearming of Germany. There was a real gap, even if it was mainly a time lag, between British and American sentiments here, swiftly and directly traceable to the difference in their wartime experiences and their physical proximity to the ex-enemy. Partly to avoid the creation of an entirely German army, partly to assimilate it if it developed, talk now began of an integrated European defense force. Thus Korea, by an irony of history, made its contribution, via Washington, to European unity.

Its immediate contribution, however, was much more to Anglo-American disunity. The initial British welcome for Truman's prompt "police action" cooled when it was realized that the U.S.A.'s Korean policy could not be entirely isolated from its China policy. Truman's orders on 27 June to the United States Seventh Fleet to neutralize Taiwan (interpreted often in Britain as affording protection to Chiang) were indicative of this. The appearance of Chinese Communist contingents in North Korea (of which warnings reached Attlee via India's prime minister, Jawaharlal Nehru) underlined the connection, and the longer the war lasted, the more emphatic the connection became. To the British the prospect of a larger conflict involving China was not only alarming in itself; it was especially worrying since, for them once again, Europe was the theater where American aid was most imperative, so that by comparison everywhere else seemed a needless distraction. Finally, as so often happens in an alliance, the weaker partner was apprehensive of what the stronger one might get involved in on his own—and no one was more inclined to act on his own than MacArthur. The net result of this was to bring on a British attack of nerves when, on 30 November, an incautious reply by Truman in a press conference seemed to carry the implication that the U.S.A. might be willing to use the atomic bomb in Korea. Revulsion at such an idea was heightened by the British failure, to date, to secure from the U.S.A. any continuation of the wartime cooperation in the atomic weapon field. Attlee flew to Washington for a hasty meeting with Truman aimed at allaying British public concern and improving cooperation. The meeting established that Truman's off-the-cuff rejoinder had been misunderstood, but also that there was, for all the differences of outlook and emphasis over the Far East, a basic identity of objectives in Washington and London. Indeed the most important disagreement was within the American ranks themselves, between Washington and MacArthur, and this could only be relieved, as it eventually was, by MacArthur's dismissal. The fact remained that the only point at which the British could make their representations was at Washington —especially since there was no real machinery of interallied consultation through the United Nations Command in Korea, which was de facto exclusively American. This meant an inescapable frustration and irritation, as long as the war lasted, between the partner who was carrying nine-tenths of the fighting and the negotiation, and the partner who, from the sidelines, could not restrain his anxiety over an operation that was seldom surefooted and was often alarming. To correct this even the

removal of MacArthur was not enough. As late as June 1952 there was
an uprush of alarm at the American action in bombing targets on the
Yalu River without informing Britain in advance, despite an agreement
to consult before such an attack was made.

The offense given was not only one-way. Throughout the war, although the British at the United Nations voted (however reluctantly)
for a "unified Korea" and for condemning China as an aggressor, they
continued to maintain diplomatic and, indeed, trade relations with Peking. Strategic materials were denied to China, but otherwise Hong Kong
persisted in its traditional role as the commercial gateway between East
and West. Indeed, if the colony was to remain in being at all, it had to
trade, and it was plausible to argue that, once it foundered, China would
take it over. And of course in relation to Britain's precarious economy
Hong Kong was important. Nor was its trading any secret: every fort-
night the U.S.A. was supplied with details of its shipments to China.
All this was true and in British eyes adequate as justification. It did not
alter the fact that, seen through American spectacles, it looked like trading with the enemy. Paradoxically the criticism did not abate with the
end of the fighting in Korea. This was because the legacy of bitterness
which the Korean War left behind was so skillfully exploited, especially
after the Republican victory in November 1952, that the sense of Communist China as an American enemy was actually heightened to the
point where a McCarthyite Congress could demand a blockade of the
China coast. In March 1953, in response to this pressure, the United
Kingdom introduced a strict licensing system for vessels going to Chinese ports. In the absence of a formal peace settlement this remained in
existence long after the signing of the Korean armistice on 27 June 1953
—down to 1958, in some cases.

Just as the Truman administration in formulating its Korean War
policy had to contend with an aberrant MacArthur and a largely paranoiac Congress, so Attlee had to take into account the left-wing Labour
lobby in Parliament and the complex pressures on Britain as the leader
of the Commonwealth with the prime responsibility for preserving its
unity. India in particular, committed to a risky neutralism and trading
heavily on the obligation of her recent raj to protect her, was insistent
in the United Nations and elsewhere on the avoidance of any course of
action hostile to Communist China. Thus, after supporting the original
United Nations intervention in Korea, she opposed or abstained from

all resolutions that involved further action and threw all her influence
behind an early cease-fire. In the tortuous negotiations over the repatria-
tion of the prisoners of war that preceded the armistice the Indians acted,
in many ways, as a pressure group for Asiatic "nonaligned" opinion
with British support on many issues where neither the British nor the
Indians could have won American agreement by themselves. And when
President Syngman Rhee compromised the armistice negotiations by devising the breakout of anti-Communist North Korean prisoners in June
1953, the fact that India, on Britain's assurance, was able to convince
Peking that this was not done with American connivance helped to restrain Chinese reactions.

India's nonalignment found no echo in the old dominions of the Pacific. Australia and New Zealand, at the time of Korea, were already
investigating the possibilities of a Pacific-wide pact which would give
them the sort of security that Europe was getting through NATO. They
supplied, of course, part of the occupation forces in Japan. In the Korean
fighting their servicemen made a substantial contribution; in the diplomacy of the war they played a smaller part, generally adopting a position midway between those of Britain and the U.S.A. They shared Britain's concern for the unity of the Commonwealth, but they were also
aware of their dependence on the U.S.A. for their security in the Pacific.
Against the grain they accepted far milder terms for Japan in the peace
treaty which fifty-two nations signed at San Francisco on 4 September
1951 than their public opinion would have wished. (Australia and New
Zealand's attitude to Japan was very like that of Britain to German rearmament at the same time.) In return for their acquiescence in Japanese
resurgence, the dominions secured American guarantees for their own
security in the form of the so-called ANZUS (Australia–New Zealand–
United States) Pact of mutual defense, also signed in September 1951.
For the U.S.A., ANZUS represented, for those who cared to emphasize
the continuities of history, an extension of the Monroe Doctrine to the
South Pacific; the language of the vital article referring to an attack on
a signatory as one which "would be dangerous" to the peace and safety
of all the others is drawn from Monroe's message. The pact was part of
a structure of Pacific defense which included similar treaties with the
Philippines (1951), South Korea (1953), Chiang's China (1954),
SEATO (1954), and eventually even Japan (1960), with commitments
less automatic than those of NATO but still constituting a comprehen-

sive net of anti-communist encirclement. For the dominions it was the culmination of a process that went back to the fall of Singapore in 1941 and the consequent inability of the United Kingdom to defend its Commonwealth kith and kin. The dependence on the U.S.A. created by the war continued into the peace as the United Kingdom's preoccupation with Europe persisted. (One of the dominions' expectations for ANZUS was that it would prevent NATO from engrossing too much of the U.S.A.'s resources of supplies and materials.) The ANZUS treaty might not give the dominions a much greater guarantee of United States protection than they would have without it, but it did give them a direct voice in Washington, either to stimulate or (as, e.g., over Korea and China) to restrain. In London ANZUS came as something of a shock, with its pointed exclusion of Britain from membership. For the first time in history a dominion (other than Canada, whose contiguity to the U.S.A. gave her a distinctive role) had entered into a vital defense arrangement from which the mother country was excluded. That this was done at America's insistence was painful—it even extended to a ban on a British "observer" at ANZUS Council meetings. But it was a logical consequence of Britain's diminished power in the region and it did not in fact entail, as some pessimists at the time forecast, a total absorption of Australia and New Zealand into the American system, even militarily. The Woomera Rocket Range set up in 1949 continued to serve a vital function for British research and development. Cooperation with Britain in Malaya was fully maintained. Indeed it could be argued that the assurance which ANZUS provided of protection in the Pacific set both Australia and New Zealand free to a degree that would otherwise have been impossible to cooperate with Britain outside the areas of their immediate domestic concerns.

13

Dwight D. Eisenhower's taking over the White House in January 1953 might have been expected to guarantee a continuance of good United States–United Kingdom relations, if not indeed a period of even closer collaboration. From the British point of view no more popular president could be imagined than the "Ike" of the war years and NATO, while in London the return in November 1951 of Winston Churchill to No. 10 restored the greatest survivor of the wartime Anglo-American partnership to his old post. With Winston went another central figure of the war years, Anthony Eden, heir apparent and foreign secretary. When Eden took over from Churchill in 1955, he was succeeded, as foreign secretary, by Harold Macmillan, who also, as minister resident in Algiers in 1942–45, had firsthand experience of Anglo-American collaboration.

It was, of course, true that Eisenhower's victory brought to power a party which Britain for twenty years had only known in opposition, and often as an isolationist opposition—the Republicans. Yet though this was bound to involve for Britain an adjustment of old habits, the feeling was general that too exclusive an identification of alliance politics with one party was unhealthy and also that for accustoming the Republicans to their new role no leader could possibly be better than Eisenhower. His nomination was itself evidence that the isolationist, "fortress America" wing of the party was in retreat, while his election gave him an overwhelming mandate for the policies of international cooperation which he had espoused as explicitly as his Democratic opponent and to which he had made a unique personal contribution.

Yet the record of Anglo-American cooperation during Eisenhower's eight years was troubled and checkered, approaching in 1956 a complete breakdown that represented the lowest point in the relations of the two countries since the 1920s. What went wrong? At the personal level it is easy to pinpoint one failure. There was one figure in the new cast who was not reassuming an old role, but was for the first time playing what was almost the lead, in a part that he had been understudying for years. That was John Foster Dulles, a lifelong advocate of American involvement in world affairs, but a lawyer whose indisputable experience in international relations had previously been confined to the councils of a party in opposition. There he had done yeoman work in committing the Republicans to an international role, but he had had very little share in the practical management of American policy either during the war years or after. He was, in this sense, the odd man out. Yet Eisenhower, recognizing the value of his long apprenticeship as "shadow" secretary of state, not only regarded his appointment as virtually automatic but gave him almost a free rein in his crucial office. Dulles as secretary of state combined the subtleties of a lawyer with the moral rigidities of a crusader. (The crusade was mainly against communism, conceived of not merely as a political creed but as a worldwide conspiracy.) This had the effect, where allies were concerned, of inspiring both distrust of his deviousness and fear of his impetuosity. The classic instance of this is to be found, unfortunately, in his relationship with Anthony Eden, his temperamental opposite number, who had weaknesses of vanity and impetuosity of his own.

Disastrous as the Dulles-Eden misalliance was, however, it does not provide the whole answer to the frictions and clashes of these years. In retrospect it seems certain that it was a mistake to try to re-create a wartime relationship in such backward-looking and exclusively personal terms. There was too much reliance on old formulas, such as "summit" meetings. (There were thirteen Anglo-American "summits" in these eight years compared with three in the eight years after Potsdam, and the observable benefits were hardly proportionate.) And even when old intimacies were restored, they were paid for in the price of tired and devitalized performances by the principal participants. It is surely significant that during his two presidential terms Eisenhower had three serious illnesses, that during his four-year premiership Churchill was out of action for three months with a stroke that took its inevitable toll, that Eden was incapacitated for six months in 1953 as well as prostrated after Suez, and that Dulles was almost continuously ill from late 1956 to his death in 1959.

Moreover, this rather worn and backward-looking leadership was having to address itself less to Europe, where the problems were familiar and on the whole manageable, than to Asia, where wartime precedents had less validity and consequent policies were more controversial. Neither the Far East nor the Middle East had been conspicuously successful areas of Anglo-American cooperation; to become so they required much more flexibility, imagination, and mutual confidence than the fifties were able to supply. In the United States in particular, issues involving the Middle or Far East were liable to attract party political pressure and controversy and to be settled more by reference to the exigencies of domestic politics than by consideration of the real local factors involved. Then again, each country had its peculiar long-range difficulties in formulating a consistent policy in these areas. Britain was having to reduce her responsibilities to match her diminished power. The U.S.A. was having to adjust to new focuses of nationalist and Communist self-assertion and to build new outposts of stability with strange allies in remote places. Ideally, each would find its own task easier if it could undertake it in collaboration with the other. Actually, that very cooperation sometimes proved so difficult as to increase rather than reduce the burden each partner carried.

The end of the Korean War came as a relief to Britain almost as much as it did to the U.S.A. But the relief was short-lived, because almost immediately a critical situation developed in an area that was to prove much more intractable than Korea, Indochina. Here the European power immediately concerned was France, as the former colonial ruler trying to maintain the structure of local self-government which she had created against the pressures of communism, indigenous and external. By the end of 1952 American aid amounted to one-third of the cost of this struggle, but still the French were losing heavily, in men and money, and were arguing that if they were to be able to pull their weight in Europe they must look to the U.S.A., and to a lesser degree Britain, for still further assistance. The concern was widespread that China might overtly intervene in the conflict; in general the British hope was that this could be averted by some kind of negotiated settlement, while the American conviction was that China could and should be deterred. Thus on 29 December 1953 Dulles announced that, in the event of an invasion of Indochina, the American reaction "would not necessarily be confined to the particular theater chosen by the communists for their operations," and on 12 January 1954 that the consequences of Chinese intervention "might not be confined to Indo-China." As the French position deteriorated, so the gap between the British and the American approaches widened. French ambivalence further complicated the picture: sometimes their emphasis fell on the search for negotiation and extrication; sometimes they sought direct and violent Anglo-American intervention, as when they pressed for an air strike to relieve their desperately beleaguered forces at Dien Bien Phu. It was support for this latter proposal by Dulles and Admiral Arthur Radford, chairman of the Joint Chiefs of Staff, who hoped to present it to Congress with British endorsement, that led Churchill to comment that "what we were being asked to do was to assist in misleading Congress into approving a military operation, which would in itself be ineffective, and might well bring the world to the verge of a major war."[1]

The idea of an armed strike was dropped, and with the change of government in Paris disengagement became the goal of French policy. This was achieved via the conference at Geneva which had originally been called to settle the future of Korea. In fact it proved impossible to get agreement on this topic, and when the conference moved on to discuss Indochina the Americans were reluctant to participate in talks that could result at best only in a compromise and in any case involved negotiating with the Communist Chinese. A disproportionate part was consequently played by Sir Anthony Eden in the final settlement, which involved a partition of Vietnam and the neutralization of Laos and Cambodia, supervision by a commission consisting of India, Canada, and Poland, and a promise of nationwide elections in 1956. The agreements obviously registered a defeat for the French and a gain for the Communists. Yet they almost certainly salvaged as much as could be expected from a situation in which all-out war offered the only alternative. As such they put Dulles in a painful dilemma. He resolved it by declining to endorse any of the agreements, while announcing that the U.S.A. "took note" of them, would not disturb the cease-fire, and would view any forceful violation of it with grave concern.

While Geneva was in progress, negotiations, at American instigation, had been going on about the organization of collective defense in Southeast Asia, initially as part of the program for saving Indochina and subsequently for preventing any further similar setbacks at the hands of the Communists. The British welcomed any support for their exposed position in Malaya but insisted on first opening the membership of any such organization to India and other Asian Commonwealth countries. To this Dulles countered by insisting that if India were to be invited, then Chiang's China, i.e., Taiwan, would have to be included as well. Reluctant approaches were finally made to India, Pakistan, Ceylon, Burma, and Indonesia. But the charms of nonalignment, together with perhaps some distrust of America's Asiatic presence, proved too strong. Only Pakistan chose to join—thus making, with Thailand and the Philippines, the only three member states which belonged to the area at all.[2] This absence of local roots bothered the British, but they were willing to make do with a Southeast Asia Treaty Organization (SEATO) which, despite all its limitations, did provide a framework for consultation and for defense of the region. SEATO thus came into existence at Manila in September 1954, with the U.S.A., Britain, Australia, New Zealand, and France as members in addition to the three indigenous states. It resembled NATO in being a mutual defense pact against the threat of communism, but its commitments are less automatic than NATO's and the military organization set up to implement the treaty bears this out. There are no counterparts to NATO's supreme allied commander and integrated forces. A council of ministers directs the organization and combined exercises take place at intervals, but there is no unified command. Indeed the closest integration of forces in the area is that provided by the Commonwealth members—the Commonwealth strategic reserve, based near Malacca and established in August 1960, to serve Australia, New Zealand, the United Kingdom, and Malaya. The guarantees that SEATO provides are not confined to its member countries; they can extend to any state which the signatories may "designate." Cambodia, Laos, and South Vietnam were so "designated." But significantly Hong Kong and Taiwan both lie outside the area south of 20°30′ to which the treaty applies. And even more significantly the treaty was not initially invoked in relation to any part of the Indochinese conflict; the closest it came to such application was when in March 1961 the SEATO council warned against *possible* consequences of subversion in Vietnam and Laos. When in May 1962 Thailand requested SEATO assistance, it was the U.S.A. which responded with 5,000 troops while Australia and New Zealand sent only token contingents and the United Kingdom only a squadron of jet fighters. And when in the autumn of 1961 the decision was taken in Washington to commit American strength to Vietnam, it was as exclusively

American as the United Kingdom's decision to aid Malaya had been exclusively British. SEATO was indeed consulted about Vietnam on several occasions in the early 1960s, but the nearest it came to action was the council agreement in April 1964 that members "should remain prepared, if necessary, to take further concrete steps within their respective capabilities of fulfillment of their obligation under the treaty."

Thus SEATO was no Asiatic NATO, morally or militarily. But at least it constituted some sort of forum for consultation and information, whereas American policy outside the SEATO area was, under Dulles, largely a unilateral affair. This was well illustrated in connection with China, the country whose handling continued to divide the U.S.A. and Britain. In February 1953 one of the first acts of the Eisenhower administration was to revoke the orders given by Truman to the Seventh Fleet in relation to Taiwan; henceforward it was not to shield Communist China from any Nationalist attack. A year later hostilities did break out between the two rivals, when the Communists started to shell the offshore islands of Quemoy and Matsu, and again there was concern in London lest America's commitment to Chiang should involve her in conflict with his enemy. This fear was heightened later in the year by the signing of the mutual security pact between the U.S.A. and Taiwan and the following January by the congressional resolution which empowered Eisenhower to protect against armed attack not only Taiwan and the Pescadores but also "such related positions" as—Quemoy and Matsu? The resolution left the question hanging in the air. This was the celebrated Dulles tactic of "brinkmanship," of leaving the enemy uncertain of how far you would go. The trouble for the leader of an alliance was that this left your allies similarly uncertain. At the time it seemed to have worked, and Chou En-lai piped down, but it left ragged nerves in London.

The unity of the alliance was also shaken in a different context on the other side of the world, in Europe. By the 1950s the movement for European unification was well under way. Its roots lay far back in history and also very near the surface in the catastrophic experiences of two world wars which impressed on the minds of serious Europeans the conviction that national sovereignties must be curbed if the Continent was to survive. Even in Britain such sentiments found echo. As early as November 1939 Attlee had gone on record with the stark dilemma, "Europe must federate or perish." After the war Churchill put himself at the head of the European movement with a speech at Zurich in 1946 urging the creation of "a kind of United States of Europe." Bevin as foreign secretary used language about "Western Union" which, while primarily strategic in its emphasis, had a political and economic thrust as well.

The United States was initially rather uninterested in such ideas, even somewhat hostile–e.g., toward Churchill's advocacy of a United Nations organization constructed on a regional basis, with Europe as one region. Gradually, however, as the U.S.A. came to accept its new postwar responsibilities to Western Europe, its position changed. The idea of a united Europe became attractive because it seemed to simplify alliance relationships: one would be easier to deal with than many, especially when those many were necessarily competitors for the U.S.A.'s favor. It was hoped that economically and politically a larger entity would be stronger and more self-sufficient, requiring less of America's manpower and money for its support. Such a belief found ready nourishment in the U.S.A.'s own national experience: had not federation been the secret of America's success? By degrees these attitudes became tinged with missionary fervor, as an increasing number of politicians and officials felt the urge to bring the federalist gospel to Europe. In 1948, the year that saw the launching of the plan for the Council of Europe, the preamble to the Economic Cooperation Act declared it to be the policy of the people of the United States "to encourage that economic cooperation in Europe which is essential for lasting peace and prosperity," while Governor Thomas Dewey, then the Republican candidate for president, promised to use the program of aid to Europe "as the means for pushing, prodding and encouraging the nations of Western Europe towards the goal of European union." When NATO required finance for rearmament, the Mutual Security Act of 1949 that provided it listed among its objectives "the economic unification and political federation of Europe."

But while the U.S.A. was becoming enthusiastic, Britain was becoming more skeptical. Some of this was that familiar phenomenon, the onset of caution which overtakes politicians when they exchange opposition for office. Some of it, for the Labour governments of 1945 to 1951, was a concern not to lose their newfound freedom to shape a socialist Britain by immersion in a capitalist Western Europe. Some of it was the result of substituting precise language for loose rhetoric; when this was done, it was discovered in Britain that while the kind of unification represented by NATO and the ERP was wholly acceptable (indeed Britain would take the lead here), and even a European consultative assembly was tolerable, surrender of powers to a European executive was not. When it came to this point, the age-old tradition of the sovereignty of Parliament reared its head. Finally, and in some ways most potent of all, it became apparent that much of the British endorsement of European unity was intended for a continental Europe across the Channel, with Britain seeing herself as a helpful neighbor, not an active member. The United Kingdom in fact was casting herself for a role parallel to that of the United States, of supporting European unity from outside. Britain, it was insisted, had a set of Commonwealth and world commitments which could not be accommodated within the framework of a European federation. The logic of such a contention was often accepted in America. It would have been more often accepted if the language of British pronouncements about Europe had been less woolly and self-contradictory.

With Korea came the second phase of NATO, the need for its reinforcement by West Germany's strength. This shifted the emphasis of American interest in European unification from the economico-political to the strategic-political. The European Defense Community (EDC) idea was devised with British encouragement as a device for incorporating German forces in NATO and so laying the specter of a revived German militarism. But British encouragement, it was soon made clear, would not involve British participation—British involvement would not be any closer than American. So when the EDC treaty was signed by France, West Germany, Italy, Belgium, the Netherlands, and Luxembourg in May 1952, Britain and the U.S.A., after close consultation, gave only a joint undertaking that "if any action from whatever quarter threatens the integrity or unity of the Community, the two governments will regard this as a threat to their own security."

It was not enough. With the rise of Gaullism in France the French Assembly dragged its feet on ratification of the treaty. In Washington frustration and irritation mounted. Dulles pursued a more forcing tactic than his predecessor. In December 1953 he threatened France with his celebrated "agonizing reappraisal" if the EDC were defeated and privately warned Britain of the risk of America going over to a policy of hemispheric defense, with emphasis on the Far East. In April 1954 Eisenhower committed the U.S.A. to keeping armed forces in Europe, including Germany, as long as the need existed, and Britain, in a concerted move, said virtually the same. The carrot was no more successful than the stick. In August 1954 the French Assembly rejected EDC. The implications of this for Britain were as grave as for Europe, now that the U.S.A. had staked so much of its European policy on German rearmament. It evoked from Eden what was perhaps the most adroit diplomatic operation of his career, devising and winning acceptance of a plan which would admit Germany to NATO on terms that would allay French fears. The secret of its success was a carefully timed announcement, whose effect Eisenhower described as "electric,"[3] committing Britain not to withdraw from the Continent the strength she then maintained—four divisions and the tactical air force—"against the wishes of the majority of the Brussels Treaty Powers." The pledge, at first glance little more than previous undertakings, in fact marked an important departure for Britain: it constituted a commitment which took Britain further into Europe than her Atlantic ally, the U.S.A., and its indefinite duration was in contrast to America's thirty-year engagement to NATO. The assurance thus provided made possible the creation of a framework of European security which would contain Germany and allay French concern. Germany entered NATO as an equal in 1955.

Eden's success in snatching victory from the jaws of EDC's defeat has been seen as further heightening the rivalry and antipathy between him and Dulles, but it was the course of events in the Middle East that finally set the two at loggerheads. Dulles's anticommunism coexisted uneasily with a strong disapproval of British imperialism. Initially, when confronted with a clash between the two principles in the controversy that arose over Iran's precipitate seizure in 1951 of Britain's oil interests, the U.S.A. allowed anticommunism (or conceivably the common interests of two oil-consuming states) to determine her policy; in brief she sided with Britain, promoted the downfall of the expropriating Iranian premier, Mohammed Mossadegh, participated in an Anglo-American consortium for marketing Iranian oil, and provided substantial interim dollar aid to get the new arrangements going.

When, however, a similar ebullition of national feeling was directed against the comparable "imperialist" presence in Egypt, no such common front developed between Washington and London. There was, to be sure, a history to the Suez affair. British concern with Egypt antedated the canal, but was intensified by it and was etched even deeper by the role which the defense of Egypt had played in British strategy during

World War II. A British military presence and untrammeled use of the canal had been axioms of British policy for nearly a century. The rise of Egyptian nationalism, sharpened by the creation of Israel, was bound to bring these axioms into question. The hope in Britain was that a hitherto exclusively British control of the area could be transformed into an Anglo-American condominium resting on an "enlightened" Arab awareness of the need for a common front against communism. There were two flaws in this attempt to transmute the old imperialism: the first was that it rested on a set of priorities different from those of Arab nationalism in general and Egyptian nationalism in particular; the second was that it required much more explicit and sustained commitments from the U.S.A. than the U.S.A. would give. The first flaw produced Nasser; the second flaw led to the complex of disasters known as "Suez."

The attempt to transform the nature of the British base in Egypt got under way in 1951—already rather late in terms of the tempo of nationalist demands—with the proposal to establish a Middle East Defence Organization (MEDO), to include Britain, France, the U.S.A., Turkey, and Egypt. The initiative was Anglo-American, and when the Egyptians rejected it, American support for the underlying concept did not disappear. What did disappear was any willingness to present the new nationalist Egyptian government with an open Anglo-American common front. The conclusion in October 1954 of an Anglo-Egyptian agreement to withdraw British troops from the Suez base and to reactivate it only if Egypt were attacked owed more to a reassessment of British strategy (in the light of the USSR's hydrogen bomb) than to any clear policy of Dulles.

Dulles's main concern at this time seems to have been the construction of a "northern tier" alliance along SEATO lines which would take the place of the ill-fated MEDO. Britain was not averse and in April 1955 joined Turkey and Iraq in the so-called Baghdad Pact. But the U.S.A., originator of the pact, would not openly endorse it (presumably because of the support in the U.S. Senate for Israel) and the United Kingdom found itself having to bear the brunt of the criticism that the pact evoked in the other Arab states, particularly Egypt. In this delicate situation the Egyptian purchase of arms from Czechoslovakia in September 1955 looked ominously like the introduction of a Communist presence behind the lines. There was no clear Anglo-American riposte to this, but some confidence was reposed in Nasser's desire for Anglo-

American assistance over his great prestige project, the Aswân High Dam. In fact it was the dam that, so to say, burst and washed away everything. Dulles, aware of Egypt's heavy arms debts, concluded that he could not recommend the project to Congress as a good investment, politically or economically, and suddenly announced as much. On 13 June the last British troops evacuated Suez. On 19 July, without consulting Britain, Dulles told the Egyptian ambassador that American participation in the Aswân project was not feasible.

From then on everyone, it seems, lost his head. On 26 July Nasser expropriated the assets of the Suez Canal Company to build the dam. Eden and Guy Mollet, the French prime minister, dismissed Nasser's assurances of not interfering with the free navigation of the canal as the worthless pledges of a latter-day Hitler with his "thumb on our windpipe." Dulles agreed that a way had to be found "to make Nasser disgorge." Eden warned Eisenhower that they "must be ready, in the last resort, to use force." Dulles did not exclude the possibility if all else failed but pressed for an international conference first. While the proposals of the conference were being put to Nasser, Dulles told the press that "the Suez Canal is not a primary concern of the United States," and Eisenhower emphasized that "we are committed to a peaceful settlement of this dispute, nothing else." When Nasser rejected the proposals, Dulles launched the idea of a canal users' association but then, to British disappointment, announced that, if the canal were blocked, "we do not intend to shoot our way through." The search for a settlement then moved to the Security Council of the United Nations, but in fact by this time the die had been cast for direct action. England and France had secretly agreed with Israel that the latter would launch an attack on Egypt and that Britain and France would intervene, ostensibly to restore order, actually to secure the canal. On 29 October the Israelis attacked Egypt. Britain and France sent ultimatums to the combatants threatening intervention if there was no cease-fire. Israel accepted its ultimatum, Egypt rejected hers. The Anglo-French intervention took place (somewhat behind schedule), most of the canal was secured (but only after it had been blocked), and the Egyptians were indeed defeated and accepted a cease-fire, but only after Britain and France had been exposed before the whole United Nations as aggressors who had to make way for a United Nations police force and who had blackened the reputation of the free world at the very moment when a united front was needed against the Soviet invasion of Hungary.

Suez remains such a monument to human folly that the disposition is very strong to blame it all on the aberrations of individual leaders—the hubris of Eden, the equivocations of Dulles, the carelessness of Eisenhower. Certainly opinion in each country was far from united behind its policymakers. One of the factors that brought Eden's ill-judged adventure to an abrupt end was the revulsion against it of a large number, perhaps a majority, of British voters. Even in the United States there was much criticism of Dulles and Eisenhower's handling of the affair. The fact remains that in each country the ranks held—at any rate long enough for the blunders to be committed. At the height of Suez—the coincidence had something to do with Eisenhower's failure to rise to the demands of the crisis—the president was reelected with a landslide majority. In Eden's cabinet only two junior ministers resigned. His majority in the House of Commons fell, but his resignation was the result of ill health, not of a parliamentary defeat. All this points to a deeper determinant of the Suez disaster than the errors of individuals or even the temporary misjudgments of majorities can provide. Not all these determinants are relevant here; many are rooted in the long history of Britain's relations with the Middle East. But as far as Anglo-American relations are concerned, the basic trouble was that in connection with the complex of issues which Suez represented there was no mutuality of interests between Britain and America. For the U.S.A. the canal was not a historic lifeline and Egypt was not a testing ground of national prestige. The prime enemy in the region was felt to be, not Arab nationalism, but Soviet communism. Consequently the major objective of American policy was to harness the Arab world to the containment of communism, and while for this purpose the lingering vitality of the British (and French) presence in the region might offer tactical advantages, in the longer run it might prove to be a decisive drawback. Of course it was true that, even from the American point of view, Nasser represented an unpredictable force which might as easily end up in the communist camp as in theirs. To this extent there was a genuine American ambivalence about the way to handle him, and it is arguable that if the Anglo-French-Israeli venture had succeeded, the U.S.A. would have accepted the result with private gratification and little public protest. Yet this oversimplifies the administration's position. There was a widespread concern in Washington, at least with respect to Africa, the Middle East, and Southeast Asia, about winning over the emerging countries of the third world, and in relation to this objective even the overthrow of Nasser would be self-defeating unless it were accomplished by a process that seemed legal and non-violent.

In all this there was nothing that Eden should not have known or could not have predicted from the signals that emanated from Washington. To fly in the face of it was not merely to ignore the difference between British and American interests in the area and go ahead on his own; it was to assert that what was at stake at Suez was more important than the Anglo-American alliance. It was no doubt true, as Eden sadly complains,[4] that what Britain tried to do at Suez was little different from what the U.S.A. had done when it contrived the overthrow of a communist-influenced government in Guatemala in 1954. The analogy might also hold for America's quasi-Suez contretemps at the Bay of Pigs in 1961. In each case Britain, however uneasy and disapproving, was careful to do nothing to hamper or publicly embarrass its ally. Unfortunately it is not enough for a national leader to discern underlying parallelisms of law and morals. He must also be responsive to the brute facts of power. And the brute facts were that Britain needed the U.S.A. more than the U.S.A. needed Britain, both in the Middle East and in the wider world. In the perfect alliance each partner takes equal account of the needs and problems of the other; in an imperfect alliance, such as the Anglo-American one had become in these years, the weaker partner pays the heavier price for ignoring the principle of reciprocity.

Initially it was indeed a heavy price. To make Britain and France desist, the Americans, as Eden says,[5] used "every resource at their command" including, so it was generally believed, private threats of economic sanctions. The serious drain of the operation on Britain's gold and dollar reserves was aggravated by American action and was undoubtedly a major factor in Eden's decision for a cease-fire. Of course the United States would have nothing to do with N. A. Bulganin's impudent proposal for a joint Soviet-American intervention to halt the fighting, and certainly Eisenhower[6] was careful not to go beyond asserting that the Anglo-French actions had "been taken in error." But at the United Nations there was American insistence on resolutions that made very few concessions to the British point of view; outside it there were calculated delays in the provision of emergency oil supplies while the canal was closed. Above all the president declined, despite his personal predilections, to receive a visit from Eden so long as any British troops remained on Egyptian soil. The action of over a hundred British Conservative members of Parliament in "deploring the attitude" of the U.S.A. as "endangering the Atlantic alliance" was merely a reciprocal indication of how sour relations had become.

Yet, considering the size of the breach, the remarkable thing is the speed with which it was repaired. Here all credit must go to Harold Macmillan, who, succeeding to the premiership after Eden's collapse, brought an inheritance (his mother was a Hoosier), a temperament, and a set of priorities eminently conducive to re-creating the lost intimacy. This was no mere trick of personality. It was rooted in a realistic assessment of British interests and requirements. Priority was given to the claims of the alliance, not only for its own sake, but as a way of helping Britain to cut her coat according to her cloth and to accelerate the transition from imperial sovereign to chairman of a multiracial Commonwealth. On the American side there was a comparable disposition to let bygones be bygones, if only because the Hungarian invasion betokened a militancy in the Soviet Union which would take quick advantage of any rift in the NATO alliance or of any vacuum in the Middle East. It was the vacuum which was first filled. On 5 January 1957 Eisenhower asked Congress to authorize economic and military aid to Middle East nations that requested it "against overt armed aggression from any nation controlled by international communism." Essentially the Eisenhower Doctrine, as it was inevitably dubbed, was an underpinning of the Baghdad Pact without the complications that joining or extending it would seem to present. In April it was quickly implemented, when King Hussein of Jordan felt his country threatened, by $30 million of aid and a contingent of United States Marines. In July 1958 when Lebanon and Jordan similarly felt themselves threatened as a result of the revolution in Iraq, a similar protective operation was launched, this time Anglo-American, American marines for Lebanon and British paratroops for Jordan. There could hardly be a clearer demonstration of Anglo-American coordination, either in planning or in execution, though it took all the skills of the United Nations to extricate the two powers from an intervention easier to launch than to terminate.

Important though this healing of the Middle East rift was, Macmillan's greatest achievement was in securing American understanding of Britain's new defense posture. This was achieved at the Bermuda meeting in March 1957, which Eisenhower later described as "by far the most successful international conference that I had attended since the close of

World War II."[7] The problem for Britain was threefold: to recover the national nerve which had been so nearly lost over Suez, to reduce the strain on the economy which the high rate of post-Korea defense (9 percent of the GNP) had imposed, and to reestablish the shattered intimacy of the Anglo-American alliance. The solution was found in coupling defense cuts with a new emphasis on nuclear deterrents and securing active American support in making these British nuclear deterrents credible. The cuts were sweeping: conscription was to be ended by 1960, thus cutting the army strength by 50 percent—including the British Army of the Rhine—and the tactical air force in Germany would be halved. This came only two and a half years after Eden's pledge of 1954. To offset it there was to be a strengthening of Britain's nuclear striking power through the V-bomber force, a deterrent which, it was emphasized, would be "European." Even if the "Europeanness" of Britain's deterrent were accepted, for NATO this could only mean a further shift of emphasis away from shield to sword, with Britain adopting, in relation to the alliance, a posture very like the American one.

As such the "new look" of British defense caused little delight in Washington, especially since it was coupled with a good deal of talk about the British deterrent being "independent"—independent, that is, of the U.S.A., giving Britain an "ultimate weapon" of her own with which to establish her own tactical priorities, preserving for her an equal and independent voice in the councils of the great powers. Yet the U.S.A. not only accepted this "new look"; at Bermuda Eisenhower actively assisted it by providing Britain with a stock of intermediate range ballistic missiles (IRBMs) as delivery vehicles for the "ultimate weapon" until such time as the V-bomber force was ready. Why was this done?

Logically, the U.S.A. could not object to a British "new look" which had been preceded by an American "new look" in 1954, when the president, with his concern for not letting military spending cripple the economy, cut the defense budget and reallocated expenditure from army to air force in a similar switch of emphasis from conventional to nuclear forces. But granted that the U.S.A. thus lost any right to protest, why did she carry acquiescence to the point of assistance? No doubt sentimental and political considerations counted for something; if this was the price for patching up the alliance, perhaps it would be worth paying. But beyond this there was a recognition that since Britain was bent on this course, it was better to accompany her than to let her go it alone.

Already in 1956 the British had been given data that helped in the development of an atomic submarine. Britain's acquisition of a hydrogen bomb (first exploded in May 1957) showed that her nuclear potentiality was a real one. It was pointless any longer to keep "secrets" from her, yet she still lagged in the possession of delivery systems. Was it not better to partner and so share control than to stand aloof and alienate confidence? After all, the IRBMs operated under a two-key system, requiring each partner's agreement for their activation.

Other considerations also supervened. In October 1957 the Russians put their earth satellite, *Sputnik,* into orbit and the margin of continental America's immunity from overseas attack shrank overnight. In 1948 the Soviet pressure on Berlin had suddenly made British bomber bases crucial for American diplomacy and strategy. In 1957 (when, incidentally, the Berlin fuse was still smoldering) *Sputnik* similarly made Britain a necessary advance missile base at a time when the American intercontinental ballistic missile (ICBM) was still only on the drawing board. Thus the Bermuda agreement was seen to have a dual aspect: the British nuclear deterrent was also an American nuclear defense. (No other NATO country was willing to offer the U.S.A. comparable facilities except, at the end of 1958, Italy and, soon after, Turkey.)

This was the background to the eventual 1958 agreement on a comprehensive exchange of atomic information that ended Britain's long exclusion. But it was also the background to new developments in Europe which while not directly involving the U.S.A. yet were closely tied in with her relations with the United Kingdom. In 1957 the movement for European unification, to which Britain had given a somewhat aloof encouragement, suddenly gathered momentum with the signing of the Rome Treaty, which came into effect on 1 January 1958, setting up the European Economic Community (EEC), the so-called Europe of the Six. Britain initially had little desire to become a member; it cut across the ties of Commonwealth and of the North Atlantic alliance. But she could not be indifferent to the creation of this new economic entity and sought to protect her interests and discharge her extra-European obligations by creating a free-trade area which would embrace all the members of the Organization for European Economic Cooperation (OEEC) including the new economic community. The attempt failed. The Six were afraid that their newfound identity would be diluted in a larger system, and Franco-British suspicions and rivalries were sharpened by Macmillan's improved and, in the sphere of nuclear armaments, exclusive relations with the U.S.A. De Gaulle felt shut out from this "special relationship" and decided in return to concentrate French efforts on an exclusive role in Europe. In March 1959 he withdrew the French fleet from NATO and in June denied NATO any nuclear stockpiling facilities unless France was allowed to participate in control. This resulted in a further concentration of United States striking power in British and German bases. The Six stood out so resolutely against a larger economic grouping that Britain's European Free Trade Area (EFTA) when it came into existence in July 1959 consisted only of the so-called Seven, the minor powers outside the EEC, "le club des sans-club"—Scandinavia, Austria, Portugal, Switzerland, and Britain. Nineteen sixty saw these trends intensified. In nuclear defense and offense Anglo-American intimacy continued, with the establishment in Britain of the Fylingdales radar system, designed to provide the U.S.A. with early warning of Soviet missiles, and of the Holy Loch base for Polaris atomic submarines. At the same time, at the Camp David meeting of Eisenhower and Macmillan in March 1960 it was agreed that the British "independent" nuclear deterrent was to be updated, the Americans agreeing to furnish, when completed, their latest Skybolt airborne missile, to be launched from Britain's own V-bombers. The French meanwhile, as the British had done earlier, were "going it alone"; they exploded their first nuclear device unaided in February 1960 and went on to create their own "force de frappe." It was apparent that these opposite tendencies could not continue indefinitely without fatal consequences for both the U.S.A. and Western Europe, but nowhere in the declining years of Eisenhower's second presidency did there seem to be the will or the capacity to resolve the problem. The long-prepared "summit" conference of Eisenhower, Khrushchev, Macmillan, and de Gaulle collapsed ignominiously in June 1960 with the shooting down of America's U-2 "spy" plane, leaving the alliance in disarray. And Britain, long used to being the economically sick man of the alliance, now found herself, incredulously, actually giving support to America in her own "dollar crisis," occasioned by the mounting deficit in the U.S.A.'s own balance of payments. True, this "dollar crisis" was very largely the reflection of the U.S.A.'s overseas expenditure in the cause of NATO, but it was nonetheless a reminder that the simple relationship of strong America and weak Europe had now become a great deal more complicated.

No sympathetic historian of Anglo-American relations can view the Kennedy years without a profound sense of promise unfulfilled and possibilities denied. The sixties were bound to bring changes in the disposition of world affairs that would impose new strains and problems on the Anglo-American relationship. But so long as Kennedy was in the White House and Macmillan in No. 10 there was a personal intimacy which could be relied upon to ease the strains and seek creative solutions to the problems; after Macmillan's retirement, followed quickly by Kennedy's assassination, the strains and the problems multipled and the personal intimacy disappeared.

The Kennedy-Macmillan rapport rested not on memories of the wartime comradeship in arms (indeed Kennedy *père* with his appeasement record had enjoyed no esteem in Britain) but upon a temperamental affinity ("They found the same things funny and the same things serious")[1] and a common approach to political problems—cool, pragmatic, and confidential. The exchange (and safeguarding) of confidences was facilitated by an unusual intimacy between the president and the British ambassador at Washington, David Ormsby-Gore (later Lord Harlech), related by marriage to both the Kennedys and the Macmillans.

Kennedy's constant concern was to escape from what he felt to be the rigid postures, both of strategy and of diplomacy, into which the U.S.A. had fallen in the closing years of Eisenhower, to refurbish the alliance, and to negotiate from strength with the Russians. Yet the changes this implied were more of form than of substance; the central policies of the Eisenhower years were not discarded. In British eyes this combination of new style and old verities was not unwelcome. They were less happy with the minor ideologically motivated (as it seemed) legacies of the fifties which survived to plague the New Frontiersmen—in Cuba the Bay of Pigs, in Southeast Asia the commitments to Laos and Vietnam.

For their own part the British had larger readjustments on hand. By the 1960s the transition from Empire to Commonwealth, which began in the interwar years with the older dominions and accelerated after World War II with the emancipation of the Indian subcontinent, had now quickened its tempo and extended its area to involve the rapid abdication of British rule throughout Africa. The 500 million out of 600 million inhabitants of the Commonwealth who in 1945 had been ruled from London had by 1963 shrunk to 27 million (out of over 700 million). This was not the result of a surrender to revolutionary independence movements so much as an intelligent anticipation of them, a brisk succession of acts of devolution designed to retain the Commonwealth as a framework of amity rather than as, in any sense, an instrument of compulsion. And when in 1961 it became apparent that this involved the adoption of racial equality as a central principle of Commonwealth membership, the withdrawal of South Africa, with its doctrine of apartheid, was accepted as a necessary and tolerable price to pay for preserving the unity of the remaining members.

The fraternal association which thus took the place of the old imperial rule had indeed already in many respects enjoyed the interest and support of the United States. In defense this was most apparent in Asia where, despite the nonalignment so attractive to India and some other Commonwealth members, ANZUS and SEATO brought New Zealand, Australia, and Pakistan into varying degrees of direct dependence upon the U.S.A. In economics all the developing nations of the Commonwealth—which is to say all save the old dominions—found it very desirable to supplement such intra-Commonwealth aid as was available by assistance from the U.S.A. By the 1960s the U.S.A. was providing directly about half the capital required for investment in the developing countries of the Commonwealth, apart from the substantial provision made by the United Nations and its related agencies, most of which was ultimately traceable to the American Treasury. With the establishment of free convertibility for sterling in 1958, the advantages which Commonwealth members derived from being members of the sterling area, based on London, also declined.

All this made for a looser relationship between Britain and the other Commonwealth members. At the same time a tighter and more exclusive relationship was growing up in Europe among the Community of the Six. Its exclusiveness presented a threat to Britain as long as she remained outside; its tightness meant that a new power bloc was coming into existence which Britain would be impotent to control. On both accounts, the arguments for British "entry into Europe," as it was popularly termed, became increasingly persuasive in the 1960s. Even the interests of the Commonwealth itself, it could plausibly be argued, were better served if Britain were "in Europe" representing their association rather than outside, helplessly looking on.

Given the weakening nature of Commonwealth links, this was plausible enough. It was not so easy to relate British entry convincingly to the strong bonds of the Anglo-American alliance (which, incidentally, were almost inextricably intertwined with the bonds that linked Britain to the oldest Commonwealth member, Canada). It was in flat contradiction to the old guideline of going into Europe as far as the U.S.A. would venture and no farther. Did it also involve abandoning whatever was "special" in the "special relationship," substituting a London-Brussels axis for the London-Washington one, putting Britain on a par with all the other allies of the United States on the continent of Europe? The Commonwealth after all was not a power association; it was a link of sentiment and an economic interest group. The sentiment could be preserved and the economic interest negotiated for in any terms Britain might make on entry. But the Anglo-American alliance, for all its unwritten character, was both a bond of sentiment and a tremendous reinforcement of British power. How and in what degree could it be maintained if Britain joined the European Economic Community?

One thing was certain under Kennedy. The United States, whatever its misgivings about the creation of a new potentially discriminatory economic unit, continued to be sympathetic to the EEC and to British membership in it. It was not only uneasy at the prospect of a Europe divided between the Six and the Seven; it was positively anxious to see the European end of the Atlantic alliance become more unified. It was tired of the intra-European rivalries, impatient to see a consolidation. But it did not want a consolidation into a "third force," independent of both the U.S.A. and the USSR, which was what de Gaulle often seemed to favor. It saw British membership of this consolidation as a guarantee that it would remain anchored faithfully to the North Atlantic alliance. For this reason, above all others, it wanted Britain in.

However, in the 1960s the place occupied in American thinking by either Europe or Britain was observably less than it had been. Three factors account for this. The first was the loss, progressive throughout the decade, of the U.S.A.'s nuclear superiority. With the development of Russian ICBMs the value of Europe as an advance bastion of American defense and the invulnerability of America herself substantially declined. The second was the rising power of China, both as a potential threat to the U.S.A. itself and as a rival to counteract the menace of the USSR. The third, which, while linked to the second, was not caused by it, was the increasing American involvement in the Vietnam War that drained her energies, sapped her morale, and alienated her both from her allies and from herself.

Initially, however, the shadow of Vietnam did not fall heavily across the relations between Kennedy and Macmillan. Though the Laos situation precipitated their first official meeting at Key West on 26 March 1961, it seemed then as if the neutralization of the country which had been envisaged at the Geneva Conference of 1954 was not beyond all hope of attainment. In July 1962 the Geneva Conference was reanimated and led to the establishment of a Laotian government of national unity. This may or may not have been stimulated by SEATO's intervention in Thailand, at the Thais' invitation, an intervention in which Britain, New Zealand, and Australia participated with an RAF fighter squadron and token infantry contingents respectively. This force withdrew six months later, in November, and represented the high point both of British intervention and of participation. By the end of 1963 both Laos and South Vietnam were becoming battle areas again.

Stubbornly unmanageable as Indochina continued to be, it was still Europe that in the early sixties dominated American thinking. Here the U.S.A. and the United Kingdom worked hand in hand. In May 1961 Kennedy confided to Macmillan the shock he sustained at his first meeting with the intransigent Khrushchev at Vienna; in August the common front of the two leaders had to be maintained in face of Russian pressure in Berlin and the construction of the Berlin Wall. At almost the same time Macmillan, after careful Commonwealth and American soundings, took the plunge and applied for admission to the EEC. "We are wholly with you," Kennedy told him.[2] Europe (which was largely to say, France) took its time over the British application. Meanwhile Russia's pressures mounted: in September she resumed nuclear tests; in October she exploded a terrifying fifty-seven-megaton hydrogen bomb. In face of this the U.S.A. felt obliged to resume atmospheric testing too, and Britain, accepting the logic of her argument, made available her Pacific possession, Christmas Island, for the American tests in April 1962. Then in October came the American-Russian confrontation over Cuba, when for days the world seemed to tremble on the edge of a nuclear war of the superpowers. At the time Britain's role outwardly appeared to be that of a hapless bystander at this "eyeball-to-eyeball" contest of the giants. We now know, however, what the delicacies of "crisis management" concealed at the time, the extent to which Britain was not merely consulted but, by the regular telephone talks of Kennedy and Macmillan and the presence of Ormsby-Gore, was intimately involved in the decisions taken. As Kennedy told Macmillan on the eve of his crucial broadcast to the nation on 22 October, "We shall have to act most closely together. I have found it absolutely necessary, in the interest of security and speed, to make my first decision on my own responsibility, but from now on I expect that we can and should be in the closest touch."[3] They were—sometimes two or three times a day by telephone—and British representations were responsible inter alia for the decisions not to call for a general NATO "alert" and to shorten the "interception line" of the naval blockade from 800 to 500 miles so as to give the Russian ships more time to reconsider their course and turn back. "We felt," to quote Macmillan, "as if we were in the battle headquarters."[4]

Cuba passed, but the fund of Anglo-American understanding on which it drew—and which it replenished—was real. It was barely a month before that fund had to be drawn on again. The Skybolt airborne missile which the U.S.A. was to furnish Britain under the 1960 Camp David agreement turned out by 1962 to be a nonstarter; mounting technical problems led the Americans to abandon its development. For Macmillan this was a shock; to lose Skybolt was to lose the "independent nuclear deterrent" on which so much had been staked. Moreover, since Robert McNamara, the U.S. secretary of defense, had gone on record in June as opposing the "proliferation" of nuclear weapons among America's allies, many were quick to see the cancellation of Skybolt as a diplomatic veto in a technological wrapping. As the final straw, its cancellation coincided with a crucial Macmillan–de Gaulle meeting over Britain's bid to enter the EEC. It seemed as if everything—diplomacy, strategy, and technology—had conspired to frustrate and humiliate Macmillan's policy.[5] On 18 December he flew to Nassau and appealed to Kennedy to act as Eisenhower would have done and, in default of Skybolt, provide an alternative. After three days of intensive negotiations it was agreed that Britain should have Polaris, the submarine-fired missile, in lieu of Skybolt, the United Kingdom to make its own warheads for the missile. Undoubtedly Kennedy gave his consent with reluctance; there was an obvious risk of upsetting all the other European allies who would be denied access to this nearly invulnerable weapon. To meet this point, the British agreed to "assign" their nuclear fleet to NATO, except when they judged their "supreme national interests" to be at stake. At the same time the Americans made an offer of Polaris to France, on similar terms. But the French (who indeed at this time had neither appropriate submarines nor warheads) would have no truck with such "interdependence." De Gaulle declined the offer. He also, for good measure, applied his veto on 14 January 1963 to British entry into the EEC. Was *post hoc propter hoc?* In the strict sense, probably not, since de Gaulle had been warned by Macmillan of his hopes and intentions when they met before Nassau. But the Nassau agreement undoubtedly reinforced de Gaulle's determination not to allow Britain into his EEC club while she enjoyed so special a relationship with the U.S.A.

The remainder of Macmillan's premiership (he resigned, a sick man, on 18 October 1963) was mainly concerned, in the Anglo-American field, with the establishment of some détente with the Russians. Here he and Kennedy, working closely together, did achieve a fair measure of success. The firm stand over Berlin was maintained, but a "hot line" of direct communication was established between Washington and Moscow, and in July the Americans, the British, and the Russians finally hammered out a treaty banning the testing of nuclear weapons. It marked the beginning of that profound reorientation of world politics which saw the USSR and China at odds, and the U.S.A. (and the United Kingdom) enjoying better relations with the two great Communist powers than these ideological giants enjoyed with each other.

In November 1963 Kennedy was assassinated, but already the shadow of Vietnam was spreading across the American political horizon. Under Lyndon Baines Johnson the darkening cloud came near to covering the whole sky. By Britain, as indeed by all the U.S.A.'s NATO allies, Vietnam was seen as America's problem. From the beginning there was skepticism about American policy there; the skepticism went back to the differences of view about the Geneva agreements of 1954. But the skepticism stopped well short of opposition or even outright criticism; the disposition was rather to adopt a stance of sympathetic nonbelligerency, in the hope that, as opportunity served, Britain might be able to act as mediator in bringing the war to a close. Britain's overwhelming concern, second only to that of not getting involved herself, was to prevent the U.S.A. from becoming bogged down in a hopeless and costly struggle that would divert her attention, her will, and her resources from her primary tasks, as Britain saw them, elsewhere. The posture of the sympathetic but hand-wringing bystander is a poor one at best from the point of view of influencing policy, but it was made even more ineffectual in these years by the fact that there was little or no real trust or intimacy between the successive administrations of Johnson and Nixon and the governments over which Alec Douglas-Home (1963–64), Harold Wilson (1964–70), and Edward Heath (1970–74) presided. Relations during these years were not bad, but they were seldom easy, warm, or confident. Some of this was attributable to the personalities involved; more of it was inherent in the situation. Britain labored under the inhibitions that are consequent upon seeing an old friend succumb to some enfeebling vice; if the U.S.A. was hooked on Vietnam, what could one do about it? The U.S.A., a weary Titan, was in no mood to admit those who evaded what she regarded as common burdens to an equal place at the council table. Moreover, a consciousness of "going it alone" in a war increasingly unacceptable at home and abroad heightened a tendency natural to Johnson and Nixon to indulge in private, secret, and indeed at times deliberately deceptive decision making. Lastly, by the very facts of geography Vietnam turned American attentions and energies increasingly away from Europe.

It was not difficult to approve the principles of United States action in Vietnam if that action was accepted as resistance to communist aggression. For some time it was possible to present it publicly, whatever private misgivings there might be, as parallel to the support that Britain was giving Malaysia in her contemporaneous struggle with Indonesia. In February 1964, after talks in Washington, Home could reaffirm support for United States policy in South Vietnam and Johnson could do the same for United Kingdom policy in Malaysia, where 54,000 British troops were involved. When six months later the Gulf of Tonkin incident drew such a forceful response from Johnson, the United Kingdom, as well as Australia, New Zealand, and Canada, gave the United States full support at the United Nations. Nor did the change in October from a Conservative to a Labour government alter this. In November the U.S.A. announced that it was sending military aid (though not troops) to Malaysia. In February 1965, when the "retaliatory bombing" of North Vietnam began on a heavy scale, both Wilson and his foreign secretary defended it in the House of Commons.

Yet the vehemence of the American bombing offensive shook public opinion in Britain and elsewhere to a degree which the government could not ignore; when the Commonwealth Prime Ministers' Conference met in June the strength of feeling displayed there led Wilson to head a commission, on which the prime ministers of Ghana, Nigeria, and Trinidad and Tobago also served, to try to negotiate a Vietnam peace. It was abortive; neither the USSR nor China (nor, of course, North Vietnam) would receive them. Nor was Johnson basically more receptive. "I won't tell you how to run Malaysia and you don't tell us how to run Vietnam" was his angry reply to Wilson in December 1964.[6] And Britain was in a poor position to press her arguments when she was reducing her own world commitments under the strain of an overloaded economy. Every year from 1964 to 1969 there was some crisis or other in Britain's finances for whose resolution she was, of course, heavily dependent on the United States, as the mainspring of the world's monetary system. It was at the worst moment in the sterling crisis of July 1966 that Johnson asked Wilson whether Britain could not send even a token force to Vietnam. "A platoon of bagpipers would be sufficient; it was the British flag that was wanted."[7] But by this time it was all that Wilson could do to keep his own Labour ranks from splitting wide open on Vietnam. When in June 1966 the Americans first bombed the outskirts of Hanoi and Haiphong, 113 Labour M.P.'s urged the government to dissociate itself completely from the war, and Wilson had to combine his "general support" for the American policy with dissociating the government from the American bombing. It was not an easy or convincing stance to maintain. Over the next two years Wilson was ceaselessly at work trying to disembarrass Britain and America of a war which he could neither endorse nor condemn, sparing no effort to win Soviet support for peace negotiations. (His hopes were exclusively centered on the USSR because by 1967 Britain's relations with China were so bad that her chancery in Peking was burned and riots were being fostered in Hong Kong.) There was a succession of peace talks—Wilson in Moscow and Washington, June–July 1966; George Brown (then foreign secretary) in Moscow, November 1966; Kosygin in London, February 1967; Wilson in Moscow and Washington, January–February 1968. Not only were they all abortive; they left in their wake an unpleasant feeling of unreality, whether because Britain was attempting a mediatory role for which she lacked the necessary leverage, or whether because Wilson, consciously or unconsciously, was being used by Johnson to give the appearance of negotiations where no negotiations were seriously intended.

Britain's impotence as a negotiator was enhanced by her declining significance as an Asiatic power. Now, in place of the old critical attitude to British imperialism, America's involvement in Vietnam led her to welcome a British presence in Asia paradoxically just at a time when Britain's economic resources were least able to sustain it. No American forces operated between Suez and Singapore; the "containment of China" policy was felt to require a British presence throughout this area to close the gap. But in 1966, in the wake of the sterling crisis of 1965, the British government put in hand a drastic review of the defense budget and imposed a firm ceiling of £2,000 million per annum at 1964 prices. This involved painful choices. The nuclear deterrent cost £180 million per annum, the maintenance of forces east of Suez £360 million per annum. Both could not be continued, and Labour in office revealed itself as reluctant as the Conservatives to give up the nuclear deterrent. With the shift of power in Indonesia from the Communists to the Nationalists the confrontation with Malaysia ended, and with it the only Asian operation in which Britain was actively involved. The decision was therefore made to abandon the Aden base by 1968, to halve the strength of British forces in Singapore and Malaysia, and to prepare for total withdrawal by the 1970s. The British Defence White Paper of 1969, the first year in a decade in which the defense estimates actually declined, was described by Denis Healey, the defense secretary, as setting "the seal on Britain's transformation from a world power to a European power." The Conservatives when they returned to power in 1970 halted this process, to keep a British presence in Southeast Asia. They withdrew from the Persian Gulf but kept treaty relations and a military training connection with the oil states there. They negotiated with Australia, New Zealand, Malaysia, and Singapore a five-power defense agreement which shared the costs and manpower of the defense of the area. So they stayed "east of Suez" (and of course in Hong Kong) but in greatly reduced strength. And they welcomed a new American naval presence in the Indian Ocean, represented by the 1972 agreement to set up a joint communications base on the atoll of Diego Garcia (expanded in 1974 to provide joint support facilities).

In Europe the American concern was mainly to halt the weakening of NATO while U.S. efforts were concentrated on the Far East. Much energy was expended on devising and promoting some device for meeting the claims of Germany and France in particular for a share in the nuclear deterrent while retaining ultimate control in American hands. Various schemes were tried—the multilateral nuclear force, the multinational nuclear force, the Atlantic nuclear force (a British idea)—but they all came to grief on the impracticality of combining multiple national sovereignties with unified control. They clashed, moreover, with the desire of both the U.S.A. and Britain as members of the "nuclear club" to see a nuclear nonproliferation treaty signed between East and West. The decision, however, of de Gaulle in 1966 to withdraw France from NATO and to require the removal of NATO installations from French soil was a reminder equally to Britain and the U.S.A. that one price to be paid for their policy might be a weakening of NATO. This came, moreover, at a time when both Britain and the U.S.A. were feeling the mounting burden of their military establishment in Germany. In 1967 they both reduced their forces there, although the Germans increased their financial contribution to the total costs. In 1968 the Nuclear Nonproliferation Treaty was signed by the United Kingdom, the U.S.A., and the USSR (though conspicuously not by France), and although the Soviet invasion of Czechoslovakia was a rude reminder of how little the essentials of Soviet imperialism had changed, the gradual easing of East-West relations continued with the opening of the Strategic Arms Limitation Talks (SALT) at Helsinki in November 1969.

Meanwhile the great American retreat from the Asiatic mainland had got under way, beginning, as now seems clear in retrospect, with President Johnson's March 1968 announcement of his intention not to seek reelection. In Britain the withdrawal from Vietnam was as welcome as the previous involvement had been distasteful, but relief was tempered with anxiety lest retreat on this front turn into a rout on all. What Britain wanted was not an abdication of American power but a redeployment of it. Unfortunately this proved impossible of full realization. A decade's experience of such strains and frustrations as Vietnam imposed leaves no corner of a nation's policy unscathed. Whatever the ultimate impact might be, President Nixon's "doctrine," as enunciated at Guam in November 1969, clearly had implications that extended to Europe as well as to Asia. To the conventional pledges of loyalty to allies and satellites "threatened by a nuclear power" it added: "In cases involving other types of aggression we shall furnish military and economic assistance when requested in accordance with our treaty commitments. But we shall look to the nation directly threatened to assume the primary responsibility of providing the manpower for its defense." Read in London, the doctrine was felt to involve a novel assertion of American independence of action with respect to her allies of a kind that previous administrations had explicitly disavowed. It seemed to imply, as one American analyst put it, "a strategy . . . that balances alliance interests against the interest in developing new and more advantageous relationships with adversaries."[8]

For this there seemed to be two reasons. The first was the deliberate American retreat from omnicompetence, from being the policeman of the world. Of this the most dramatic manifestation was the withdrawal from Vietnam itself. More ominous still was the consequential reduction in the total fighting power of the United States—the slide into mere parity in nuclear force with the USSR, the cut in troop numbers from about 4.25 million in 1970 to 2.5 million in 1973, and in expenditure from 11 percent of the gross national product in 1967–68 to less than 7 percent in 1972–73, and of course the ending of the draft in July 1973. For Europe there was a very direct corollary, spelled out by Senator Mike Mansfield with increasing emphasis over a decade in his annual amendments for cuts in American troops stationed in Europe. Each year the pressure mounted in the Senate, held off only by counterpressure from the White House (and the USSR).

The burden of alliance, moreover, was economic as well as military, and here too America proved vulnerable where once she had been regarded as invincible. In 1971 (though there had been premonitory warnings before) the United States felt with full force the shock wave of a balance-of-payments crisis of the kind which had been only too familiar for Britain. But while the maladies of the pound had been troublesome for the dollar, the sickness of the dollar proved critical for the monetary systems of the entire free world. No longer was the dollar the sun around which, like planets, the lesser currencies revolved; for a moment, in the critical months of August to December 1971, it seemed more like a meteor streaking downward in the sky. The sudden desperate measures —the suspension of convertibility, the 10 percent import surcharge, the 10 percent cut in foreign aid—all signified that the U.S.A. was no longer exempt from the vagaries of fortune which beset lesser powers and was no more able than they, in such a crisis, to resist the initial *sauve qui peut* reaction. For a brief and alarming period in 1971 it looked as if the U.S.A., amid the ruins of the dollar-centered Bretton Woods system, had turned her back on the economic liberalism and interdependence which that system implied (especially since the crisis measures were adopted without consultation with even her closest ally). By the end of the year the worst immediate effects of the American crisis measures had been corrected, but the shock effects did not disappear. (A second devaluation followed within fourteen months, in February 1973.) American confidence had suffered a severe blow and the first casualty of it was, understandably, American economic liberalism. The freeing of world trade to which Kennedy had tried to impart a permanent momentum became much less obviously a primary American interest, and the old voices of protectionism became insistent once again.

Second only to the relative decline in American power was the revision of American diplomatic priorities. The world of the seventies was notable for the maturing of the Soviet and Chinese leadership, the deepening of their mutual hostility, and the opportunity this afforded to the U.S.A. to establish a modus vivendi with each. In place of a simple bipolarity into which the alliance with Britain and Western Europe fitted as neatly and inevitably as fingers into a well-made glove, there was now a considerably more complex balancing of relationships between the consolidated superpowers, into which the semiconsolidated Europe that Britain was entering did not slot with any preordained precision. In and of itself the "normalization" of American relations with China was very welcome in Britain, not only as a long overdue relaxation of Asiatic tensions but also as a removal of a twenty-year-old source of Anglo-American friction. Similarly the whole network of détente measures with the USSR was warmly cheered as the realization of objectives for which Britain had worked as hard as the U.S.A.—particularly the A.B.M. treaty and Interim Agreement on Strategic Offensive Arms of May 1972 and the four-power agreement on Berlin of June, not to mention the long, slow, but still rewarding negotiations on strategic arms limitations and mutual balanced force reductions. But below the genuine appreciation of the achievements of President Nixon's diplomacy of negotiation ran a strong undercurrent of concern about the recurrent indifference to consultation with his allies which accompanied it. Dr. Henry Kissinger, initially the president's adviser on foreign affairs and then from 1973 secretary of state, who was already on record as believing that consultation "works best [sic] in *implementing* a consensus rather than in *creating* it,"⁹ was regarded as a particular offender in this respect. This appeared to be borne out by the administration's behavior over the unveiling of the new China policy, the change of voting habits in the United Nations that was its corollary, and the economic crisis measures of 1971, all of which had particular and immediate implications for Great Britain and on all of which consultation was largely or wholly nonexistent.

But of course it was not only the American end of the Anglo-American relationship which had shifted by the seventies. Britain too had made a historic break with her past. She refused to take de Gaulle's ban on her entry into the European Economic Community as final. Labour, when in office, knocked again on the door. At the end of 1967 the French again applied their veto. But in 1970 de Gaulle was succeeded by Pompidou and Wilson by Heath. Negotiations begun late in that year were brought to a successful conclusion in 1972 and Britain joined the Community on 1 January 1973. It was certainly a historic step, yet it was not easy to be sure what it was a step to. The Europe Britain joined was much more of an economic trading unit, much less of an embryonic political federation, than had been envisaged in the fifties. To avert French alarm that Britain would be a "Trojan horse" for America inside the Community, relatively little was said, in the long British debate over entry, about its implications for what Heath called the "natural relationship" of Britain and the U.S.A. It was a basic British assumption that the essentials of this would not be affected. On the American side benevolent endorsement of British entry persisted under Johnson and Nixon much as it had before. Yet as the Community prospered and America faltered under her own balance-of-payments problems, it was observable that economic anxieties about the Community's behavior and Britain's participation in it steadily mounted. The two principal targets of American concern were the Community's agricultural policies and the preferential trading arrangements it accorded to its associated states. Yet there was already a very considerable American economic penetration of the EEC—a $7,000 million direct investment in Britain alone—and it was plausible to argue that already in the 1960s America had benefited on balance from the economic integration of Europe. Moreover, Britain, more than any other member of the EEC, retained after entry a concern that most nearly matched America's both over agriculture and over trading preferences.

Besides, there was American concern over its politics and diplomacy. In particular there was a mounting anxiety in Congress over the drain on American dollars and manpower represented by the 300,000 U.S. troops still stationed in Europe. The executive, for its part, while beating off repeated congressional moves to reduce this commitment, was worried at the extent to which Europe, especially with a highly self-assertive France, was insensitive to Kissinger's diplomatic strategies. This became very apparent in 1973 with Kissinger's rather patronizing proclamation of a "year of Europe" and a call for a new Atlantic Charter that would redefine the principles of the alliance in a way which would unify its military, political, and economic objectives. In October the outbreak of the Arab-Israeli war graphically demonstrated how far from unified the alliance was. Kissinger's unilateral proclamation of an American nuclear alert to counter Russia's pressure in the Middle East was accompanied by a refusal by Britain and other NATO powers to place their bases at America's disposal for air lifts of arms to Israel. With this went the new and sudden strains that followed on the Arabs' deployment of their oil weapon. No doubt the oil challenge was a threat to every NATO member but in such disparate degrees that no common front could be presented—certainly not thrown up overnight. France, it is true, was alone in her stubborn refusal to seek any basis of common action; yet it was Germany more than Britain that kept the rest of the EEC in line with a modified American strategy and averted an open split on the issue of framing a common energy policy. Even so there was American resentment that the nine Community countries made their own approach to the Arabs.

From these disagreements (significantly perhaps, as at Suez, largely Middle Eastern in their origins) came President Nixon's public insistence that if Europe wanted U.S. cooperation in defense it must cooperate on the economic and political fronts as well. This was a crude and embarrassing splutter of an administration about to enter on the last phase of its ignominious collapse and in fact it was quickly followed by retractions, by Kissinger's abandonment of the search for a new Atlantic Charter and by a mutual commitment to future consultation, timed to coincide with the twenty-fifth anniversary of NATO. In all this Britain was involved as much as but not conspicuously more than her European partners and the strains on Anglo-American relations were not distinctively or exclusively painful. Yet, whatever the irritation that American unilateralism or impatience might provoke, British policymakers had to admit that the ambiguities in the condition of western Europe made real difficulties for American diplomacy as well as recoiling on Britain in her search for a stable posture in a shifting world. Heath's dramatic plunge into Europe in January 1973 produced no immediate solutions for Britain's problems, and indeed Britain's deepening economic crisis facilitated the return to power in 1974 of a Labour party grown skeptical of a European utopia.

Much of the concern that the U.S.A. was now feeling over a potentially restrictionist Europe resembled the anxieties which prompted Labour to "re-negotiate" Britain's terms of entry to the European Community. But behind the new calculus of Britain's profit and loss loomed a modified British concept of the Community itself, according to which integration would proceed at a pace compatible with the full maintenance of Britain's association with the U.S.A. This did not necessarily imply any exclusive association; it was, for example, very similar to the attitude which successive West German governments had adopted whenever a contradiction threatened between NATO and Community objectives. Nor was it easy to predict what the precise shape of the British-European-Atlantic relationship would be, with Britain, in whatever form, necessarily "in" Europe and the U.S.A. inescapably "in" NATO. But one thing was certain; it would not be determined by import levies on soy beans or even currency realignments. It would ultimately depend on the strength of historic cultural and political ties in a world where the pressures for change must still take account of the need for continuity.

Notes

1 Introduction

1. For an analysis and anthology of these see Arnold Wolfers and Laurence W. Martin, *The Anglo-American Tradition in Foreign Affairs* (New Haven, 1956).

2. Ibid., p. xxi.

2 1776–1812: The American Revolution and After

1. *Correspondence of George III*, ed. Sir John Fortescue (London, 1927–28), 4: 350 f.

2. Ibid., 6: 429–30.

3. See Bradford Perkins, *The First Rapprochement* (Philadelphia, 1955).

4. Rufus King MSS cited in Bradford Perkins, *Prologue to War, 1805–1812* (Berkeley, 1961), p. 58.

5. Ibid., p. 305.

6. Maurice Smelser, *The Democratic Republic, 1801–15* (New York, 1968), p. 219.

3 1812–1860: The Young Republic

1. R. G. Albion, *The Rise of New York Port, 1815–1860* (New York, 1939), p. 38.

2. *The Anglo-American Connection in the Early Nineteenth Century* (Philadelphia, 1959).

3. This, incidentally, was not confined to direct Anglo-American trading. Britain's worldwide nexus of credit and finance was at the disposal of American traders over most of the world.

4. Sydney Smith, *Humble Petition to the House of Congress at Washington* (1842).

5. For further exemplification of this see Frank Thistlethwaite, *The Great Experiment* (Cambridge, 1955), especially the chapter entitled "The Atlantic Outlook, 1790–1850." Also Charlotte Erickson, "British Immigrants in the Old Northwest, 1815–1860," in *The Frontier in American Development,* ed. David M. Ellis (Ithaca and London, 1969). Britain, though outstanding, was not, of course, unique among European countries in having America as, in this sense, a frontier; see Walter Prescott Webb, *The Great Frontier* (Boston, 1952) and, for a specific example of European-Western interaction, Morton Rothstein, "The American West and Foreign Markets, 1850–1900" in *Frontier in American Development,* ed. Ellis.

6. See Thistlethwaite, *Great Experiment,* chaps. 2–5, for details.

7. P. Guedalla, ed., *Gladstone and Palmerston* (London, 1928), p. 208.

8. Bradford Perkins, *Castlereagh and Adams* (Berkeley, 1964), p. 327.

9. Samuel F. Bemis, *A Diplomatic History of the United States* (New York, 1936), p. 283.

4   1860–1865: The American Civil War

1. A cable had been laid and used in 1858, but it functioned only for a few weeks. It was 1866 before a permanent link was established.

2. For the attitude of the Lancashire workingmen, in the districts most affected by the famine, see Mary Ellison, *Support for Secession: Lancashire and the American Civil War* (Chicago, 1972).

3. At Newcastle on 2 October 1862: "Jefferson Davis and other leaders of the South have made an army; they are making, it appears, a navy; and they have made—what is more than either—a nation."

4. Quoted in Samuel Flagg Bemis, *Diplomatic History,* p. 381.

5   1866–1895: America and Victorian England

1. There was a further reason for this. As the major sea power, Britain was very happy to accept, in return for an identical pledge from the U.S.A.,

a strict interpretation of a neutral's duty not to equip or release a naval vessel likely to play a belligerent role.

2. Bemis, *Diplomatic History,* p. 413.

3. R. C. K. Ensor, *England, 1870–1914* (Oxford, 1936), p. 19.

4. James Bryce, *The American Commonwealth* (London, 1888), chap. 96.

5. Sir Lionel had guilelessly responded to what he imagined to be a private correspondent's inquiry for his advice on how to vote in the presidential election, only to find his reply reproduced and headlined as "The British Lion's Paw Thrust into American Politics."

6. They also paid the bills for some of the eighteen British newspapers which Carnegie bought and ran in the radical interest.

6   1895–1914: Imperialism

1. "The Great Aberration," as Samuel F. Bemis called it (*Diplomatic History,* chap. 26).

2. See R. G. Neale, *Britain and American Imperialism, 1898–1900* (Brisbane, 1965) on this.

3. Bradford Perkins, *The Great Rapprochement: England and the United States, 1895–1914* (New York, 1968; London, 1969), p. 276.

7   1914–1919: The First World War and the First World Peace

1. In most Allied-American relationships Britain's maritime and commercial preponderance made her the spokesman and pacemaker for the entente. The terms *Allies* and *Britain* are therefore often interchangeable in what follows.

2. And even then Britain agreed to support the market up to ten cents a pound, rather than inflict, as it were, a "cotton famine" in reverse upon the American South.

3. There was also, of course, in 1914–18 no impressment issue.

4. It took 209 in all.

8   1919–1939: Isolationism and Neutrality

1. By June 1922 Congress had reduced the official strength of the army to 175,000 men. In fact by 1923 its actual strength was only 115,000.

2. *The Gathering Storm* (Boston and London, 1948), pp. 254–55.

3. W. L. Langer and S. E. Gleason, *The Challenge to Isolation, 1937–40* (New York and London, 1952), p. 25.

9   1939–1945: World War II—Intervention and Alliance

1. See Churchill's own description of it in *Their Finest Hour* (London and Boston, 1949), p. 23: "My relations with the President gradually became so close that the chief business between our two countries was virtually conducted by these personal interchanges between him and me. . . . In all, I sent him 950 messages and received about 800 in reply." A reading of the correspondence provides a unique insight into the Anglo-American partnership during the war years. The imbalance in the letters exchanged is indicative not merely of Churchill's greater assiduity as a correspondent but also of the roles of the two men, the one necessarily the suitor, the other the wooed.

2. *Their Finest Hour*, p. 409.

3. At Boston, on 30 October 1940. The America First Committee, the isolationist reply to William Allen White's committee, had come into being two days after the destroyer bases deal was signed.

4. Winston S. Churchill, *The Grand Alliance* (London and Boston, 1950), pp. 606–7.

5. To avoid confusion with the later United Nations Charter, it is important to remember that this was a statement of war aims, based largely on the Atlantic Charter, and a mutual undertaking to wage all-out war on the Axis. It was drawn up by Roosevelt and Churchill during the latter's visit to Washington at Christmas and the New Year 1941–42 and subsequently signed by the governments of twenty-six countries.

6. "Combined" acquired a technical meaning in World War II, to signify specifically any agency of Anglo-American cooperation.

7. William H. McNeill, *America, Britain and Russia: Their Cooperation and Conflict, 1941–1946* (London, 1953), p. 17.

8. See, e.g., H. Duncan Hall and C. C. Wrigley, *Studies of Overseas Supply* (London, 1956), p. 205.

9. W. S. Churchill, *Triumph and Tragedy* (London and Boston, 1953), p. 429.

10   1946–1948: Postwar and Cold War

1. Worse still, by saying so in Stalin's presence.

2. He was to regret it later. Dean Acheson records him as saying "in

later years" that he had come to think of it as "a grave mistake" (Dean Acheson, *Present at the Creation* [New York, 1969], p. 122).

3. The American draft had originally spoken of "markets."

4. Acheson, *Present at the Creation,* p. 133.

11   1948–1950: NATO, Marshall Aid, and the Special Relationship

1. Additional members were admitted later—Greece and Turkey in 1951, West Germany in 1954.

2. *The Forrestal Diaries,* ed. Walter Millis (New York, 1951), p. 392 (London, 1952, p. 372).

3. Ibid. (New York), p. 491 (London, p. 460).

4. A good deal less enthusiasm was shown in Britain for the appointment of an American admiral as supreme allied commander Atlantic (SACLANT).

5. *The Papers of Senator Vandenberg* (Boston, 1952; London, 1953), p. 361.

12   1950–1952: East Asian Problems and the Korean War

1. It was also significant that the U.S.A., so active in promoting in the United Nations Charter the doctrine of international trusteeship for dependent territories, devised the novel category of "strategic trust territories" supervised by the Security Council, where the great power veto operated. This was made applicable to the formerly Japanese mandates of the Marshall, Caroline, and Mariana groups of islands which the U.S.A. had acquired in the course of the fighting.

2. Canada, Australia, New Zealand, and South Africa withheld recognition.

3. Acheson, *Present at the Creation,* p. 390.

13   1952–1960: The Eisenhower Years

1. Anthony Eden, *Full Circle* (London, 1960), p. 105.

2. Even Malaya, when it attained independence in 1957, did not choose despite her firm anticommunism to continue the SEATO membership that she had indirectly enjoyed under British rule.

3. Dwight D. Eisenhower, *Mandate for Change* (New York, 1963), p. 406.

4. Eden, *Full Circle,* p. 566.

5. Ibid., p. 558.

6. Though not his vice-president, Richard Nixon, who on 2 November announced: "For the first time in history we have shown independence of Anglo-French policies towards Asia and Africa which seemed to us to reflect the colonial tradition. This declaration of independence has had an electrifying effect throughout the world."

7. Dwight D. Eisenhower, *Waging Peace* (New York, 1965; London, 1966), p. 124.

14   1960–1974: Uncharted Waters

1. Arthur M. Schlesinger, *A Thousand Days* (New York, 1965), p. 377.

2. Harold Macmillan, *At the End of the Day* (London, 1973), p. 17.

3. Ibid., p. 182.

4. Ibid., p. 220.

5. For a classic analysis of this breakdown in the machinery of the alliance see Richard E. Neustadt, *Alliance Politics* (New York, 1970).

6. Harold Wilson, *Our Days in Power* (London, 1971), p. 80.

7. Ibid., p. 264.

8. Robert W. Tucker, "The American Outlook: Change and Continuity," in *Retreat from Empire?* ed. Robert E. Osgood (Baltimore and London, 1973), p. 64.

9. Henry Kissinger, *The Troubled Partnership* (New York, 1965), p. 227.

Supplementary Reading

The most comprehensive single-volume history of Anglo-American relations is H. C. Allen, *Great Britain and the United States, 1783–1952* (Odhams Press, London, 1954). J. B. Brebner, *North Atlantic Triangle: The Interplay of Canada, the United States and Great Britain* (Yale University Press, New Haven, 1945) traces an often neglected aspect of the relationship from 1492 to 1942. Accounts of major phases and developments will be found in the principal diplomatic histories of the United States; Richard W. Leopold, *The Growth of American Foreign Policy* (Knopf, New York, 1962) is especially valuable, particularly for its treatment of the present century.

Strategic relations are explored in Gerald S. Graham, *Empire of the North Atlantic: The Maritime Struggle for North America* (University of Toronto Press, Toronto, 1958), with emphasis on the eighteenth century, and in Kenneth Bourne, *Britain and the Balance of Power in North America, 1815–1908* (Longmans, London, 1967), with emphasis on the nineteenth.

Economic relations, perhaps because of their very intimacy and intricacy, have been nowhere comprehensively surveyed, but aspects of them have been treated in L. H. Jenks, *The Migration of English Capital to 1875* (Knopf, New York and London, 1927), N. S. Buck, *The Development of the Organization of Anglo-American Trade, 1800–1850* (Yale University Press, New Haven, 1925), R. W. Hidy, *The House of Baring in American Trade and Finance: English Merchant Bankers at Work, 1763–1861* (Harvard University Press, Cambridge, 1949), and Dorothy R. Alder, *British Investment in American Railways, 1834–1898* (University Press of Virginia, Charlottesville, 1970). The large themes of British emigration and immigration in their multiple ramifications similarly defy comprehensive treatment. Stanley C. Johnson, *A History of Emigration from the United Kingdom to North America* (Routledge, London, 1913) concentrates on organized schemes of emigration. Wilbur S. Shepperson, *British Emigration to North America* (Blackwell, Oxford, 1957) focuses on the export of this human capital in the early Victorian period. For its reception in the U.S.A. see Rowland T. Berthoff, *British Immigrants in Industrial America* (Harvard University Press, Cambridge, 1953) and chapters in Donald Fleming and

Bernard Bailyn, eds., *Dislocation and Emigration: The Demographic Back-ground of American Immigration,* Perspectives in American History, vol. 7 (Harvard University Press, Cambridge, 1973). A distinctive political rela-tionship is examined in Henry Pelling, *America and the British Left: From Bright to Bevan* (A. and C. Black, London, 1956).

The intermingling of the two cultures has similarly defied comprehensive summary, but many revealing insights are to be found in Allan Nevins, *America through British Eyes* (Oxford University Press, New York, 1948). The Anglo-American connection has proved a fertile theme for fictional treatment. Charles Dickens in *Martin Chuzzlewit,* Anthony Trollope in *The American Senator,* and Henry James, almost passim, provide notable exam-ples of the genre.

The immediate consequences of independence may be studied in Samuel F. Bemis, *Jay's Treaty* (Macmillan, New York, 1923) and Vincent T. Har-low, *The Founding of the Second British Empire, 1763–1793* (Longmans, London, 1952).

For the social, economic, and cultural background to the period between Independence and the Civil War see Frank Thistlethwaite, *The Anglo-Amer-ican Connection in the Early Nineteenth Century* (University of Pennsyl-vania Press, Philadelphia, 1959). One area of particularly close intellectual interplay is studied in Howard Temperley, *British Anti-Slavery, 1833–1870* (Longmans, London, 1972). Our understanding of the diplomatic relations of the newly independent United States and its newly rejected "mother coun-try" has been given a precision and form hitherto lacking as a result of the definitive studies of Bradford Perkins: *The First Rapprochement: England and the United States, 1795–1805* (University of Pennsylvania Press, Phila-delphia, 1955), *Prologue to War, 1805–1812* (University of California Press, Berkeley, 1961), and *Castlereagh and Adams, 1812–1823* (Univer-sity of California Press, Berkeley, 1964).

For the war of 1812 see Julius W. Pratt, *The Expansionists of 1812* (Macmillan, New York, 1925), Reginald Horsman, *The Causes of the War of 1812* (University of Pennsylvania Press, Philadelphia, 1962), and Harry L. Coles, *The War of 1812* (University of Chicago Press, Chicago, 1965).

The period between Ghent and Sumter can be further studied in R. W. Van Alystyne, *The Rising American Empire* (Oxford University Press, New York, 1960); J. Fred Rippy, *Rivalry of the United States and Great Britain over Latin America* (Johns Hopkins Press, Baltimore, 1929); Dexter Per-kins, *The Monroe Doctrine, 1823–1826* (Harvard University Press, Cam-bridge, 1927) and *The Monroe Doctrine, 1826–1867* (Johns Hopkins Press, Baltimore, 1933); Norman A. Graebner, *Empire on the Pacific* (Ron-ald Press, New York, 1955); Frederick Merk, *The Oregon Question* (Bel-knap Press, Cambridge, 1967); and Wilbur D. Jones, *The American Prob-lem in British Diplomacy, 1841–1861* (Macmillan, London, 1974).

For the Civil War see the relevant chapters in Allan Nevins's epic, *The Ordeal of the Union* (8 vols., Scribners, New York, 1947–71), especially the last four volumes, entitled *The War for the Union*. Ephraim D. Adams, *Great Britain and the American Civil War* (2 vols., Longmans, London, 1925) is still a valuable source. See also Donaldson Jordan and E. J. Pratt, *Europe and the American Civil War* (Oxford University Press, Oxford, 1931), F. L. Owsley, *King Cotton Diplomacy* (University of Chicago Press, Chicago, 1931; 2d ed., 1959), and Martin B. Duberman, *Charles Francis Adams, 1807–1886* (Houghton Mifflin, Boston, 1961).

The effect on Anglo-American relations of America's emergence as a world power is traced in Alexander E. Campbell, *Great Britain and the United States, 1895–1903* (Longmans, London, 1960), Charles S. Campbell, *Anglo-American Understanding, 1898–1903* (Johns Hopkins Press, Baltimore, 1957), R. G. Neale, *Britain and American Imperialism, 1898–1900* (University of Queensland Press, Brisbane, 1965), John A. Ferguson, *American Diplomacy and the Boer War* (University of Pennsylvania Press, Philadelphia, 1939), R. H. Heindel, *The American Impact on Great Britain, 1898–1914* (University of Pennsylvania Press, Philadelphia, 1940), and Bradford Perkins, *The Great Rapprochement: England and the United States, 1895–1914* (Atheneum, New York, 1968).

No comprehensive study of Anglo-American relations during World War I exists. A wealth of insight and information will be found in Arthur S. Link's magisterial life of Wilson (Princeton University Press, Princeton, N.J., 1947–) and, in smaller compass, in his *Woodrow Wilson and the Progressive Era, 1910–1917* (Harper, New York, 1954). See also the incisive study by Patrick Devlin of Woodrow Wilson's 1914–17 diplomacy, *Too Proud to Fight* (Oxford University Press, London and New York, 1974). Daniel Smith, *The Great Departure: the United States and World War I* (Wiley, New York, 1965) provides a brief survey and a good bibliography. Reference should also be made to Laurence W. Martin, *Peace without Victory: Woodrow Wilson and the British Liberals* (Yale University Press, New Haven, 1958) and Seth P. Tillman, *Anglo-American Relations at the Paris Peace Conference of 1919* (Princeton University Press, Princeton, N.J., 1961).

On the interwar years see Robert E. Ferrell, *American Diplomacy in the Great Depression* (Yale University Press, New Haven, 1957). The copious literature for Franklin Roosevelt's presidencies is usefully assessed in the bibliographies to Robert A. Divine, *The Reluctant Belligerent: American Entry into World War II* (Wiley, New York, 1965) and Gaddis Smith, *American Diplomacy during the Second World War, 1941–1945* (Wiley, New York, 1965), both of which provide good outline accounts of the period. Anglo-American relations enter into every aspect of the diplomacy of these years, but special mention must be made of *The American Speeches of Lord Lothian* (Oxford University Press, Oxford, 1941), Theodore A. Wilson, *The First Summit* (Macdonald, London, 1971), William H. McNeill, *America, Britain, and Russia: Their Cooperation and Conflict, 1941–1946* (Oxford University Press, London, 1953), Robert E. Sherwood, *The White House Papers of Harry Hopkins* (2 vols., Harper, New York, 1948), and Winston S. Churchill, *The Second World War* (6 vols., Houghton Mifflin, Boston, 1948–53).

The distinctively British connections of American policy since World War II are examined in H. G. Nicholas, *Britain and the U.S.A.* (Johns Hopkins Press, Baltimore, 1963). For particular aspects see Richard N. Gardner, *Sterling-Dollar Diplomacy* (Oxford University Press, Oxford, 1956), Max Beloff, *The United States and the Unity of Europe* (Faber, London, 1963), Coral Bell, *The Debatable Alliance* (Oxford University Press, London, 1964), Leon D. Epstein, *Britain—Uneasy Ally* (University of Chicago Press, Chicago, 1954), Margaret Gowing, *Britain and Atomic Energy, 1939–1945* (Macmillan, London, 1964), Richard G. Hewlett and O. E. Anderson, *History of the United States Atomic Energy Commission* (2 vols., Pennsylvania State University Press, University Park, Pa., 1962–69), Andrew J. Pierre, *Nuclear Politics* (Oxford University Press, London, 1972), Henry L. Roberts and Paul A. Wilson, *Britain and the United States: Problems in Cooperation* (Harpers, New York, 1953), Bruce M. Russett, *Community and Contention: Britain and America in the Twentieth Century* (M.I.T. Press, Cambridge, 1963), and Richard Neustadt, *Alliance Politics* (Columbia University Press, New York, 1970). Ian S. McDonald, *Anglo-American Relations since the Second World War* (David & Charles, Newton Abbot, 1974) is a useful collection of documents.

Index